What is Classical Liberal History?

What is Classical Liberal History?

Edited by
Michael J. Douma and Phillip W. Magness

LEXINGTON BOOKS
Lanham • Boulder • New York • London

Published by Lexington Books
An imprint of The Rowman & Littlefield Publishing Group, Inc.
4501 Forbes Boulevard, Suite 200, Lanham, Maryland 20706
www.rowman.com

Unit A, Whitacre Mews, 26-34 Stannary Street, London SE11 4AB

Chapter 1: Portions of this chapter were originally published as Scott M. Shubitz, "Liberal Intellectual Culture and Religious Faith: The Liberalism of the New York Liberal Club, 1869–1877," *The Journal of the Gilded Age and Progressive Era* 16, no. 2 (April 2017): 183–205.

Chapter 7: A portion of this chapter was previously published in Jonathan Bean, "Introduction," *in Race and Liberty in America: The Essential Reader*, ed. Jonathan Bean (University Press of Kentucky, 2009): 1–12.

British Library Cataloguing in Publication Information Available

Library of Congress Cataloging-in-Publication Data Available

ISBN 978-1-4985-3610-3 (cloth : alk. paper)
ISBN 978-1-4985-3611-0 (electronic)

♾ ™ The paper used in this publication meets the minimum requirements of American National Standard for Information Sciences—Permanence of Paper for Printed Library Materials, ANSI/NISO Z39.48-1992.

Printed in the United States of America

Contents

Acknowledgments

The editors would like to thank the anonymous peer reviewers who provided invaluable comments on early drafts of the book and the editors at Rowman & Littlefield who were a pleasure to work with. Michael Douma would like to thank Bruce Caldwell, Peter Boettke, Fred Smith, and George Nash for useful comments.

Jonathan Bean would like to thank all those who reviewed and commented upon earlier drafts, including David Bernstein, Richard Epstein, Robert Weems, Paul Moreno, Roger Clegg, and Andrew Barbero. I am also grateful for my loving wife, Tina Bean, who supported me in this endeavor, even as my keyboard clicking filled the air with words that eventually landed on these pages.

Hans Eicholz would like to thank his friends and colleagues, historians G. M. Curtis and Peter Mentzel for enduring his interminable discussions on these themes through the years. He would also like to acknowledge the assistance of his former mentor, the late Joyce Appleby who had commented on and encouraged an earlier essay on historicism and a review of Bernard Bailyn's work that proved highly informative in this project.

Lenore T. Ealy would like to thank the dozens of intrepid individuals who have participated since 2001 in the programs of the Project for New Philanthropy Studies, the Fund for the Study of Spontaneous Orders, and the Philanthropic Enterprise, initiatives founded by Richard Cornuelle (1927–2011) to foster scholarly deliberation to help us understand voluntary social processes as well as market processes.

Introduction

Michael J. Douma

This book is designed to generate new ideas and new ways of thinking by reviving a neglected historical tradition, classical liberal history. In doing so, we hope not only to call attention to the best elements of the classical liberal tradition but also to call upon historians to reflect on the importance of this tradition to the history and practice of their own discipline.

Modern historiography reflects a diverse and overlapping set of epistemological positions, methods of inquiry, and approaches to research. In American academia, historiography began in a conservative vein. Conservative historians tend to write histories of nations and biographies of statesmen and great figures who serve as moral models for preserving the best of society. Conservatives see in the past a morality tale and lament the destruction of ordered systems which they hope to resurrect at least in part. By the turn of the 20th century, however, progressive history had come to dominate the preparation and practice of American historians. This approach to historical study arose toward the end of the 19th century, alongside the development of the new "social" sciences. Progressive historians, like their counterparts in sociology, political science, and economics, tended to see the role of their professions as helping to direct society on a path toward a better future. Such presentist and political purposes have also characterized the alternative Marxist and other collectivist models of history (e.g., feminist histories) which are based on the propositions that all people belong to a class, that their actions are shaped by their material circumstances, and that therefore we must study people as groups to understand how the past is necessarily moving us through different stages of development. More recently, postmodernist historians have challenged the possibility that historians can arrive at "objective" facts with the implication that history is itself a political act written only to serve power.

This book seeks to offer an alternative approach by illuminating what may be called "classical liberal" history. Like progressive, Marxist, feminist, postmodernist, or conservative historians, historians self-consciously working in the classical liberal tradition seek evidence from the past to explain how the world is structured. Unlike these other approaches to historical research, however, classical liberal historiography is based upon the principle of methodological individualism central to the classical liberal tradition. While classical liberal historians do not reject out of hand the study of nations, political parties, social or minority groups, they recognize that these collectives do not act on their own, but consist rather of the ideas and actions of their individual members. Classical liberal history is the study of individual action in the past. Guided by a general set of assumptions about human nature (i.e., that humans seek to better their circumstances, that they act on their subjective desires to satisfy ends, that they inhabit a world of trade-offs and scarcity) classical liberal historians see acting individuals as the basic units of historical investigation.[1] Classical liberal history begins with the recognition of the inherent worth of the individual and presents individuals as the starting point for historical inquiry and concern. Moreover, because in the classical liberal tradition human action is conceived of as voluntary action, classical liberal historians are especially attuned to examining the economic, social, political, and cultural conditions, and institutions that preserve the widest sphere for human liberty.

Classical liberals have no monopoly on the study of liberty nor its definition, but they do give exceptional weight to liberty as a concern of their analysis and they do define liberty in ways that differ from the conservative or progressive conceptions of the term. In short, classical liberals value negative liberty over positive liberty. Negative liberty is best defined as "freedom from external impediments deliberately imposed."[2] Positive liberty, on the other hand, is not a "freedom from" but a "freedom to," as when one is enabled to make certain actions. Classical liberals tend to be skeptical of positive liberties, especially when they are imposed by government. The boundaries between these and other conceptions of liberty, however, are not always clear, and in fact may overlap in certain ways. Following Jacob Levy, we might break down classical liberal concerns of liberty into two categories: (1) ideas about the threat of tyranny through central planning and bureaucracy, and (2) worries about threats to liberty from "customary, local, religious, traditional, and decentralized authority," or what Levy calls a pluralist liberalism and a rationalist liberalism. These two threats to liberty identified by classical liberals seem to press back against progressivism's impositions on the one hand, and the lingering injustices of conservative orders on the other hand. Classical liberal history is a record of the attempts to define and encourage individuals' freedom from these outside threats, and to understand the economic, political, social, and cultural limitations to complete, unlimited freedom.

Any conceptual category begs for a definition, and "history" is no exception. How we define history determines how we write it, and what purpose it has. Obviously, historians make choices of what we write about and how we write about it. Classical liberal historians believe that history is a rational inquiry into the past and an attempt to reconstruct and try to understand human decision-making through the trail of evidence that the past has left us. And yet classical liberal historians tend to acknowledge that interpretation of this evidence is not an exact science, and that it is not the goal of historical study to discover universal laws of human behavior not to defend the assumed inevitability of progress toward greater liberty. Classical liberal historians believe that we should choose to write about salient, relevant issues of human freedom and unfreedom such as the rise and fall of slavery, the origins of constitutional limits on government power, and the growth of markets that bring prosperity. What we write about matters.

Moreover, how we write history matters. History is not an exercise in literary fiction; it requires correspondence to things that really happened in the past. At the same time, only a naïve mind would call for a "neutral" or "objective" historical account uninfluenced by the subjective concerns and perceptions of the historian. Nevertheless, because evidence of the past cannot interpret itself, and because the aim of historical writing is to expand our stock of knowledge about the past, good historians believe that we must aim to get our facts straight and our narratives to cohere, while always standing open to reconsider our views of the past. By recognizing that history presents claims that should be subject to empirical falsification, we retain a means to constantly check and test their accuracy.

Classical liberal history is thus both a methodological and ethical approach to doing history that has been shaped by the classical liberal orientation itself. It operates, first of all, within a tradition of the scholarly ethic that historians owe their subjects. We must study the past with a sense of philanthropy, that is, with attention and love for what it means to be human. This ethical orientation compels us to treat evidence on its own terms, not our own. This orients us fundamentally to an anthropological understanding of human persons possessed of dignity, reason, passion, interests, and an inalienable moral responsibility that can be fulfilled only to the extent that we are free. One consequence of such an outlook is that we treat our subjects through a principle of charity, seeking to understand rather than to judge. When historians poorly handle evidence, willfully misinterpret it, or allow presentist judgments to shape too much of their interpretations of the evidence, they diminish the public trust in their discipline. This is why classical liberal historians reaffirm these liberal scholarly principles of openness, debate, empiricism, and charity.

The principles of liberal openness and debate are essential for all historical discourse. This is why a central tenet of classical liberal history is dissatisfaction with narratives that claim certainty or completeness, or which shut off all attempts to present alternative perspectives. Classical liberal historians are skeptical of grand claims, and skeptical above all of prediction, which falls outside of the realm and purpose of proper history. The complexity and great unknowns of history teach us to be humble in what we claim for truth and foster a scholarly approach rooted in epistemic humility. While others might look to the past for knowledge to implement in policy or justify political action, classical liberals are more likely to use the past to show how policies intended to do good might fail—not predicting that they *will* fail, but being open to the ways policies may or *may not* "do good." On the topic of prediction, the liberal view opposes the teleology of Christian or Marxist history, or even certain Whig antecedents of our own intellectual traditions. Most classical liberals believe that history is not a great march, that there is no discernable grand theory, and that we should beware those who claim that there is. It might be best, they think, if we follow J. G. A. Pocock or Reinhardt Kosseleck and think of histories in the plural, or, if we follow John Lukacs, and think of history as an engagement between a participant and the empirical evidence.

What we are framing as classical liberal history is a broad tradition, with strong philosophical roots and active present-day practitioners. One might include in this later list such scholars as the economic historians Deirdre McCloskey, Niall Ferguson, Raymond de Roover, and Robert Higgs; the historians of Europe: Alan Charles Kors, Richard Pipes, and Ralph Raico; American historians: Larry Schweikart, Kevin Gutzman, Allan Kulikoff, Jeffrey Hummel; legal historians: Stephen Halbrook, Randy Barnett, David Bernstein, and Philip Hamburger. This list includes many people who diverge in opinion on a number of issues, and many who would not self-consciously call themselves classical liberals or classical liberal historians. The editors and many of the contributors to this book believe that the increasing domination of collectivist ideals in the scholarly training and practices of academic historians makes the present an auspicious time to delineate more explicitly what can be construed classical liberal history.

Many historians, regardless of their politics, are working partly in the classical liberal tradition, even if they don't recognize it. This is because liberalism and the historical profession grew up side-by-side in the 19th century, so many of their methods and goals overlap and complement each other. The liberal view of history first emerged in the 18th century, when liberals sought protection from monarchy and tyranny by developing constitutional opposition to autocratic rule. Classical liberal history came into force in the 19th century, and it developed in tandem with nationalist projects in Europe.

Writers like Droysen in Germany, Croce in Italy, Fredericq and Pirenne in Belgium, and Hume in England, all focused on liberty in their nations. These early generations of liberal historians, ever concerned with political theory, told stories of how liberty had emerged and how it could be protected. They praised heroes of liberty, condemned acts of predation upon it, and they inspired progress toward the development of free societies. As histories of national freedom became a common genre, scientific standards demanded fair readings of the sources. In Germany, where the historical profession was most developed, the classical liberal view of history was often paired with rigorous archival work and the historicist emphasis on the uniqueness and unrepeatability of historical events.

We believe that historians across the profession can benefit from better understanding both the history of the classical liberal tradition and the approach to historical study that has emerged out of that tradition. The conservative tradition of historical thought, for example, can appreciate methodological individualism and the classical liberal opposition to central planning. It can learn to better apply principles of neoclassical economics and appreciate the importance of subjectivity and subject value in history. Eschewing discussions of philosophy of history, conservatives often write about what history is *for*, but not what history *is*. According to conservatives such as Russel Kirk, Edmund Burke, Eric Voegelin, and Christopher Dawson, the past is a source of wisdom and moral understanding. In this view, history is useful for structuring society along certain moral and political ends. A chief goal of conservative historians is to recognize order and purpose, both human and divine. It should not come as a surprise then that many major conservative historians (we might add to the list above Owen Barfield and Harry Jaffa) were primarily political philosophers, not trained historians. There are also conservative historians like R.G. Collingwood and Herbert Butterfield, who were concerned more with historical methods than politics. While the modern conservative approach to history is nowhere well-defined and systematized, it seems to have a few essential elements: (1) influence of the Christian view of the world and a general acceptance of teleology, (2) preference for ideas over materialist explanations of history, (3) a belief that history teaches us about wisdom and even divine wisdom, and (4) that ordered society is preferable to disordered society. The second point most strongly overlaps with the classical liberal approach. Less important in conservative history, but still sometimes visible are the classical liberal themes of freedom, checks on political power, and tolerance.

Progressive historians could also benefit from an introduction to classical liberal history because they share many of the same values (tolerance, rights, free speech, etc.) and scientific assumptions. Progressive historians seek to study conflicts in the past, particularly to highlight the failures of the market

economy and successes of government regulation. Like conservatives, progressives look to the past to find examples of order, not the organic order
of tradition, but the imposed order of the cognitive elite. For progressives,
written history serves to justify particular actions. Progressive history from
Charles Beard and Vernon Parrington on the American side, to Geoffrey
Barraclough in England all tend toward history that is useful for present
politics. It is possible to agree with a philosopher like the conservative R.G.
Collingwood, and admit that all history is present thought, or with Barraclough, that all history must have contemporary relevance, and still not be a
progressive. But some progressives have been all too willing to use history to
serve present ideological ends.

Even when broadly historicist, progressives have retained a belief in
teleology. Serving this narrative of progress all too often becomes the aim,
rather than the end of progressive history. Classical liberals are not immune
from falling into the same trap, but because they have less faith in the application of top-down solutions, they are less confident in the ability to apply
past knowledge to directly solve present-day social problems. From the
writings of F.A. Hayek, they have learned to recognize that any individual
can only possess a small fragment of available and relevant knowledge,
and that it is the conceit of the planners to think that they can implement
singular top-down solutions. Rather, classical liberals believe that history
teaches humility and does not readily give us answers about how we should
behave. While classical liberals study and praise great historical processes
that bought human flourishing, and conservatives study and praise great
statesman and national power, progressives prefer to highlight the errors and
evils of Western civilization.

Classical liberal and progressive historians can also often be distinguished
by whether they treat historical change as contingent or as part of a necessary process. The former, for example, tend to write of improvement, while
progressives speak, of course, of progress. The difference is subtle but significant. Improvement is the measureable distance between the present and
the past. Progress, however, is the general direction of development toward
some usually generally conceived but often ill-defined goal.

Classical liberal historians have an affinity for borrowing theory from other
disciplines, particularly economics and political science. From economics,
they have adopted a recognition of spontaneous orders (the patterns resulting
from human action, but not human design), and an awareness of unintended
consequences. They have concluded that a necessary prerequisite for prosperity is the freedom of individuals to maximize their own advantage through
barter and trade. They have also imported from the toolbox of the economist
such ideas as subjective value theory, marginalism, opportunity costs, and the
ever-present reality of the scarcity of goods. Any historical explanation must

obey the rules of economics. Aiming at the improvement of society, instead of just its preservation (conservative) or its destruction (Marxist), classical liberals have had an inherent interest in political theory (such as in forms of federalism, or public choice voting analysis), even as they express skepticism of the claims of politicians.

A large part of classical liberal history written today confronts and challenges reigning interpretations of history that disparage individual freedom or fail to tell an accurate or coherent story. Others can be defined as classical liberals because they have chosen to write about liberty itself, including studies of freedom across the world, in particular nations, or even in political movements. Classical liberal history writing also seeks to expand the possible array of historical interpretations of a given event or historical process, so that those traditionally opposed to individual freedom might reconsider their views. Across the board, these historians write to celebrate positive cultural developments, the growth of prosperity, and individual successes. But, they also criticize the growing power of the State and the trend toward group identity politics at the expense of individual freedom.

Histories of liberty promise to re-direct the historical discourse into themes that a classical liberal historian finds more appropriate and rewarding. The history of liberty may be broad such as David Schmidtz and Jason Brennan's *The History of Liberty*, or it may focus on important figures such James Otteson's works on Adam Smith, or it may chart the political course of liberal ideas like Arthur J. Ekirch's *The Decline of American Liberalism*, or Louis Hartz's *The Liberal Tradition*. A subset of this type of history is the history of libertarianism like Brian Doherty's *Radicals for Capitalism: A Freewheeling History of the Modern American Libertarian Movement*. The study of liberty is also an implicit theme in most works of slavery, abolitionism, emancipation, immigration, civil rights, and technological progress.[3]

Works of this type may be written (and often are written) by people unfriendly to liberty (particularly negative liberty—"freedom from coercion"). In fact, many works on, for example, the role of capitalism during the industrial revolution, are concerned with liberty, even if their greater concern is equality or order, or something else entirely. Since classical liberal historians view the study of liberty as the most important and relevant concern of history, they tend to welcome books such as David Hacket Fisher's *Liberty and Freedom*, Joyce Appleby's *History of Capitalism*, and Eric Foner's *History of American Freedom*, even if these authors are sometimes opposed to liberal values. At least they are talking about topics of common interest and importance. As these examples illustrate, those studying the history of classical liberalism do not always embrace the term "classical liberal historian." Indeed, the history of classical liberalism can and should be written by historians of all ideological persuasions.

A third type of classical liberal history writing is open, meaning that it doesn't directly argue for a particular interpretation of an event, but rather presents multiple interpretations, sometimes through primary sources, allowing the audience to wrestle with ideas or perhaps come to their own conclusions. The process of encouraging open debate on multiple views of history is itself affirming of classical liberal openness to ideas. In the classroom, multiple views can be presented on spectrum or a matrix to encourage debate and further understanding. Unlike confrontational classical liberal history, this type of open inquiry allows the audience to discover an interpretation of the past through engagement with curated materials. It does not preach to the crowd like the confrontational works, but may win new recruits or get fence-sitters to commit to a new view. Regardless, by opening up debate, the open method naturally challenges reigning interpretations, promotes the liberty of free-flowing discussion and debate, and encourages people to arrive at more considered, thought-out conclusions.

Finally, classical liberal history is not "neoliberal" history. Neoliberalism has been an ill-defined, amorphous term used to deride a range of ideological opponents. Those who call themselves classical liberals today stress their connection with their liberal heritage on both the right and left of the political spectrum. In this sense, it is also much broader than simply libertarianism, which is largely a late 20th-century invention. Neoliberalism is usually conceived of as a right-wing ideology, attached—often haphazardly—to an array of figures and concepts including Milton Friedman, the Chicago School of Economics, Ronald Reagan and Margaret Thatcher, Augusto Pinochet, and even Donald Trump. It is also applied to capitalism in general, and state capitalism in particular, or is essentially synonymous with globalization. The term's use in a growing but often disjointed academic literature is almost exclusively pejorative, with few if any serious claimants using the term or its purported characteristics to identify themselves.[4] Far from advancing scholarly understanding, this approach serves little more than to poison the well of inquiry—to define one's opponents with a priori assumptions of evil motivations, secret affinities for dictators, and quasi-conspiratorial designs for the world. The resulting literature on neoliberalism, itself often highly polemic and sure of its own position and yet simultaneously starved of evidentiary rigor, becomes little more than a destructive bludgeon to shut down further inquiry.

This present collection is about what classical liberal history is, and what it is not; this book is also an attempt to describe what classical liberal history writing should be going forward.

While many of the contributors to the book identify as classical liberals, some do not, and some even reject the usefulness of the term. Regardless of how we define ourselves, we are fundamentally interested in exploring those aspects of the past that illustrate the vital importance of human thought, decision, and freedom to explain the unfolding of events. We are committed to the proposition that moral and intellectual decisions are at the very center of any story worthy of the name history, for without choice there is no story to tell. It is in this sense then we may be seen as belonging broadly to that tradition of scholarship that is classically liberal. But in a still wider sense we believe that neglect of this important aspect of the human condition, of Liberty in thought and deed, has eroded the standards of evidence necessary to sustain historical inquiry. Voluntary associationalism, fallibilism and humility, we suggest, are at the root of the historical enterprise and must not be abandoned. We offer these essays then as a way of reopening a critically important discussion of the nature of the human being and the kinds of analysis and evidence required to interpret his/her past.

CHAPTER DESCRIPTIONS

Each of the contributors to this book were asked to summarize the historiography of a sub-field or theme of historical research. They were asked to then explain the contribution of classical liberals to this historiography and explain what historians in the field should focus on next.

The book opens, ironically, with a chapter that challenges the coherence of the concept of classical liberalism in American history. The author, Scott Shubitz (Gordon State University), argues that classical liberalism is a concept formed by Progressives and conservatives in the early 20th century in an attempt to project onto the past a narrative to justify their own political agendas. The dominant narrative of a free-market classical liberalism, Shubitz finds, is more imagined than real. Shubitz warns of the all-too-real chance that we can define the past from a platform that is too firmly situated in the present. Nineteenth-century liberals were a different lot than what we might imagine. Shubitz' presentation raises questions that we expect will not only continue to be contested among historians of classical liberalism, but that will challenge us to continue to refine the potential meanings of classical liberal history.

Lenore T. Ealy (President, The Philanthropic Enterprise) offers a reflection on some of the epistemological and methodological problems that arose with the development of classical liberal thought. These problems can be seen in the successive methodological battles in which classical liberals have found it necessary to engage both in justifying their approach to creating a science of human action and in their working out of the historical, moral, and political implications of this science. Ealy suggests that as classical liberal thought has developed into a distinct intellectual tradition that now seeks to narrate its own theory and history, its adherents have largely ignored addressing what may be the central historical puzzle that classical liberalism is challenged to solve. In failing more intentionally to address Alexis de Tocqueville's call for a new science of association as an indispensable guide to human action in the democratic age, classical liberal scholars have as yet missed the opportunity to formulate a paradigm of social and political thought capable of garnering epistemic authority that might help democratic societies become less vulnerable to the paradoxical situation through which excessive individualism generated by equality of conditions produces despotic government.

Chapters follow in a roughly chronological order, even if these contributions tend to be more thematic than chronologically focused. Phillip Magness (Berry College) takes on the New History of Capitalism school for its intellectual inconsistencies and pejorative approach to its subject, and suggests ways in which classical liberals are better armed to engage this subject on a definitional and methodological basis. Much of this new wave of literature is prescriptive, rather than descriptive. Its rejection of much of the toolbox of the economics profession, ignorance of earlier cliometric approaches, and inability to define capitalism leaves practitioners of the New History of Capitalism ill-equipped to do more than insert political presumptions in place of researched conclusions.

Anthony Gregory (PhD candidate, University of California-Berkeley) offers a provocative assessment of how classical liberals have approached the topic of civil liberties in historical research. His chapter offers, at once, a measured criticism of the mythologies that civil liberties conceptually infuse into classical liberal treatments of the past as well as a challenge to take up the topic with greater nuance. He suggests a renewed attentiveness to the messiness of a common law tradition that classical liberals often accept as a timeless principle without due scrutiny, urging scholars instead to historicize our treatment of particular civil libertarian issues of the past and present. This path urges greater engagement with past conceptualizations of race, as well as subjects that distorted—and arguably continue to distort—the theoretical conceptualization of a robust system of civil liberties.

David Beito (University of Alabama) investigates the relationship of Progressivism and Classical Liberalism in the Progressive Era and the New Deal. This period has been essential ground for informing political views of history. In the period, a transition was underway as those who feared government power gave way to those who wished to use government power to re-shape society. Classical liberalism in the Progressive Era was unable to shed a host of associated beliefs like separation of church and state and universal natural rights that seemed old-fashioned in a new forward-looking and pragmatic century. The welfare state took over from mutual-help organization, and the support for big-government solutions became entrenched in the 1930s. Beito offers the classical liberal counterfactuals, the roads not taken, which are often left out of historical accounts of the period. Historians must learn to adequately tell both sides of the controversies of the period.

Jonathan Bean (Southern Illinois University-Carbondale) argues that the historical study of civil rights deserves to incorporate the classical liberal emphasis on natural rights, individual freedom, colorblind law, constitutionalism, and market capitalism. Because the field of civil rights history is almost entirely dominated by the left, it forgets and neglects the greater classical liberal tradition that rights-language emerged from. The result is that historians over-emphasize the role that radical communists played in the civil rights movement, and "whiteness" interpretations are used to explain why workers did not organize along class lines. The forgotten aspects of civil rights history include the role of religion in attacking slavery and promoting anti-discrimination laws, the individualism that introduced right-to-work legislation, a legal structure that maintained that laws should apply equally, regardless of color, and, finally, the role of the market in undermining racism by punishing those who act on irrational prejudices. Even more importantly, classical liberals were actors, both individually and through voluntary associations that fought segregation and argued for liberal immigration policies.

Hans Eicholz (Liberty Fund) seeks to shed light on the course and development of modern social history, especially as it relates to questions of personal agency and context. All too often, modern social history has presented itself as the grand scientific alternative to intellectual and biographical narrative, and for a time, it did indeed appear that social historians would sweep the field to the exclusion of intellectual and political narratives. But, social history, as Eicholz explains, carried with it the seeds of its own destruction. When everything is socially constructed, thought and choice are dead, and to this day, the ghosts of materialism still haunt the theoretical understanding of social historians even as they now invoke phrases like discourse and meaning. This latter "linguistic turn" is however the product of a series of controversies that current social historians resolutely refuse to acknowledge: the Hobsbawm-Hartwell-Thompson debates concerning how to interpret the rise of wealth in the early Industrial Revolution in England. As Eicholz demonstrates, it was Hartwell's challenge to both that prompted the move to subjective assertions about the nature of class that have yet to be substantiated.

Sarah Skwire (Liberty Fund) adds a chapter on classical liberal feminist history. She argues that the race, class, gender paradigm does not have to be Marxist, deconstructionist, or postmodernist, but that it fits well into the empowering, liberating agenda of classical liberalism. The dominant line in feminist history sees the state as a necessary tool for the advancement of women's causes. Skwire reminds us that most of the social and economic gains women have made in the past few centuries have come from their own initiatives that lie outside of the state, and often run against state power. She then gives helpful direction for those who wish to write feminist history from the classical liberal perspective. Areas of study such as peace studies, the history of taxation, and marriage law would be good places to start. A focus on "rights," an essentially liberal theme, is essential in the history of feminism.

Leonid Krasnozhon (Loyola University New Orleans) and Mykola Bunyk (Lviv Regional Institute of Public Administration) describe how classical liberals played a vibrant role in Russia and the Ukraine, despite the reigning Marxist orthodoxy in the 20th century. The authors focus on particular neglected liberals like Mykhaylo Drahomanov, a historian who rejected the materialist dialectic of history as too simple and crude, while looking to social change to explain historical developments. They also present a history of the Ukrainian Mykhaylo Tugan-Baranovsky, who was influenced by Carl Menger's theory of marginal subjective value in his search for a way to combine socialism and the market. Krasnozhon and Bunyk provide inspiration for liberals to look to unlikely places to find their history in action.

In the penultimate chapter, Matthew Brown (University of Illinois) uses insights from Adam Smith to show how liberals might explore the history of modern economic growth. Many histories of the origins of the modern economy rely on overly stylized episodes in the historical narrative that make the story easy to tell, but untrue to history. Focusing on major labeled events, for example, leads to outcomes being confused for causes. The study of causation and origins needs to be more focused on a process-oriented understanding of both economic and social changes. And major social and economic changes such as the rise of capitalism of the "great divergence" need to be explored with the tools of both economists and social historians, when in practice they are seldom combined.

Alberto Garín (Universidad Francisco Marroquín) closes with a warning about how attempts to create common history, history ostensibly belonging to us all, are logically impossible and necessarily exclusive. First of all, Garin challenges the view that the nation is the natural container of history. Common history is also put into service of regional minority groups and political parties to define themselves against others. Garin gives advice about how to avoid generalizations, anachronisms, anecdotes, hagiography, and elite paper sources. For Garin, liberal history is the same as good history. It is scientific not in the sense that it has a body of laws, but scientific in its dedication to standards of evidence and precision of explanation. Grand, general histories are histories written at low resolution to apply broadly. High resolution historical narratives bring out the uncomfortable nuances and encourage debate as much as inclusion. Honesty, not comfort, should be the goal of history. For freedom to persist, and for free inquiry to continue, we must be honest above all.

As these chapters demonstrate, the goal of classical liberal history is the study of those events and processes which can tell us something about human nature and the development of society, so that what we learn can better inform us about how we can maximize individual and collective freedom and prosperity. The contributions in this book demonstrate some of the range of issues that interest classical liberal historians.

Classical liberal historians have defended market economies and the rights of free speech. They have warned against the failures of government intervention in the economy, highlighted individual successes, described the conditions that made the rise of private property and free exchange possible, analyzed the nature of political regimes and statecraft, recorded the historical atrocities of collectivist thinking, warned against corporate interference in the government, rejoiced in the liberation of people from slavery, serfdom, and oppression, and charted the importance of ethics in operating good business. Research on these themes is far from closed, and the arguments far from settled. There is much work left to be done. This research cannot be successful without considering liberty.

After all, what is history without liberty? For the Austrian economist, Ludwig von Mises, history literally was the story of liberty, and by definition it could be nothing else. That is to say, when we write history, we are charting free, individual choices made against the backdrop of the material world. While circumstances certainly influence action, only individuals can have the freedom to choose what action to take. In this light, culture is the free expression of free people, the sum patterns of how people have given meaning to their lives. Each moment, a moment of liberty, reveals real choices that matter. It is the task of any historian to understand that moment of freedom, that human choice. History teaches us to recognize freedom and unfreedom, to guard against tyranny and corruption. Historical narratives give us the justification of who we are and why we act in certain ways. Historical understanding is the bulwark against which evil and ignorant flail.

Now, classical liberal historians must do more than tell the story of liberty. They must also provide young scholars with the tools of analysis to become critical and creative historians. Skills such as foreign languages, the patience to interpret, the ability to make analytic connections, and above all, clear writing, are necessary. If this school of thought is to make a larger impact, it needs to build a network of classical liberal historians, with institutions and infrastructure for research and dissemination of ideas. If the historical profession is to remain relevant to the needs of individuals and societies, it must re-engage with the classical liberal tradition. It is this tradition, following in the footsteps of J. S. Mill, that recognizes open, vigorous debate as the core of healthy historical interpretation.

NOTES

1. Ludwig von Mises would add that history is literally the story of individual human actions, choices made within the confines of society and the environment. Ludwig von Mises, *Theory and History* (Yale University Press, 1957).

2. David Schmidtz and Jason Brennan, *The History of Liberty* (Wiley-Blackwell, 2010), 17.

3. Brian Doherty, *Radicals for Capitalism: A Freewheeling History of the Modern American Libertarian Movement* (New York: Public Affairs, 2007). George H. Smith, *The System of Liberty: Themes in the History of Classical Liberalism* (Cambridge Univ. Press, 2013). David Schmidtz and Jason Brennan, *A Brief History of Liberty* (Wiley-Blackwell, 2011).

4. Boas, Taylor C., and Jordan Gans-Morse. "Neoliberalism: From new liberal philosophy to anti-liberal slogan." *Studies in Comparative International Development* 44.2 (2009): 137–161.

Chapter 1

Beyond *Laissez-Faire* and State Power

A Critical Look at the Transformation Thesis and Classical Liberalism in Nineteenth-Century America

Scott Shubitz

In a 2006 article, historian William J. Novak commented upon the preoccupation with "the dramatic transformation in liberal ideology" among scholars of American political thought.[1] This transformation, noted Novak, had for decades dominated (and still dominates) the careers of many scholars. The shift, explained by Novak, was one of "classical liberalism to democratic social welfarism" and occurred between the years 1880 and 1920. At the center of this transformation was the evolution of liberal thought from a worldview devoted to limited government and the free market, to a worldview devoted to the regulatory and welfare state.[2] The origin of the "transformation thesis" and how it has obscured the development of liberal thought in the United States is the subject of this chapter.

In this chapter, I argue that "transformation thesis" misrepresents nineteenth-century American liberalism—what we commonly think of as "classical liberalism"—by not recognizing its diverse variety of advocates. In this, I argue for understanding classical liberalism as a label for many broadly related movements that addressed the problems and context of nineteenth-century America.[3] But before we can better identify what these movements had in common, we need to move beyond seeing classical liberalism as only a form of nineteenth-century free market ideology. Viewing classical liberalism this way does a huge disservice to historical actors such as protectionists, secularists, liberal religionists, and opponents and advocates of a strong state, all of whom carried the "liberal" banner at one time or another. Nineteenth-century American classical liberalism, then, should not be defined by a single cause, movement, or political agenda. Classical liberalism cannot be understood by examining Google Ngram graphs, as one scholar has recently attempted.[4] American classical liberalism of the nineteenth century was tolerant, intolerant, pragmatic, and ideological, and all at the same time. I believe that once we critically examine the transformation thesis, we will better be able to understand this diversity and draw conclusions about its character.

Before reviewing how historians and others have shaped our understanding of classical liberalism, we must first face the difficult task of defining classical liberalism. Here, I define classical liberalism as a variety of movements, unified by a constellation of ideas such as intellectual tolerance, a commitment to inquiry, and a broadly defined commitment to liberty. However, American classical liberalism is generally understood in two distinct ways. First, it is the tradition of thought associated with self-government, rationalism, and the idea of the autonomous individual that dates to at least the seventeenth century and has roots far back as Ancient Greece and Rome. Second, classical liberalism is understood as a transatlantic movement that flourished during the long nineteenth century and was focused on undermining absolutist monarchical power, established religion, and mercantilist economic systems. Historians generally suppose that this second type of classical liberalism was dead by the 1930s, but experienced a revival in the ensuing decades. Complicating our understanding of "classical liberalism," though, is that the term did not exist until at least the 1920s, when political reformers and historians began to differentiate it from the then-emergent modern political liberalism. This new liberalism was, as it is now, associated with the rise of the regulatory and welfare state.[5] This new liberalism has traditionally been understood to have evolved to answer the needs of an urban and industrial society in the years around the turn of the nineteenth century. This is important, as I believe liberalism is best defined not by an absolute, transcendent commitment to certain ideas, but by how certain broad commitments—for instance to the idea of freedom and tolerance—are manifested by individuals within specific historical contexts.

SECULARISM AND LIBERALISM (1865 TO 1910)

For the origins of classical liberalism in the United States, we must look to religion. Indeed, for most of the nineteenth century, liberalism in America was associated with liberal Christianity. The first self-identified American liberals were dissenting Congregationalists in New England who left mainstream congregationalism as part of the emerging Unitarian movement during the first decades of the century. By 1805, Congregationalism in New England was in great turmoil, as liberal theologians like James Freeman challenged traditional New England Calvinist thought, including the belief in the Trinity, predestination, and the sinful nature of man.[6] After 1805, it was increasingly clear to observers that dissenting Congregationalists wielded more power in Boston and its vicinity than they ever had before. That year, liberal theologian

Henry Ware assumed the Hollis Chair at Harvard, and with this promotion he tipped the scale of power at the school in favor of then-evolving Unitarianism. Over the course of the next decade, Unitarian-leaning Congregationalists like Andrews Norton and William Ellery Channing increasingly dominated powerful religious institutions such as leading Boston-area churches and Harvard College.[7] Orthodox Congregationalist theologians responded with a defensive stance. In 1807, they formed Andover Theological Seminary to try to counter the religious liberality associated with Unitarianism emerging at Harvard and elsewhere.[8] During the first two decades of the century, Unitarians gained the name "liberals" for their "liberality" in following Calvinist doctrine.

At the heart of the division between orthodox Congregationalists and Unitarians was the Unitarian commitment to a broad conception—or "liberal" view—of what it meant to be a Christian. Unitarians like William Ellery Channing rejected religious creeds and embraced "liberality" in religion. Channing argued that Christians should have a wide latitude in interpreting scripture. No specific idea or doctrine, apart from the divinity of Christ, was required for someone to call himself or herself a Christian. For Channing, liberality was an important part of his faith and worldview. Channing asserted that "the word liberality expressed[d] the noblest qualities of the human mind, freedom from local prejudices and narrow feelings," and the enlargement of "views and affections." Unitarians in Channing's circles accepted all who received "Jesus Christ as their Lord and Master" as Christians. This liberality also led Channing and other early Unitarians to "reject all tests or standards" or creeds of faith or character.[9] In many ways, this broad-minded approach to ideas would come to characterize and even define liberal thought for the rest of the century.

After the 1830s, some religious liberals in Channing's movement committed themselves to the abolition of slavery. Religion, it goes without saying, informed their view of abolition. Rejecting the literalism that proslavery opponents used to sanction the institution of slavery in the South, Channing pointed to the "general tenor and spirit" of the New Testament, which he believed condemned slavery. This was despite the literal sanction of the institution throughout the Old Testament.[10] Thus, in a very imperfect way, leading Boston Unitarians (but not the denomination as a whole) formed the core of the antislavery cause in Boston and its vicinity. This liberalism by the 1840s and 1850s, was rooted in religious toleration but also connected to the abolitionist movement. Because of these origins, by 1860, American liberalism was a forward-looking, tolerant worldview associated with freedom of religion, freethought, and liberty in general.[11]

By Reconstruction, liberalism had evolved along with American Unitarianism toward a secular footing. Liberals increasingly took on a commitment to open-mindedness, the free exchange of ideas, and the pursuit of knowledge. Due to this, in the decades after the Civil War, American liberalism contrasted remarkably with European liberalism. Whereas European liberalism was largely defined by free trade, limited government, and laissez-faire, American liberalism was not. American liberalism, by and large, lacked political and economic prescriptions.[12] An English observer noted how American liberalism differed from liberalism in Europe. American liberalism, the observer noted, was largely associated with secularism, rather than with the economic and political policies of British liberals—namely liberals associated with the Liberal Party. The author wrote that in England the terms "Liberal," "Liberalist," and "Liberalism," "have a politico-partisan meaning which they do not have in the United States."[13]

One of the best examples of this sort of American liberalism was the thought of former Unitarian minister Francis Ellingwood Abbot. In his influential 1873 tract the "Nine Demands of Liberalism," Abbot outlined the goals of many post–Civil War liberals.[14] He championed a secular society free from the power and influence of organized religion. Abbot also helped establish the National Liberal League, which championed secularism, fought Sabbath laws and censorship, and offered an alternative to Anthony Comstock's Christian moralism. Much like Abbot, members of freethought groups like the New York Liberal Club (active from 1869 to 1877) were dedicated to the pursuit of knowledge and the free exchange of ideas. Discussions at the New York Liberal Club, in particular, reflected a growing association between liberalism and secularism during the 1870s and 1880s.

Some liberals, including many in the New York Liberal Club, went further. Rather than simply championing a commitment to tolerance or freethought, they embraced irreligion. One American observer of liberalism in the 1880s articulated the idea of liberalism as secularism when he noted that "Liberal ideas and Christianity were not compatible."[15] Examples like this abounded during the 1870s and 1880s.[16] During the 1880s, Robert G. Ingersoll, popularly known as the "Great Agnostic," was regularly championing this conception of liberalism.[17] Historians themselves noted this connection by the 1890s. In an 1897 lecture, historian John Fiske equated "liberal thought" and "freedom of thought."[18]

While liberalism as secularism was taking root in the American mind, some liberals also expressed an interest in what we would today define as economic leftism. Liberals with the National Liberal League, the New York Liberal Club, and other groups often supported the causes of organized labor, labor reform, and government regulation of industry. These and other liberal calls for a stronger regulatory state were heard so loud that some periodicals, most notably the individualist anarchist magazine *Liberty*, associated with Benjamin Tucker and Lysander Spooner, could be found blasting liberals as enemies of freedom for their call for a more activist state.[19] But still, by the end of the century, this leftist reform–oriented nature of liberalism was only a minor part of its character, and was dwarfed by most liberals' almost single-minded commitment to secularism and free inquiry.

REVISIONISM

The years after the turn of the century initiated a period of revisionism in which the transformation thesis became established as historic fact. By the second decade of the twentieth century, scholars, historians, and others were at work reimagining America's liberal past as one defined by laissez-faire. Both people on the right and on the left of the political spectrum participated in this revisionism. Both sides of the political spectrum had the same goal in this endeavor: they embraced the transformation thesis to better legitimize their own intellectual positions. For those on the emerging progressive left, they could claim that classical liberalism was incompatible with the needs of a modern urban and industrial society. Thus, the *idea* of dramatic transformation in liberal thought made practical sense. At the same time, those on the political right championed the idea of transformation as a way of bolstering their policy initiatives and resistance to progressivism.

At first, people on the political left were more proactive in the historical revisionism of liberalism. Their work was aided by the fact that some liberals during the 1870s and 1880s had linked the terms "progressive" and "liberal" as well as "radical" and "liberal." The first major effort to reimagine the history of liberalism was launched in 1914 by journalists associated with the magazine the *New Republic*. Journalists there, led by editors Herbert Croly and Walter Lippmann, began to use the term liberal to refer to political left-ism in the United States. Croly and others in his circle, though, were primarily focused on initiating a new liberal movement rather than in exploring the complexities of America's intellectual history.

During the decade that followed Croly and Lippmann's effort to champion a new liberalism, progressive politicians associated with the Democratic Party increasingly billed themselves as liberals. By the late 1920s, Al Smith, Robert La Follette and Franklin Roosevelt referred to themselves or were labeled by others as liberals. The election of 1928 was the first election in which the term "liberal" was widely and almost universally used to refer to the reformist or "progressive" politics of the left. By this point, liberalism had entered the American vernacular to describe the distinct political and economic ideology of the American left.

At the same time, Americans on the political right were also trying to claim the liberal mantle for themselves. Those on the right identified liberalism as an ancient movement rooted in opposition to the absolute power of European monarchies and the Catholic Church. This history stretched back to before John Locke, and was championed in the eighteenth century by thinkers like Adam Smith and Frederic Bastiat. Liberalism, in this view, was tied to the ideas of limited government, individual rights, and free markets. But for revisionists on the right, liberalism now represented opposition to the abuses of the ever-growing welfare state in twentieth-century America.

In response to the work of Croly and others, some journalists and others on the right began to argue that the left had "expropriated" the term liberal and changed its "true" meaning.[20] One contributor to *The American Magazine* summoned the spirit of Gladstonian Liberalism and blasted the "grotesque" trend of rebranding liberalism to fit the agenda of the radical left.[21] Another great example of this was Albert Jay Nock, who in a 1934 unpublished article "Liberalism, Properly So Called," noted that "Liberalism is now motivated by principles exactly opposite to those which originally motivated it."[22] A year later, Samuel Orace Dunn, a journalist and railroad expert, noted that the liberalism of contemporary liberals was contrary to the spirit of liberalism.[23] For Nock, Dunn, and others like them, liberalism was associated with the ideas of limited government, free markets, and individual liberty. During the 1920s, supporters of the policies of presidents Harding, Coolidge, and then Hoover tried to reclaim the idea of liberalism for themselves. In 1922, Vice President Calvin Coolidge referred to America as leading the world in "a great Liberal movement."[24]

While Nock was working to re-establish the "proper" meaning of liberalism, the concept of "classical liberalism" began to appear in British and American journals.[25] These journals distinguished "classical liberalism" from "liberalism" by proposing that there had been a great transformation of liberal thought. In America, E. L. Godkin was one of the earliest and loudest to lament this supposed transformation. In 1900, he noted the "eclipse" of "true Liberalism" by a new liberalism that was closely aligned with socialism.[26] In the British context, this was true. The Liberalism of the Liberal Party in Britain had indeed undergone a transformation from 1890 to 1910; The rise of the "New Liberalism" eclipsed an older Liberalism championed by earlier liberals like William Gladstone. This transformation was followed by a sustained decline in the power of the Liberal Party from 1910 to 1930 as its platform increasingly mirrored the Labour Party's agenda.[27] However, Godkin—Irish by birth—was plugged into transatlantic intellectual currents and assumed that the same trends characterized American intellectual culture. The transformation thesis, then, was largely bolstered by a myopia that conflated British liberalism and American liberalism.

As a concept, classical liberalism mostly made its debut in academic and intellectual circles. Several historians in the 1930s put the narrative of classical liberalism and its transformation to print. The narrative was the one we are all familiar with: American liberalism of the nineteenth century was dedicated to limited government, laissez-faire, and individual rights. This liberalism reigned during a period of unparalleled industrial growth and urbanization and lent itself to excesses of the wealthy at the expense of the lower classes. Ultimately, classical liberalism failed because it did not offer answers to the problems of a modern industrial society, namely poverty, inequality, and the plight of industrial workers. This was, undoubtedly, a very compelling narrative for progressive historians writing during the two or three decades after the turn of the century.[28]

HISTORICAL REVISIONISM

One of the most well-known academic revisionists was the historian Vernon Parrington—noted for his (1928) 3-volume *Main Currents in American Thought.* In a 1928 letter, Parrington admitted to purposefully "warping" the term liberal to give it political and social meaning that it did not have before. He purposefully sought to associate it with "radical" politics. He did this through the simple substitution of words in his *Main Currents.* In the first draft of his *Main Currents* Parrington had used the word "radical" throughout the text to describe left-wing political movements. However, on his next draft, he substituted "radical" for "liberal."[29] The impact of this was substantial; Parrington's work served as the foundation for two generations of historians on the left who sought to define liberalism as a leftist movement in the context of a modern industrial society.[30]

By the end of the 1930s, Parrington's narrative was firmly entrenched in the historical imagination. A decade of New Deal liberalism and the left's embrace of the term now married "liberalism" to the idea of the regulatory state and the emerging welfare state. Progressive historians during the 1930s propagated this concept in myriad of works. Harold U. Faulkner's 1931 book *The Quest for Social Justice, 1898–1914,* for example, argued that around the turn of the century reformers around the nation took a new approach toward government, switched gears, and embraced social reform and the idea of social justice.[31] In 1937, Walter Lippmann, champion of reformist liberalism and a founding editor at the *New Republic*, published his *The Good Society*, in which he promoted the transformation thesis and set the date for the transformation of liberal thought around 1870.[32]

In 1939, Louis Filler further developed the narrative of the transformation of classical liberalism to modern liberalism. In his, *Crusaders for American Liberalism*, Filler offered the typical conflict-driven progressive narrative.[33] Filler's liberals were moved, emotionally, in the face of the social inequities

of the late nineteenth and early twentieth centuries. With "the rise of Theodore Roosevelt," these liberals, who had earlier embraced some of the older
classical liberal ideas of their parents, gave themselves over to the movement
for social reform; Filler's liberals became muckrakers. Emboldened by moral
courage and outraged by inequity, the first twentieth-century liberals broke
with the old laissez-faire liberalism of the nineteenth century and pioneered
a new liberalism.[34]

During the postwar period, historians of all ideologies and political persuasions continued to promote the transformation thesis.[35] Historians of
the postwar period, driven by a quest for unity and consensus in the face
of cold war–related anxiety, put the progressive's narrative to a new use. A
classic example of the application of the transformation thesis was Richard
Hofstadter's 1948 *The American Political Tradition*.[36] In his book, Hofstadter
argued that American political thought was built on the shared "belief in the
rights of property, the philosophy of economic individualism, the value of
competition" and to an extent, the virtues of capitalism. These ideas, per Hofstadter, characterized "the central faith" of the American political tradition.[37]
But Hofstadter and other historians of the postwar era altered the progressive's account of the history of American liberalism. For Hofstadter and others during the period, the transformation of liberalism in the years following
1900 was more about solving problems and uniting American society than
about conflict with the champions of laissez-faire. The new liberals merely
sought to meet the demands of an emerging urban and industrial society, and
sometimes, they were acting out of simple status anxiety.[38]

In the hyper-paranoid, anti-Communist, climate of 1950s America, classical liberalism was defined as everything anathema to the Soviet Union. While
classical liberalism was antiquated and did not answer the needs of a modern
industrial and urban people, it did demonstrate the American commitment to
freedom. Louis Hartz's 1955 *The Liberal Tradition in America*, is perhaps
the most iconic academic work of this period to immortalize the narrative of
transformation. For Hartz, American society was a liberal society universally
devoted to individualism, freedom, equality, and capitalism. Hartz argued that
due to the absence of feudal and aristocratic institutions, the liberal tradition
dominated American politics. In his 1955 *The Decline of American Liberalism*,
historian Paul Ekirch echoed a similar note, but enshrined the old liberalism—
classical liberalism—as an idea responsible for American freedom and prosperity. Ekirch, unlike Hartz and most of his contemporaries, mourned the decline
of classical liberalism and saw its demise as one ushering in a period where
American liberty and freedom were under attack.[39] In many ways, Ekirch's
book is one of the clearest and simplest examples of the transformation thesis.

By the early 1960s, historians, like those two decades before, continued
to echo the idea of a dramatic transformation in liberal thought at the turn

of the century. One of these was Charles Forcey, who in 1961 published his *The Crossroads of Liberalism.* Forcey again reinforced the notion that nineteenth-century liberalism—classical liberalism—was characterized by a commitment to "individual rights and laissez faire." For Forcey, it was in the second decade of the century that the old liberalism gave way to a new liberalism. This new liberalism was committed to "the conviction that only the conscious, co-operative use of governmental power can bring reform."[40] Forcey, though, focused on the actual moment of the transformation from the old to the new liberalism. For Forcey, writers at the *New Republic*—Herbert Croly, Walter Lippman and Walter Weyl—were instrumental in the development of American liberalism. Croly and his associates not only abandoned old liberal ideas and helped develop new liberal ideas but they also shared and promoted those ideas and influenced presidents Roosevelt and Wilson. Fundamentally, the transformation of liberalism, in Forcey's view, was a highly intellectual endeavor.[41]

The rise of the New Left during the 1960s compounded earlier trends, but initiated a new period of revisionism that began to push reformist liberalism back beyond the turn of the century. During the 1960s, the main example of this was the framing of the abolitionist movement as a parallel to the modern civil rights movement. Ronald G. Walters has noted that "in the 1960s in particular there were numerous books and articles point out parallels between the anti-slavery movement and the civil rights struggles of the 1950s and 1960s." James McPherson's 1964 *The Struggle for Equality*, perhaps most exemplified this trend. In his book, McPherson argued that abolitionists continued their work after emancipation but shifted their efforts to African American civil rights. McPherson expanded upon his argument in his *The Abolitionist Legacy*, in which he showed that abolitionists, and their descendants, furthered their fight for equal rights into the twentieth century with the founding of the National Association for the Advancement of Colored People.[42] Later studies on abolitionism, like Lawrence J. Friedman's 1982 *Gregarious Saints: Self and Community in American Abolitionism,* echoed this focus on civil rights and political equality championed by historians during the 1960s.[43] At the same time, other historians, like Joyce Appleby, explored the roots of liberalism and its association with capitalism in seventeenth-century Western Europe.

LIBERTARIANISM

While liberal historians searched deeper into the nineteenth century for modern liberalism's origins, a new wave of classical liberal scholarship, associated with the emerging libertarian movement during the 1970s, sought to "rediscover" nineteenth-century America's classical liberal history. This

wave of scholarship was driven not by historians, but by economists seeking to ground their work in the historical record. In his 1962 *Capitalism and
Freedom*, Milton Friedman echoed the transformation thesis, noting that
"Beginning in the nineteenth century, and especially after 1930 in the United
States, the term liberalism came to be associated with" the "readiness to rely
primarily on the state rather than on private voluntary arrangements." Freedmen,
like earlier scholars, was pushed by his conflation of American and English
intellectual history as well as historical revisionism to embrace the transformation thesis.[44] Partially due to late twentieth-century liberal historians' use
and treatment of the abolitionists and other mid-to-late nineteenth-century
liberals, these scholars (the few that there were by the 1970s and 1980s) went
in search of oft-neglected liberal heroes for their movement. Libertarian historians after the 1970s, who sometimes donned the label of classical liberal,
began to focus on radical reformers like Lysander Spooner, Josiah Warren,
Ezra Heywood, and Benjamin Tucker. These radicals were, unlike their more
pragmatic liberal contemporaries, more ideologically driven and committed
to anarcho-individualism.

This new wave of scholarship added to the legitimization of the old narrative originally put forth by revisionists at the turn of the century. But as
the narrative of nineteenth-century liberalism served the political ambitions
of progressive historians half a century before, it also served the politics of
classical liberal historians or libertarians in the 1970s and after. Libertarians
embraced this narrative to anchor their ideology in the mythos of a classical
liberal tradition in America. In the end, though, classical liberal scholars, just
as the progressive historians had done half a century before, diminished the
contributions of religious liberals and liberalism's religious roots during the
nineteenth century.

Another movement in the academe during the 1970s and after further influenced scholars to conflate British and American liberalism in the nineteenth
century. Robert Kelley's 1969 *The Transatlantic Persuasion: The Liberal-
Democratic Mind in the Age of Gladstone,* initiated a movement in which
historians focused more on transatlantic intellectual exchange. Kelley argued
that Canada, Great Britain, and the United States "constitute a continuing
community with common life and therefore a common history." And this he
did, by arguing that all three nations shared an inherited worldview, which
included the thought of Adam Smith, among others. Other historians followed Kelley's transatlantic approach. According to James T. Kloppenburg,
American progressives and their European counterparts rejected the "atom-
istic empiricism, psychological hedonism, and utilitarian ethics associated
with nineteenth-century liberalism." In the United States, men like Herbert
Croly, Walter Lippmann, and John Dewey, like their European counterparts,
jettisoned old ideas that were "no longer useful," transformed liberal theory

into progressive theory, and "turned the old liberalism into a new liberalism." These men helped to ultimately transform liberalism from what we now know as classical liberalism to modern reformist liberalism.[45] Kloppenburg also recognized that there were important differences and distinctions between progressive reform movements from nation-to-nation. In his *Atlantic Crossings: Social Politics in a Progressive Age*, Daniel Rodgers has also contributed immensely to the idea that the transatlantic exchange of ideas helped influence the development of American political thought. While these studies of the transatlantic character of liberalism certainly provide us with much insight about the Atlantic World's intellectual history, they hold problems in that they reinforce the problem of transposing the history of liberal thought in Europe on America. They focus on a handful of elites—outliers I would call them—like E. L. Godkin who were proponents of British liberalism in the United States. While British and/or European liberalism certainly influenced American liberals and liberalism during the nineteenth century, focusing on it blinds us to the unique character of American liberalism—one that was much less political and even ideological in nature. In short, the transatlantic or global perspective makes it harder to spot nuance and difference between American liberalism and its European counterpart(s).

By the 1990s and 2000s, historians began to challenge at least part of the narrative of liberal history initiated around the turn of the century. Newer work has suggested a more gradual transition from classical liberalism to modern (progressive) liberal thought. This work has also undermined the myth of laissez-faire hegemony.[46] Historians have looked to late nineteenth-century America—the once unquestioned territory of laissez-faire liberalism—for the roots of modern reformist liberalism. One of the best examples of this is Elizabeth Sanders' *Roots of Reform: Farmers, Workers, and the American State, 1877–1917* (1999). In *Roots of Reform* Sanders argues that late nineteenth-century American agrarian movements were central to shaping the reform movements that came later. She argues that rather than being dedicated to the ideology of individualism, populists were firm believers in state solutions to economic and social problems.

Others have also looked back to this earlier period for the roots of reformist liberalism. In Gill J. Harp's *Positivist Republic: August Comte and the Reconstruction of American Liberalism, 1865–1920* (1995), Harp argues that the ideas of August Comte made a substantial impact on the thinking of key individuals, including Lester Ward and Herbert Croly, who would go on to influence modern reformist liberalism. David Greenstone also looked back to the post–Civil War period. In his *The Lincoln Persuasion: Remaking American Liberalism* (1993), Greenstone argued that modern liberalism emerged from the fires of the American Civil War and represented the union of two conflicting types of liberal thought. Most recently, in her

The Reconstruction of American Liberalism, 1865–1914, Nancy Cohen has argued that the post–Civil War period brought the issue of the conflict between democracy and corporate capitalism front and center. This conflict challenged liberals to re-examine their ideas and to find ways to maintain previous values (private property and individual liberty). Postwar liberals grappled with these problems and soon embraced new ways to reconcile corporate capitalism and democracy. They did this by discovering a new, larger, role for the state in society—the regulatory state. Recent treatments of the questions surrounding classical liberalism and liberalism have been helpful in understanding the idea of liberalism. Newer interpretations have also challenged the idea that reformist liberalism appeared suddenly out of the darkness of a laissez-faire "classical" liberal landscape. This is constructive, but most of these interpretations still take the narrative of transformation for granted.

CONCLUSION

Historians of classical liberalism should do three important things to move this historiography forward. First, they should more critically examine the transformation thesis. At the center of this project is the question of the idea of laissez-faire dominance of nineteenth-century American liberal thought. Second, they need to measure their enthusiasm for transatlantic intellectual history and avoid letting it overshadow the unique characters of liberal thought on both sides of the Atlantic. While we can speak of transatlantic liberalism during the century—and the importance of actors like E. L. Godkin in spreading it—we should avoid speaking of a coherent movement, as this suggests that actors in different countries shared a specific platform and had nearly identical visions.[47] Importantly, when we focus on men like Godkin, we ignore those like Francis Ellingwood Abbot—perhaps one of the best representatives of American liberal thought during the 1870s. Third, historians of classical liberalism should cast a wider net for liberals and move beyond the circumscribed group that classical liberal historians of the 1970s focused on. While Lysander Spooner, Benajmin Tucker, and their kind are fascinating characters, they, arguably, do not define mainstream American liberal thought during the late nineteenth century. Finally, these points reinforce how classical liberal historians need to move beyond a focus on economics and consider the compelling work of historians of American religion.

Ultimately, the career of the concept of classical liberalism is an interesting and complex one. By imagining the idea of classical liberalism as a grand intellectual tradition that cuts across time and space and includes figures as diverse as John Locke and Ludwig von Mises, scholars have helped us better organize the way we think about the past. However, while constructing the past and embracing ideas like the transformation thesis, we've forgotten how historical actors viewed liberal thought during their own time. Thus, we've lost our understanding of the true dynamism of nineteenth-century American liberalism. By taking a critical eye toward the transformation thesis, we will see that nineteenth-century American liberalism—classical liberalism—was a truly diverse intellectual phenomenon. By doing this, we also empower historical actors who saw themselves as liberal but have been left out of narratives of liberal thought. In the end, though, this is not easy as we're left with a much less convenient view of classical liberalism—a view that does not rubberstamp our ideological viewpoints. What we gain, however, in terms of a more dynamic and challenging view of the past, may inspire us to pose new and truly innovative research questions.

NOTES

1. Portions of this chapter were originally published as Scott M. Shubitz, "Liberal Intellectual Culture and Religious Faith: The Liberalism of the New York Liberal Club, 1869–1877," *The Journal of the Gilded Age and Progressive Era* 16, no. 2 (April 2017): 183–205.

2. William J. Novak, "The Not-So-Strange Birth of the Modern American State: A Comment on James A. Henretta's 'Charles Evan Hughes and the Strange Death of Liberal America,'" *Law and History Review* 24, no. 1 (Spring 2006), 193–199.

3. I urge us to critically examine interpretations like that of Ralph Raico, who argues for the existence of only a single liberalism dedicated to private property and free markets, and who, seemingly rejects the idea of classical liberalism outright and the validity of modern liberalism. Ralph Raico, *Classical Liberalism and the Austrian School* (Auburn, AL: Ludwig von Mises Institute, 2012), 1.

4. Daniel B. Klein, "A Plea Regarding 'Liberal,'" *Modern Age* 57, no. 3 (Summer 2015): 7–16.

5. For more, see: Alan Brinkley, "The Late New Deal and the Idea of the State," in *Liberalism and Its Discontents* by Alan Brinkley (Cambridge: Harvard University Press, 2000), 37–62.

6. Unitarians levied their challenge to Calvinism from two places. While one group, predominantly English in character and best represented by dissenter Joseph Priestly (but included James Freeman) was theologically Socinian, the other group which was based in New England was theologically Arian. Socinianism rejected the doctrine of the Trinity, the divinity of Christ, and the concept of predestination. Arians rejected the Trinity and believed that the son of God, Jesus, was subordinate to God. Ultimately, the largest difference between the two was belief in the divinity of Christ. Peter Tufts Richardson, *The Boston Religion: Unitarianism in its Capital City* (Rockland, ME: Red Barn Publishing, 2003), 3.

7. David Robinson, ed. *William Ellery Channing: Selected Writings* (New York: Paulist Press, 1985), 39.

8. John Fletcher Hurst, *History of Rationalism: Embracing a Survey of the Present State of Protestant Theology* (New York: C. Scribner and Co., 1865): 539–541.

9. Robinson, ed. *William Ellery Channing: Selected Writings*, 62–63.

10. E. Brooks Holifield, *Theology in America: Christian Thought from the Age of the Puritans to the Civil War* (New Haven: Yale University Press, 2003), 497–498.

11. Amy Kittelstrom has recently written on this theme. See: Amy Kittelstrom, *The Religion of Democracy: Seven Liberals and the American Moral Tradition* (New York: Penguin Books, 2016).

12. There were several exceptions, though. The Liberal Republican Party of the early 1870s is perhaps the best well known. The party emerged in 1870 as an alternative to what was widely believed to be a corrupt Republican Party. In the Liberal Republican Party, some Northern Democrats, disenchanted Republicans, and others united to offer an alternative to the incumbent Grant in 1872. However, despite its name, the Liberal Republican Party bore limited resemblance to either British liberalism at the time or what we remember as classical liberalism. For more on the Liberal Republican Party, see: Andrew L. Slap, *The Doom of Reconstruction: The Liberal Republicans in the Civil War Era* (New York: Fordham University Press, 2006).

13. "Liberalism," *The Humanitarian Review* VI, no. 1 (January 1903): 210.

14. Francis Ellingwood Abbot, "The Nine Demands of Liberalism," *The Index* (April 1872), 1.

15. *Truth Seeker*, February 1, 1875.

16. *The Proceedings and Addresses at the Freethinkers' Convention Held at Watkins, New York, August 22nd, 23rd, 24th, and 25th, 1878* (New York: D.M. Bennett, 1878), 203–206. *Humanitarian Review* 6, no. 1 (January 1903): 210.

17. *Secular Thought*, January 8, 1887.

18. *New York Times*, February 9, 1897.

19. Kelly B. Gertrude, "The 'Liberal' Love of Government," *Liberty (Not the Daughter but the Mother of Order)* 3, 23 (February 1886), 1. "Liberals and Liberty," *Liberty (Not the Daughter but the Mother of Order)*, 2, 2 (October 1882), 2. "Do Liberals Know Themselves?" *Liberty (Not the Daughter but the Mother of Order)*, 1, 14 (February 1882), 2.

20. I have several articles that support this assertion. See Harold Stearns liberalism in America for proof of old type of liberalism.

21. "The Interpreter's House," *The American Magazine* 73, no. 5 (1912): 635–640.

22. Albert Jay Nock, "Liberalism, Properly So Called," in *The State of the Union: Essays in Social Criticism* by Albert Jay Nock (Indianapolis, IN: Liberty Fund, 1991), 276–284.

23. Samuel O. Dunn, "Modified Laissez Faire," *The Annals of the American Academy of Political and Social Science* 178, (March 1935): 142–147.

24. "Our Poise Regained, Declares Coolidge," *The New York Times*, January 17, 1922, 3.

25. F.A. Hayek, "Planning Away Our Liberty: From the Contemporary Review London Topical Monthly," *The Living Age* (June 1938): 290. "Liberals in Decay,"

The New York Times, April 28, 1922. "Are There Any More Liberals?" *The Youth's Companion* 98, 35 (August 28, 1924): 572.

26. E.L. Godkin, "The Eclipse of Liberalism," *The Nation* (August 1900): 105.

27. William Clarke, "The Decline of English Liberalism," *Political Science Quarterly* 16, no. 3 (September 1901), 450. For more on this process, see Michael Freeden, *The New Liberalism: An Ideology of Social Reform* (London: Oxford University Press, 1986) and J. A. Thompson, "The Historians and the Decline of the Liberal Party," *Albion: A Quarterly Journal Concerned with British Studies* 22, no. 1 (Spring 1990): 65–83.

28. Faulkner uses the terms about nine times; he uses them to describe religious liberalism nearly as much as political liberalism. In his *Decline of Laissez Faire, 1897–1917*, however, notably, Faulkner rarely referred to the terms "liberal" and "liberalism."

29. David W. Levy, "'I Become More Radical with Every Year': The Intellectual Odyssey of Vernon Parrington," *Reviews in American History* 23, no. 4 (December 1995), 667.

30. Parrington's *Main Currents* influenced the following generation of American intellectual historians and was cited by Richard Hofstadter, Clinton Rossiter, Hannah Arendt, and many more. Parrington's Main Currents won the Pulitzer Prize for history. Robert Skotheim and Kermit Vanderbilt called Parrington's *Main Currents* "one of the notable events in the writing of American history of ideas." Charles Beard and Stanley Williams lauded the importance of *Main Currents*. For more on the importance of *Main Currents*, see Robert A. Skotheim and Kermit Vanderbilt, "The Mind and Art of a Historian of Ideas," *The Pacific Northwest Quarterly* 53, no. 3 (July 1962): 100–113.

31. Notably, Faulkner rarely referred to the terms "liberal" and "liberalism." This perhaps owed to the fact that during the mid-1920s, historians and others were just then beginning to employ the term liberal to describe America's political tradition. Faulkner uses the terms about nine times; he uses them to describe religious liberalism nearly as much as political liberalism.

32. Walter Lippmann, *The Good Society* (Boston: Little, Brown & Company, 1937). Also see: Frank H. Knight, "Lippmann's *The Good Society*," *Journal of Political Economy* 46, no. 6 (December 1938): 864–872.

33. Taught at Antioch College—Institution dominated by Unitarians.

34. One of the best examples of this narrative was offered by British politician and sociologist Leonard Trelawny Hobhouse in his 1911 book *Liberalism*. Hobhouse was an advocate of the new reformist approach to liberalism. Needless to say, Hobhouse was writing from a British perspective, and his views do not necessarily represent American thought in its complexity.

35. Sidney Fine, *Laissez Faire and the General Welfare State* (Ann Arbor: The University of Michigan Press, 1956), 126.

36. Some have criticized the idea that Hoftstadter should be defined by consensus. See: Daniel Joseph Singal, "Beyond Consensus: Richard Hofstadter and American Historiography," *The American Historical Review* 89, no. 4 (October 1984), 976–1004.

37. Louis Hartz, *The Liberal Tradition in America: An Interpretation of American Political Thought Since the Revolution* (New York: Harcourt, Brace & Company), 3–15.

38. Richard Hofstadter, *Age of Reform: From Bryan to F.D.R.* (New York: Vintage Books, 1955).

39. Arthur A, Ekirch, Jr., *The Decline of American Liberalism* (London, Longmans, Green and Company, 1955).

40. Charles Forcey, *The Crossroads of Liberalism: Croly, Weyl, Lippmann, and the Progressive Era, 1900–1925* (New York: Oxford University Press, 1961), xiii–xiv.

41. Others have continued to explore Forcey's thesis. Edward A. Stettner's *Shaping Modern Liberalism: Herbert Croly and Progressive Thought* and a slew of other books have since focused on the second decade of the twentieth century as the moment in time that gave birth to modern American reformist liberalism. However, both Forcey and Stettner adhere to the narrative of a "transformation" in liberal thought—something that upholds the idea that nineteenth-century liberalism was classical liberalism and was defined can be singly defined by a commitment to laissez-faire.

42. James M. McPherson, *The Struggle for Equality: Abolitionists and the Negro in the Civil War and Reconstruction* (Princeton: Princeton University Press, 1964), James M. McPherson, *The Abolitionist Legacy: From Reconstruction to the NAACP* (Princeton: Princeton University Press, 1975), and Ronald G. Walters, *The Antislavery Appeal: American Abolitionism after 1830* (Baltimore: Johns Hopkins University Press, 1976), 146. Also see: Howard Zinn, "Abolitionists, Freedom Riders, and the Tactics of Agitation," in *The Antislavery Vanguard: New Essays on the Abolitionists*, ed. Martin Duberman (Princeton University Press, 1965), 417–451, Staughton Lynd, *Intellectual Origins of American Radicalism* (New York, 1968), Aileen S. Kraditor, *Means and Ends in American Abolitionism: Garrison and His Critics on Strategy and Tactics, 1834–1850* (New York, 1967), Bertram Wyatt-Brown, "The New Left and the Abolitionists: Romantic Radicalism in America," *Soundings* 44 (R1971): 147–163, Bertram Wyatt-Brown, "New Leftists and Abolitionists: A Comparison of American Radical Styles," *Wisconsin Magazine of History* 53 (Summer 1970): 256–268, Lawrence J. Friedman, "Antislavery Utilitarianism: A New Perspective," *Reviews in American History* 16, no. 1 (March 1988): 29–30, and Louis S. Gerteis, *Morality and Utility in American Antislavery Reform* (Chapel Hill: University of North Carolina Press, 1987).

43. Lawrence J. Friedman, *Gregarious Saints: Self and Community in American Abolitionism, 1830–1870* (Cambridge University Press, 1982).

44. Milton Friedman, *Capitalism and Freedom* (Chicago: University of Chicago Press, 1962), 4–6.

45. James T. Kloppenberg, *Uncertain Victory: Social Democracy and Progressivism in European and American Thought, 1870–1920* (New York: Oxford University Press, 1986), 298–299.

46. William Novak, *The People's Welfare: Law and Regulation in Nineteenth Century America* (Chapel Hill: University of North Carolina Press, 1996).

Chapter 2

Classical Liberalism and the "New" History of American Capitalism

Phillip W. Magness

Over half a century has passed since F. A. Hayek called attention to an "emotional aversion to 'capitalism'" within the history profession. He traced this criticism to a persistent belief that the industrial-competitive mechanisms of the modern era reached a sustained and unprecedented state of economic expansion at the expense of society's weakest members. If the economic enrichment since the Industrial Revolution was achieved on the backs of the poor, the economically ravaged, and the exploited, it is but a short step to brush aside the empirically attested abundance of "capitalism" as a tainted good. Both then and now, such zero-sum thinking depends upon an almost intentional myopia that constructs its evidence selectively to fit its already-accepted diagnosis of capitalism's ills. Yet its persistence constitutes the "one supreme myth which more than any other has served to discredit the economic system to which we owe our present-day civilization."[1] Perceptions of the past—including mistaken ones—are a heavy epistemic weight upon policy decisions in the present.

Simultaneously alarming and prescient, Hayek's description still rings true on many counts. Inequality in particular retains a persistent place in historical treatments of economic events, including a tendency to view the allocation of society's wealth as an end onto itself, or as a destabilizing causal mechanism behind a multitude of other social ills, as opposed to a measurement of other factors of growth and fiscal policy. While the topic is itself unobjectionable and even a necessary tool for assessing the distributional effects of economic outcomes, the historical study of inequality is almost always paired with prescriptive political arguments for redistributive policymaking or vindications of past examples of the same.[2]

The history profession's attention shifted away from economic history in the second half of the 20th century, ceding this turf to an increasingly quantitative economic history subfield housed in economics departments. Mainstream historical interest in economic matters resurged with a vengeance following the financial crisis of 2008. The product is a loosely defined assemblage of economically themed research, sometimes referred to as the "New History of Capitalism" (NHC).[3] Although branded with the moniker "new," a number of its defining elements are not all that novel. While it would be a mistake to attribute ideological uniformity to this growing subfield, the core characteristics of Hayek's half-century-old diagnosis are abundant in this recent body of literature. Several leading works of NHC scholarship approach "capitalism" as a cohesive societal order or system, and an eminently blameworthy one at that. Themes of physical expropriation, distributional inequality, labor mistreatment, and economic exploitation linger in the background of much of this work, and—perhaps above all other concerns—attempts to causally link slavery to the emergence of a capitalist economic "system" are particularly strong.

In so doing, the distinctive feature of the NHC genre is not actually its claimed revival of a neglected set of topics that never really left the discussion. Historians have long studied questions of economic inequality and distribution, and the socioeconomic dimensions of slavery have been a preeminent focus of historical attention for decades. Rather, what distinguishes recent works under the NHC moniker is their aggressive embrace of what Hayek diagnosed over half a century ago as a latent bias of academic historians. In attempting to study "capitalism," these works often begin from aggressively anti-capitalistic priors and peddle in the practice of infusing their authors' own ideological distastes for "capitalism," often broadly construed yet poorly defined, to long-familiar topics of historical study.

The tensions between NHC and classical liberalism are numerous and warrant consideration in detail, though one general development since Hayek's time suggests that capitalism's defenders enjoy an improved scholarly position in the present day even as the growth of the NHC movement portends invigorated hostilities. The intervening decades have yielded a vibrant scholarly literature on what Deirdre McCloskey has termed the "Great Enrichment"—the historically unparalleled expansion in the wealth and well-being of ordinary human lives that has occurred since roughly 1800. The attributed causes of this process are multifaceted and sometimes in tension with each other, though its major characteristics are situated somewhere between an emerging ethical and cultural valuation of economic production in the late 18th century, the existence of favorable legal and institutional characteristics, the improved access to and dissemination of requisite knowledge for productive processes, and the broader influence of the enlightenment upon the intellectual environment of the early industrial revolution.[4] Each offers a plausible interpretation of what might be called a capitalist age, for lack of a better term, rejecting the zero-sum disposition of recent NHC contributions and calling our attention to its empirically undeniable abundance.

A distinctive characteristic of the history of the "Great Enrichment" is its natural interaction with a number of classical liberal insights, particularly from economics. Its story rests upon an empirical observation of rapidly improved human well-being and attempts to discern its causal mechanisms not from any narrative plan or singular ideology, but through spontaneously organized exchange in a favorable cultural and institutional environment. Its story is not premised upon an idealized conception of "capitalism" or the denial of historical experiences in its wake, injustices among them, but rather the humility to ask whether such a diverse array of events can be legitimately ascribed to a single system.

Capitalism was not proclaimed, adopted, imposed, or arrived at as a moment in time. In the classical liberal sense, capitalism simply refers to a set of conditions and circumstances that are favorable to voluntary human inter-actions and that are distinguished by their absence of a centralized design. It describes a number of attributes in an economy—a freedom in the exchange and movement of goods and people, a general recognition of the validity of private property and a stable and discernable system of contracts built upon it, a cultural environment of toleration for choice and celebration of discovery, and a worldview that—at least in its professed values—deprecates forceful predation, whether by other economic actors or the power of the nation-state. A classical liberal history of capitalism is therefore a history of the conditions that permit free exchange and discovery, and with them the witnessed results of the past two hundred years.

The divergence between this conceptualization and the emerging NHC literature is profound. It presents two distinctive stories: a classical liberal capitalism as a descriptive term for spontaneously ordering interactions of the past, and an ideological capitalism that quite literally serves as a light-ning rod for faults and blame in interpreting the past's many ills. What fol-lows in this discussion is a brief examination of some of the main features and themes of the NHC literature and its tensions with the former classical liberal conceptualization. What this framing portends for the historical discussion of capitalism remains to be seen, and will likely attract much scholarly attention in the coming years. As this discussion will highlight, many of the differences between the two approaches stem from a disciplin-ary divide between historians and economists. One consequence of this divide may be seen in a number of profound methodological and defini-tional imprecisions afflicting the recent NHC genre, setting up the condi-tions in which strong ideological priors have become a primary motive for this line of research.

BETWEEN DIVERGENT PATHS

The study of history in the latter part of the 20th century was distinguished
by a methodological divide between an older approach rooted in evidentiary
empiricism and an emergent attention to social history, and particularly that
of group identities on racial, class, and gender lines. Few subfields were more
directly affected by this divide than economic history. Once an interdisciplin-
ary domain that attracted collaborative conversations between economists
and historians, the subfield was largely swept up in the "cliometric revolution" that took hold in the early 1960s. In some sense an extreme form of
quantitative empiricism in its own right, the cliometric approach saw the
emerging tools of statistics, econometrics, and economic modeling applied
to historical analysis. Social history in turn pulled the attention of many
traditional historians away from an ever-specialized discussion of economic
matters, albeit with occasional forays on a topic-by-topic basis. Slavery was
one such example where the methodological pathways between economics
and historians diverged sharply.[5]

Some of the earliest cliometric work applied heavy data analysis to the
ever-topical question of slavery's economics, and particularly its profitability. The economic theories of a century prior had conventionally asserted an
intuitive tension between slavery and capitalism premised on free labor. In
addition to its moral dimensions, slavery removed the economic incentive of
the slave to better his product and introduced a number of inefficiencies to its
productive processes—particularly those measured in lost opportunity.[6] The
empirical investigation of slavery's profitability in the second half of the 20th
century shifted this discussion. While the new empirical literature did not
establish slavery's immunity from the economic inefficiencies with which it
had been charged, and sometimes punted on this question entirely, it did show
the economic viability of plantation production in the late antebellum. The
economists, it seems, had uncovered a reason in profitability that explained
slavery's persistence. The evidence, at least on that point, ran counter to a
somewhat wishful 19th-century belief among some abolition-minded economists that the plantation system, if left to its own devices, would be outcom-
peted and die a natural death.

In a sense, the study of the economic dimensions of slavery is a micro-
cosm for the subsequent compartmentalization of economic history onto
divergent trajectories.[7] The cliometric end of this genre peaked with Robert
Fogel and Stanley Engerman's landmark *Time on the Cross* in 1973, notable
for the outpouring of respondents it provoked among historians and economists alike as well as its controversial but data-driven substantiation of the
plantation system's profitability. This last point instigated something of a sea
change in economic history, as it ran counter to both elements of an existing

historical literature on slavery and the aforementioned conventional assumptions of economic thought about slave labor in the 19th century. Curiously, the ensuing debate over slavery's profitability—and with it an oft-implied but sometimes contested claim of slavery's economic efficiency—was never quite settled, though conflicting claims of victory persist among the cliometric economists and traditional historians alike.[8]

It is likely no coincidence that the slave economy is a central focus of NHC scholarship.[9] The causal relationships implied by much of this literature are remarkably fluid, such that capitalism is simultaneously an enabling prerequisite of large-scale (and race-based) plantation slavery, as distinct from the ancient world institution, as well as its most visible beneficiary—an economic system propelled to modernity upon the backs of the slaves. In either case, many NHC scholars advance a politically tinged subtext that effectively saddles capitalism with both cause and credit for slavery's economic output and therefore, by implication, its moral price tag.

The themes of these contributions differ somewhat, with emphases that range from tracing the global reach and economic uses of plantation-derived products to the specific labor practices that were deployed to extract production from enslaved persons. The method of analysis is largely rooted in social observation and an archive-sustained story. Market-wide data interpretation takes a back seat to multi-method narrative. At its best, historical work of this type teases observations about slavery's production from the stories of individual plantations and shippers, the testimonies of former slaves where they exist, and the descriptive indicators of life on the plantation. The economic reach of slavery's output and other plantation-linked activities in shipping, finance, and production thus become the evidence of slavery's own centrality to the economic system in which it operated.

Despite methodological differences in assembling its evidence and interpreting its findings, a recurring feature of the NHC literature is that it arrives at one strikingly similar position as the economists. Both largely agree on slavery's profitability.[10] And both advance a rejection of at least the simplified forms of the older classical economic—and, to some degree, classical liberal—conclusion that slavery was unsuited for industrial capitalism on account of its comparative inefficiency to free labor.

It is all the more curious that several primary works of the NHC literature in the last five years appear to be only nominally aware of, or at least inattentive to, the discussions surrounding older cliometric and derivative economic investigations of the same topic, even where they drifted into the debates of the mainstream history profession in the 1970s and 1980s.

To the contrary, much of the NHC work on slavery seems to be enamored with its own claims of novelty—of telling a "never told" story that has in fact appeared many times before, and that even bears a striking resemblance to the old "King Cotton" arguments that were advanced by proslavery radicals and Confederate nationalists in the 19th century. Consider the following excerpt from an 1856 tract:

> Slavery is not an isolated system, but is so mingled with the business of the world, that it derives facilities from the most innocent transactions. Capital and labor, in Europe and America, are largely employed in the manufacture of cotton. These goods, to a great extent, may be seen freighting every vessel, from Christian nations, that traverses the seas of the globe; and filling the warehouses and shelves of the merchants over two-thirds of the world. By the industry, skill, and enterprise employed in the manufacture of cotton, mankind are better clothed; their comfort better promoted; general industry more highly stimulated; commerce more widely extended; and civilization more rapidly advanced than in any preceding age.[11]

But for slight idiosyncrasies of tone and terminology, this cotton-centric accounting of global political economy at the middle of the 19th century could be mistaken for the primary arguments of NHC historians Sven Beckert and Edward Baptist. Beckert, for example, describes a cotton-centric "war capitalism" that extends its reach into "insurance, finance, and shipping" as well as "public institutions such as government credit, money itself, and national defense." Baptist depicts a cotton-driven economic empire where slavery's reach encompasses everything from shipping, to "insurance and interest paid on commercial credit," to the "purchase of land, the cost of credit for such purchases, the pork and the corn bought at the river landings," to "money spent by millworkers and Illinois hog farmers, the wages paid to steamboat workers, and the revenues yielded by investments made with the profits of the merchants, manufacturers, and slave traders who derived some or all of their income either directly or indirectly from the southwestern fields" to the clothing and toolmakers who supplied the plantations to, of course, the vast sums of money invested in the slaves themselves.[12]

NHC scholars have not simply stumbled into a long-running debate about the efficiency of slave labor. They have also somewhat accidentally adopted an economic interpretation that finds its primary historical champions in the late antebellum bluster of James Henry Hammond, and the failed economic strategy of the Confederacy's diplomatic overtures to Europe.[13]

The ensuing NHC-cliometric divide has become pronounced and, at times, embittered.[14] Based on the sheer weight of evidence, the data-driven economic historians have often gained the upper hand by highlighting basic errors of empirical interpretation. Economists Alan Olmstead and Paul Rhode severely chastised the NHC literature for misusing historical cotton production data, including statistics that were derived from their own work. In another revealing indicator of the divide, economist Bradley Hanson noted a basic conceptual misunderstanding in NHC scholar Edward Baptist's attempt to calculate the percentage of the antebellum United States' gross domestic product that derived from slavery. Unaware of basic national-income accounting practices in differentiating input costs from final goods, Baptist inadvertently double- and perhaps triple-counted cotton-derived products until he reached an empirically unsupported figure that attributed nearly half of the United States' economic output in 1836 to plantation slavery.[15]

While episodes of this sort point to a specific shortcoming in the NHC literature, itself enabled by a predisposition toward "evidence" that appears to confirm a central link between slavery and capitalism, they also show the failure of even basic economic insights to penetrate the process of peer reviewing mainstream historical works that make economic claims. While it might be tempting to fault the confirmation biases of the historians' engagement with data, and the ideological undertones of their work suggests as much, another part of the problem derives from the methodological rift with the economists.

Cliometric research comes with a steep learning curve that can, at times, render its findings inaccessible to scholars who lack intensive training in advanced econometric techniques and statistical analysis. This obstacle extends well beyond the economics of slavery, leading to cases where parallel but divergent literatures emerge on either methodological divide of the same historical subject, largely in isolation from each other. For a simple illustration, consider the widespread enthusiasm that most historians show for Franklin Roosevelt's New Deal as an effective and necessary response to the Great Depression. Almost unbeknownst to them, a parallel literature in economic history largely holds that many of these same policies as well as other lesser known "relief" measures inadvertently impeded recovery and likely prolonged the Great Depression.[16]

The divide often produces competing claimants to accuracy, even where less dissimilar positions result. Economists embrace data as a benchmark of social-scientific methods to test and validate specific claims about the past. The traditional historians in turn retort, with some validity, that the data-heavy modeling on the other side of the divide has its own limitations. For one, it can artificially constrain historical inquiry to topics where identifiable quantitative metrics exist. There are no serialized archives of the trade volume of the Ostrogothic Kingdom after all, though much else might be said about the economies of late antiquity and early medieval Europe from surviving manuscript sources and even archaeological evidence. Second, the overly cliometric emphasis of some economic history outlets often comes at the expense of the deep contextual detail that narrative historians utilize to interpret events—a point that Baptist has enlisted to his defense in the slavery debate.

These concerns are neither recent nor unfamiliar to the number crunchers of the economics profession's historical subfields. Some two decades ago, economic historian Avner Greif cautioned that the dominant framework of the neoclassical model is self-limiting in its extension to historical events. In searching for markets to analyze, it imposes ahistorical theoretical assumptions about individual preferences, technology, factor endowments, and market institutions to historical events. Grief noted the effects of this emphasis upon economic history in the period since the cliometric revolution. It appeared in the neglect of "issues that were traditionally the focus of economic historians" before the emergence of quantitative dominance. Lost were historical inquiries into "the nature and role of nonmarket institutions, culture, entrepreneurship, technological and organizational innovation, politics, social factors, distributional conflicts, and the historical processes through which economies grew and declined."[17]

The persistence of the problem is highlighted in the recent resurgence of historical attention to these same topics, as seen in the NHC literature and parallel tracks. Yet the challenge we've witnessed is largely one of traditional historians who are steeped in contextual detail about economic events but ill-equipped to engage them with economic tools, hence Baptist's confusion-laden foray into national-income accounting. The NHC literature at its worst accordingly becomes not a renewed exercise in qualitative economic history, but a somewhat haphazard misapplication of social history tools to the complex economic events of the past.

The resulting picture may seem mired in its inflexibility. On one side, we find a self-limiting methodological rigidity that restricts its subject matter's accessibility to non-specialist audiences and self-limits the deployment of economic analysis to unconventional topics that are not easily quantified. On the other, we find a sea of abundant but cluttered detail and endless direction, yet also one where the only vessels are navigating by picking out bits and pieces of flotsam based on their resemblance to a strong and imported ideological prior that largely distrusts market capitalism itself.

Curiously, the classical liberal historian may be uniquely situated to operating across the rift in the history of capitalism. The conceptual toolbox of thinking economically—of grounding oneself in the concepts of scarcity, of tradeoffs, of incentives, and of institutional political economy—provides an interpretive grounding that addresses the limitations of both sides. What might we find when we examine the effects of the institutional constraints of constitutions, the robustness of private property, and the conflict-adjudicating mechanisms of a legal system upon the economic events of the past? What happens when historical actors are scrutinized for their susceptibility to the same patterns of political economy that we witness among state actors in the present? How well do historical economic events since 1776 comport to or break from the original Smithian project of finding the underlying nature and causes of the wealth of nations? In short, a classical liberal approach to the history of capitalism might consider taking economic insights to topics that exist beyond the methodological barriers of cliometrics and yet are also neglected, or erroneously serviced, by historians who lack or even eschew and caricature economic intuition.

SLAVERY AND CAPITALISM: FRIEND OR FOE?

Despite enjoying a common and in some ways concurrent intellectual history with the emergence of capitalism, a classical liberal history of capitalism must also grapple with a related ailment of its subject's historical treatment that has become increasingly pronounced in the recent years. Capitalism suffers from a definitional problem. While the persistence of market-hostile ideological frameworks in historical scholarship is in some ways a culprit, it is also the case that these new historians of "capitalism" simply lack a cohesive definition of the term and stumble from there into imprecision. The worst instances devolve into a dereliction of meaning itself, with the usage of the term "capitalism" taking on an almost intentionally pejorative character in the absence of anything more substantive.

A number of scholars have commented upon the pronounced "definitional elasticity" of recent historical work on capitalism, particularly within the NHC literature. Several NHC practitioners have in turn embraced this reluctance to define the term as a virtue of their approach. To quote NHC historian Seth Rockman, this line of study "has minimal investment in a fixed or theoretical definition of capitalism." Characterizing his approach as a process of inductive discovery, he openly concedes a willingness to let the term "float as a placeholder." Rockman further promotes a "capitalism" that is loosened from its conventional association with specific eras such as the Industrial Revolution, obviating questions of a pre-capitalist society or its causal role in transitions from an earlier state.[18] Louis Hyman echoes these sentiments even more forcefully in a recent Journal of American History roundtable on the subject: "Simply defining capitalism is a bad idea. It is too deductive."[19]

This curious state of affairs has received some pushback from other historians. In the same roundtable discussion, Scott Marler suggested that this aversion to a definition was self-defeating in that it shirked an admittedly complex but historiographically important question. Tom Cutterham similarly criticized the "rather troubling" implications of Rockman's aversion to definitions precisely because they strip capitalism of its grounding in time. "If there was no transition to capitalism, if nothing can properly be called pre-capitalist, then has it simply always been here?" he asks. The result is to turn capitalism into an overly broad term, wherein it becomes impossible to "point to anything that was ever not capitalism."[20]

The NHC struggles with an adequate definition of capitalism create additional oddities, including contradicting its own claimed premise. Instead of inductively teasing out the historical mechanisms of capitalism, these definition-averse historians have created the conditions of a never-ending cycle of "discovering" something that is never quite fully revealed or specified.

Far more problematic though is a second and less-noticed implication of adopting an intentionally vague terminology. Even while claiming to eschew definitions of "capitalism," many of these same historians have in fact imported a certain semiotic fluidity to their deployment of the term. The result is not only to broaden its meaning, but to do so selectively and in ways that are vulnerable to the importation of intentionally disparaging characteristics.

Consider Rockman's example. In the very same sentence he touts the "disavowal of theoretical definitions" of capitalism as a necessary feature of its open inquiry, he announces quite confidently that NHC scholarship has shown "slavery as integral, rather than oppositional, to capitalism."[21] One cannot specify the characteristics of capitalism for even modest conceptual clarity, and yet slavery is already admitted as an integral characteristic of capitalism. A rather awkward doctrine, this!

Internally conflicted assessments of this type are not limited to Rockman. NHC historian Sven Beckert is even more brash in his assault on "capitalism's illiberal origins." At once evading a definition for capitalism and yet aggressively infusing it with specific—and damning—attributes, he pinpoints slavery as the "beating heart of this new system"—a system built not on property rights "but a wave of expropriation of labor and land."[22] Beckert too is quite certain that capitalism and slavery are not oppositional. Or as he approvingly paraphrases Walter Johnson's parallel argument in River of Dark Dreams, "slavery [is] not just as an integral part of American capitalism, but ... its very essence."[23]

Issues of definitional rigor and consistency extend deep within the NHC literature, and Beckert offers his own addendum. By little more than reinventing terminology, he blends the attributes of 18th-century imperial mercantilism—that aggressively managed symbiosis of economic interests and nationally minded state policies to drive expansion and industry—into market capitalism under the new moniker "war capitalism" and proceeds as if the two are unified, both in character and culpability for slavery and a host of other ills.[24] The pronounced adversarial tension that historically existed between market capitalism and the mercantile political agenda is almost entirely lost in the process, even as the past's participants in the intellectual contests between them would have balked at any attempt to blend the two together.

The abusiveness of the historical distortion exhibited in Beckert's move is no small point. It inverts the very premise of capitalism's most famous and influential exposition. Composed as a retort to the prevailing mercantilist economic theories of his day, Adam Smith's *Wealth of Nations* was also a far-reaching assault upon industrial protectionism in the name of national "wealth," upon public-private enterprises undertaken through the privileged arrangements of law and government access, upon militaristic imperialism and colonialism, and upon slavery itself.[25] Beckert's version of "capitalism," still wavering between a definition that is at once equivocal in its characteristics and yet selectively infused with the certitude of an "essence" chained to slavery, has effectively become the same horde of demons that the primary intellectual father of modern capitalism specifically contested and condemned in his seminal work.

Nor is Beckert anomalous in this practice. Johnson similarly invents the phrase "racial slave capitalism" to describe a program of white supremacist mercantile internationalism. The features of this "system" unite agriculture and industry around the steam transport of cotton through a vast and globally minded system of state collusion and a vigorously regulated color bar.[26] The resulting concoction is simultaneously part Friedrich List, part Henry Clay, part J. D. B. DeBow, and part George Fitzhugh, yet few of its ingredients are quintessentially capitalistic in the Smithian sense and many are explicitly antithetical. A large economic literature empirically establishes and expands upon the economic costs of a discriminatory legal regime, as well as the tendency of market forces to rub against statutorily entrenched racial codes.[27] Smith himself saw this tension at play in slavery, observing that the entire system was sustained upon the political assistance its beneficiaries afforded to themselves. Thus the slaveowners "will never make any laws mitigating their usage; whatever laws are made with regard to slaves are intended to strengthen the authority of the masters and reduce the slaves to a more absolute subjection."[28]

This specific criticism is not offered to suggest that Smith retains a perpetual license upon determining the attributes of the economic system he described. Even the term's acquisition of its modern properties postdates his lifespan. Yet the pronounced dissimilarities between Smithian capitalism and what the NHC literature takes to be its subject matter point to another opportunity for classical liberal historians to unclutter the discussion. A history of capitalism attempted without the benefit of an intellectual history of capitalism arrives in strange and even self-contradictory positions, among them the odd state of affairs where capitalism becomes, by little more than a sleight of hand and twist in terminology, the very same practices of 18th-century political economy that Adam Smith and the other celebrated theorists of capitalism specifically argued against.

ANTI-CAPITALISM AS A HISTORICAL METHOD

There appears to be another twist at play in the definitional fluidity of the NHC, and it is here that the old Hayekian criticism's application to the modern literature becomes most salient. While selectively non-committal phrasings and ahistorical inversions of terminology can serve as a mechanism to insulate a claim about the past from the sort of falsifiable testing that economic historians prefer, they also contrast with a consistent theme of the NHC genre found in its recurring portrayal of capitalism as an explicitly illiberal system, or one of uncontested illiberal by-products. Beckert openly states as much in asserting the "illiberal origins" of modern market capitalism, and the larger NHC genre exhibits an almost singular preoccupation with forging a friendship between capitalism and slavery; and segregation; and colonialism; and exploitation, degradation, and violence, all chalked up to "market failure" or worse.[29] For all these attempts to forge—and force—an association between capitalism and a multitude of social wrongs and problems, a parallel neglect extends to the historical critics of capitalism as they saw the Smithian system unfolding in the world around them.

Seeing the now-disputed adversarial economic relationship between capitalism and slavery, many classical economists in the 18th and 19th centuries openly advanced abolitionist arguments in their works.[30] Less noticed as a historical point however is the frequency with which their contemporary advocates of economic regulation, of planned economic nationalism, and even slavery itself also perceived capitalism as a threat. A number of these anti-capitalist witnesses are noteworthy not only for their defenses of illiberal institutions and practices, but also as forbearers of many of the same arguments against unchained markets—against the much-caricatured capitalist notion of laissez-faire—that persist to the present day.

Consider the case of Thomas Carlyle, the Scottish historian and social commentator who penned a now-notorious essay that blamed the economic decline of the British West Indies on emancipation. His 1849 lamentation took direct aim at what he famously dubbed the "dismal science"—a "rueful" enterprise "which finds the secret of this universe in 'supply-and-demand,' and reduces the duty of human governors to that of letting men alone," which is to say laissez-faire. To Carlyle, this new science of economy had joined itself to the "sacred cause of black emancipation, or the like, to fall in love and make a wedding of it" to yield "dark extensive moon-calves, unnameable abortions, wide-coiled monstrosities, such as the world has not seen hitherto."[31]

This bombastic slur was no passing criticism, but rather a sustained assault on market capitalism. Carlyle saw cause for alarm in the "multifarious devices we have been endeavoring to dispense with governing" in deference

to markets where the two collided. He denounced the "superficial specula-
tions, of laissez-faire, supply-and-demand" not only in its affinity for emancipation, but as a blamed cause for other ills of the day—for the Irish famine,
as he extended his doctrines in the immediate wake of the 1849 essay.[32] In
two decades' time, with abolition achieved not only in Britain's colonies but
the United States, he placed market capitalism at the center of blame for a
society "fallen vulgar and chaotic" to the simultaneous forces of black equality and "cheap and nasty"—his term for an over-commodified marketplace of
unimpeded trade and what he saw as culturally degrading commercialism.[33]

A parallel witness may be seen in the previously referenced late antebellum theorist of the slaveocracy, George Fitzhugh. A self-described Carlylean,
Fitzhugh was also an avowed anti-capitalist. Political economy, which "may
be summed up in the phrase, 'Laissez-faire,' or 'Let alone'" was but a "false
philosophy of the age."[34] These principles, he asserted in another text, "are
at war with all kinds of slavery." Capitalism represented a competitive race
to the bottom of wages in Fitzhugh's mind, and slavery was its well-ordered
antithesis. Yet slavery was not Fitzhugh's only concern. He devoted chapters
in both of his major works to lambasting the cause of free trade. Its intellectual champion Adam Smith was, to him, an "absent, secluded, and unobserv-
ant" thinker who "saw only that prosperous and progressive portion of society
whom liberty or free competition benefitted, and mistook its effects on them
for its effects on the world." Just as revealing is Fitzhugh's antidote to this
perceived state of affairs:

> But [the South] does not let alone. She builds roads and canals, encourages
> education, endows schools and colleges, improves river navigation, excludes, or
> taxes heavily foreign show-men, foreign pedlars, sellers of clocks, &c. tries to
> build up by legislation Southern commerce, and by State legislation to multiply
> and encourage industrial pursuits. Protection by the State Government is her
> established policy - and that is the only expedient or constitutional protection.
> It is time for her to avow her change of policy and opinion, and to throw Adam
> Smith, Say, Ricardo & Co., in the fire.[35]

Fitzhugh's political recommendation is, with no small irony, strikingly similar to the managerial-mercantile platform that the NHC literature rebrands
as "war capitalism" or "slave capitalism." Beckert offers a parallel rejection
of "liberal, lean state" 19th-century Britain, depicting instead a plantation
slavery-fed and cotton-driven "capitalist" empire with "a powerful and
interventionist bureaucracy, high taxes, skyrocketing government debt, and
protectionist tariffs," with "turnpikes and canals," and with conscious state
policies to drive economic growth.[36] While the NHC literature diverges
sharply from Fitzhugh in condemning the viciousness of slavery, its representation of the slave economy largely shares and emphasizes these same

features: an assertion of the plantation system's economic prowess and
dynamism, as distinct from classical economic criticisms that saw it as an
inefficient and institutionally rigid throwback, and a mutual identification of
slavery as the primary driving engine of economic industrialization taking
place around it and in its wake. Fitzhugh also differs by including a more can-
did admission about his own adversaries. They are one and the same with the
capitalist intellectuals that much of the NHC literature now carelessly lumps
into an extension of Fitzhugh's slave-based economic system.

ANTI-CAPITALISM AND PROGRESSIVE HISTORY

Carlyle's influence and reputation have diminished since his lifetime, and
Fitzhugh was always considered something of a crank beyond the fire-eaters
of the slave-owning political class. Parallel manifestations of anti-capitalism
nonetheless transmitted into subsequent intellectual movements at the root of
American progressivism.

To some degree, the modern roots of anti-capitalistic historical writing are
products of intellectual histories about older theorists of capitalism. Richard Hofstadter's classic 1944 assault on the claimed "social Darwinism" of
Herbert Spencer and other laissez-faire theorists of the late 19th century still
looms large in the history profession's conceptualization of pre-progressive
era models of capitalism. Hofstadter's text is not without flaws as more recent
works on Spencer have suggested, but neither is it without nuance. At points
he takes a more progressive strain of "Darwinian collectivism" to task even
as the thrust of his work targets the "individualist" varieties of laissez-faire
capitalism.[37] A curious feature of the more recent historical literature is that
it retains Hofstadter's disapproving depictions of Spencerian laissez-faire
capitalism and inflates them to the point of caricature, placing them at the
source of historical racism, exploitation theory, and most pre-welfare state
social ills. At the same time though, a profound inattention may be observed
in parallel treatments of progressive economic causes that resonate among
anti-capitalists despite carrying profoundly illiberal racial and social baggage
in their respective histories.

One noteworthy expression appeared among a group of politically progressive economists in the late 19th and early 20th centuries who consciously
set out to supplant economic non-intervention with "scientific" correctives
that aimed to alleviate a host of economic ills attributed to low wages and
unemployment, distributional inequality, and regulatory laxity. This out-
wardly progressive counter to laissez-faire coalesced in the late 19th century
around a group of economists and other social scientists who shared common
intellectual roots, many of them having trained under the "younger" German

Historical School at the Universities of Halle and Heidelberg. Though a new infusion to the classical-aligned American economics scene of the 1880s, these progressive reformers could trace their intellectual lineage back to the older neo-mercantile political economy of Alexander Hamilton and its subsequent transmission to Germany in the early decades of the century.[38] The progressives used their academic work to advance a broad range of reformist causes, including labor unionization, work hour regulations, product safety regulations, anti-monopoly laws and trustbusting, "scientific" tariff targeting for strategic industries, redistributive taxation, and even the minimum wage. At the root of the movement was a widespread belief in the deployment of "scientific" managerial expertise to advise and design policies in areas where the unfettered free market fell short—where capitalism "failed" in their eyes.

The underlying rationale of progressive era economics is not far removed from similar progressive causes of today, including those championed by modern historian-advocates who are often drawn to these historical topics by political affinities and their own areas of interest. Indeed, the same NHC literature that condemns capitalism for an "integral" relationship with slavery a generation prior appears to hold the turn-of-the-century progressive rejoinder to laissez-faire in consistently high esteem. It entails a comparatively less developed body of work, though the thrust is highly approving of the progressive economic positions advanced by these historical figures.[39] Topically, there is little new to it save the investigation of unturned detail. The historiographical habit of portraying the progressive era as a corrective to the "excesses" of a hands-off Gilded Age is as old as it is oversimplified, yet it is also finding a comfortable embrace in recent NHC work.

The political economy of the progressive era warrants mention though for the complication it reveals, both historically among an identifiable group of capitalism's critics and in the present among historians who openly align with the causes they championed. Progressive scientism led its practitioners in a number of less-enlightened directions that are also just beginning to receive historical scrutiny. The product shows a selectivity of blame in the larger attempt to link capitalism to slavery's illiberal terms, juxtaposed against a polite inattention that sets in with issues that reflect poorly upon the liberality of progressive causes.

Classical liberal engagement with the history of capitalism should note the illiberal dimensions of progressivism in a growing body of recent work on the downsides of "scientific" planning. The same mind-set that prompted the progressives to enlist state tools to counter the perceived "market failures" also saw, and for parallel rationales, an aggressive role for the state in the correction of other perceived social ills. Progressivism's faults extend directly into the realm of eugenics, of forced sterilization of the "unfit," and of an assortment of pseudo-scientific theories of racial biology and psychology. They include the use of minimum wage laws and work hour regulations to exclude black and immigrant laborers from the turn-of-the-century workforce. They include racially discriminatory and pseudo-scientific drug policies, the legacies of which persist in the prison system of our own time. They also show numerous instances where the segregationist strictures of Jim Crow found a welcome partnership not in capitalism, but among its critics and "reformers." Some of the figures are relatively obscure—Richard T. Ely, John R. Commons, and Simon N. Patten to name a few.[40] Others like Woodrow Wilson are well known for infusing progressivism into mainstream political economy into the present day, again on terms that sought to correct capitalism's claimed defects.

No less a source than John Maynard Keynes developed his original attack on market failure upon a eugenic argument for population controls. The "laissez-faire" of nature and heredity was, to him, as problematic as taking the same approach to an unregulated economic order.[41] While his and other progressive affinities for these causes dissipated among their heirs, there legacy as a matter of direct historical association with other more persistent causes remains politely overlooked—an oddly selective omission for a historical profession that has gone to extreme lengths to attach free market thinkers of the same era to a far flimsier affinity for Social Darwinism.[42]

One possible counter for classical liberals is to investigate the little-studied resistance to scientific racism, eugenicism, and similarly blameworthy causes within the works of capitalism's historical defenders. Ludwig von Mises' answer to Keynes' eugenically tinged call for the "end of laissez-faire" is particularly revealing for its sounder positioning of the contesting causes of the day: "He who rejoices that peoples are turning away from liberalism, should not forget that war and revolution, misery and unemployment for the masses, tyranny and dictatorship are not accidental companions, but are necessary results of the antiliberalism that now rules the world."[43]

These examples offer just a few cases in which pronounced strains of illiberalism have emerged among the historical critics of capitalism, both left and right. They offer an avenue of research in need of further exploration as a way of contextualizing history's capitalism as it was seen and lived by persons who charged it with varying degrees of defect. Their relevance to the current state of the field is further affirmed though in the comparative inattention their own ethical shortcomings have received within an NHC literature that is simultaneously all too eager to write faults into the core of the capitalist economic system—even where historical expositors of capitalism like Smith (or later figures such as Richard Cobden, J. E. Cairnes, and Edward Atkinson) specifically assailed the very same faults.

THE FUTURE OF HISTORY AND CAPITALISM

In offering these brief remarks on the emerging and still-fluid dimensions of the history of capitalism, much more remains unanswered about the trajectory of scholarship on this topic. Research from the NHC genre has grown in appeal and acclaim within the profession, yet its foundations, as noted, have many cracks in terms of how it engages the very concept of capitalism, how it defines its terminology, and the persistent issue of inattention to complicating evidence and methods from other lines of study. Moreover, the thrust of its message does not seem to be very far removed from the anti-capitalistic biases that Hayek diagnosed half a century ago, save for a marked increase in the intensity of expression. In some areas such as its treatment of slavery, the NHC literature has almost unwittingly revived a strain of anti-capitalistic arguments from the late antebellum itself and adapted them to historical analysis, minus of course the embrace of slavery.

Where this leaves the classical liberal historian of capitalism is in some ways dependent upon the topic being studied in an immensely broad field. But as a general principle I will suggest taking up the role of historical interlocutor through the joint tools of economic reasoning and evidentiary empiricism. Rather than offering a broad-based theory of capitalism, replete with claims of defined systems and normative judgments of what they should or should not achieve, a scrutinizing alternative might eschew the push to define "eras" of capitalism and its antecedents entirely. Rather, we might turn our analysis to simply discerning patterns of human choice amid conditions of scarcity, subject to what we can discern from an evidentiary basis about the values and institutional constraints surrounding a past decision.

The search for a larger systemic narrative of the past may be an unavoidable encounter. But here too the search for the larger narrative's mechanisms can also function as its own test for the specific performance of these features, and recurring patterns that might be discerned from each. As a means of inquiry, we may make no promise that capitalism will perform as an ideal system and offers no claim of inoculation against past injustices, of which there is no shortage. Instead the classical liberal historian only seeks to understand them empirically as they are examined against the causal mechanisms of human exchange, both theorized and witnessed in similar circumstances of the past.

NOTES

1. Hayek, F.A. 1954. *Capitalism and the Historians,* Chicago: University of Chicago Press. 9–10.
2. For recent examples of inequality research that received both praise by historians and attention for their prescriptive calls for redistributive taxation, see Saez,

Emmanuel, and Gabriel Zucman. "Exploding wealth inequality in the United States." Washington, DC: Washington Center for Equitable Growth, October 20 (2014); Piketty, Thomas. 2014. *Capital in the 21st Century.* Cambridge: Harvard University Press.

3. Jennifer Schuessler. "In History Departments, It's Up With Capitalism." *New York Times,* April 6, 2013; Jeremy Adelman and Jonathan Levy. "The Fall and Rise of Economic History." *Chronicle of Higher Education,* December 1, 2014.

4. See in particular North, Douglass C., and Robert Paul Thomas. *The Rise of the Western World: A new economic history.* Cambridge University Press, 1973; Mokyr, Joel. *The Gifts of Athena: Historical origins of the knowledge economy.* Princeton University Press, 2002; Mokyr, Joel. *The Enlightened Economy: An Economic History of Britain 1700–1850.* Yale University Press, 2009; McCloskey, Deirdre N. *Bourgeois Virtue.* John Wiley & Sons, Ltd, 2006; McCloskey, Deirdre N. *Bourgeois Dignity: Why economics can't explain the modern world.* University of Chicago Press, 2010.

5. An interesting assessment of the opinions of economic historians on slavery and a number of other issues may be found in Whaples, Robert. "Where is there consensus among American economic historians? The results of a survey on forty propositions." *The Journal of Economic History* 55.01 (1995): 139–154; For a review of the literature on slavery, profitability, and the divisions between historians and economists, see Hummel, Jeffrey Rogers, "Deadweight Loss and the American Civil War: The Political Economy of Slavery, Secession, and Emancipation" (October 1, 2012). Available at SSRN:https://ssrn.com/abstract=2155362, Chapter 1.

6. Several abolitionist works advanced this notion as a critique of slavery on the eve of the Civil War. See Atkinson, Edward. *Cheap Cotton by Free Labor.* A. Williams, 1861; Olmsted, Frederick Law, and Arthur Meier Schlesinger, ed. *The Cotton Kingdom: A Traveller's Observations on Cotton and Slavery in the American Slave States: Based Upon Three Former Volumes of Journeys and Investigations by the Same Author.* Da Capo Press, 1996.

7. Conrad, Alfred H., and John R. Meyer. "The economics of slavery in the ante bellum South." *The Journal of Political Economy* (1958): 95–130; North, Douglas. "The State of Economic History." *American Economic Review* 55 (1–2) (1965): 86–91; Fogel, Robert William, and Stanley L. Engerman. *Time on the cross: The economics of American Negro slavery.* Vol. 1. WW Norton & Company, 1995. See also Hummel 2012, Introduction and Chapter 1.

8. Hummel 2012, Introduction.

9. See in particular Johnson, Walter. *River of Dark Dreams.* Harvard University Press, 2013; Baptist, Edward. *The half has never been told: Slavery and the making of American capitalism.* Basic books, 2014; Beckert, Sven. *Empire of cotton: A global history.* Vintage, 2015; Schermerhorn, Calvin. *The Business of Slavery and the Rise of American Capitalism, 1815–1860.* Yale University Press, 2015; Beckert, Sven, and Seth Rockman. *Slavery's Capitalism: A New History of American Economic Development.* University of Pennsylvania Press, 2016.

10. Whaples 1995.

11. Christy, David. *Cotton is King: Or, The Culture of Cotton, and Its Relation to Agriculture, Manufactures and Commerce; and Also to the Free Colored People; and to Those who Hold that Slavery is in Itself Sinful.* Derby & Jackson, 1856. Chapter V.

12. Beckert, 2015, p. 52; Baptist, 2013, 321–322.

13. Speech of James H. Hammond, March 4, 1858, *Congressional Globe,* 35th Congress, 1st Session, Appendix, p. 70. If the plantation system was as intractable from the global economy as the NHC literature claims, then the Confederacy's diplomatic strategy might have assured rapid intervention in the American Civil War from the European beneficiaries of its yield. As it happened, the strategy was largely a failure. Owsley, F. L. (1959). *King Cotton Diplomacy.* University of Alabama Press.

14. See in particular Marc Parry, "Shackles and Dollars," *Chronicle of Higher Education,* December 8, 2016; Murray, J. E., Olmstead, A. L., Logan, T. D., Pritchett, J. B., & Rousseau, P. L. (2015). "Roundtable: The Half Has Never Been Told: Slavery and the Making of American Capitalism. By Edward E. Baptist." *The Journal of Economic History* 75 (03): 919–931; Clegg, John J. "Capitalism and Slavery." *Critical Historical Studies* 2.2 (2015): 281–304; Edward E. Baptist, "Correcting an Incorrect "Corrective," *The Junto,* November 4, 2015, https://earlyamericanists. com/2015/11/04/guest-post-correcting-an-incorrect-corrective/; Olmstead, Alan L., and Paul W. Rhode. "Cotton, Slavery, and the New History of Capitalism." (2016), working paper, http://web.law.columbia.edu/sites/default/files/microsites/law-economics-studies/olmstead_-_cotton_slavery_and_history_of_new_capitalism_131_nhc_28_sept_2016.pdf

15. Olmstead and Rhode, 2016; Bradley A. Hanson, "The Back of Ed Baptist's Envelope," October 30, 2014, http://bradleyahansen.blogspot.com/2014/10/the-back-of-ed-baptists-envelope.html

16. Friedman, Milton, and Anna Jacobson Schwartz. *A Monetary History of the United States, 1867–1960.* Princeton University Press, 2008; Cole, Harold L., and Lee E. Ohanian. "New Deal policies and the persistence of the Great Depression: A general equilibrium analysis." *Journal of Political Economy* 112.4 (2004): 779–816; Higgs, Robert. *Depression, war, and cold war: Studies in political economy.* Oxford University Press, 2006, Chapter 1.

17. Greif, Avner. "Cliometrics after 40 years." *The American Economic Review* 87.2 (1997): 400–403.

18. Rockman, Seth. "What Makes the History of Capitalism Newsworthy?" *Journal of the Early Republic* 34.3 (2014): 442.

19. "Interchange: The History of Capitalism." *Journal of American History* 101: 503–536.

20. Tom Cutterham, "Is the History of Capitalism the History of Everything?" *The Junto,* September 2, 2014, https://earlyamericanists.com/2014/09/02/is-the-history-of-capitalism-the-history-of-everything/

21. Rockman 2014, 444.

22. Beckert 2014, 37.

23. Sven Beckert, "Slavery and Capitalism," *Chronicle of Higher Education,* December 12, 2014.

24. Beckert 2014, xvi.

25. See in particular Adam Smith, 1776. *An Inquiry into the Nature and Causes of the Wealth of Nations.* Book III, Chapter II and Book IV, Chapter VIII.

26. Johnson 2013, 14.

27. Becker, Gary S. *The economics of discrimination.* University of Chicago press, 1957; Hutt, William H. *Economics of the Colour Bar, The.* London: Institute of Economic Affairs, 1964.

28. Adam Smith, *Lectures on Jurisprudence* (Liberty Fund, 1982) 81.

29. Beckert 2014, 37.

30. Atkinson, 1861; Cairnes, John E. *The Slave Power: Its Character, Career, and Probable Designs.* New York, 1862.

31. Carlyle, Thomas. "Occassional Discourse on the Negro Question," *Frasers Magazine for Town and Country*, February 1849. See also Levy, David M. *How the Dismal Science got its Name: Classical economics and the ur-text of racial politics.* University of Michigan Press, 2002.

32. Carlyle, Thomas (1850). *Latter Day Pamphlets.* London: Chapman & Hall., 34.

33. Carlyle, Thomas. *Shooting Niagara: And After?* Chapman and Hall, 1867.

34. Fitzhugh, George. *Cannibals All! Or Slaves Without Masters.* Richmond: A Morris. 1857, 79.

35. Fitzhugh, George. *Sociology for the South: Or the Failure of a Free Society.* Richmond: A. Morris (1854): 7, 10, 188.

36. Beckert 2015, xv, 78.

37. Leonard, Thomas C. "Origins of the myth of social Darwinism: The ambiguous legacy of Richard Hofstadter's Social Darwinism in American Thought." *Journal of Economic Behavior & Organization* 71.1 (2009): 37–51; Zwolinski, Matt, "Social Darwinism and Social Justice: Herbert Spencer on Our Duties to the Poor," (April 13, 2015). Camilla Boisen and Matthew Murray, eds., *Distributive Justice Debates in Social and Political Thought: Perspectives on Finding A Fair Share* (Routledge, 2015).

38. For a related history of both Hamilton's transmission to the German Historical School, and its continued influence upon the historical profession, see Eicholz, Hans L. "Hamilton, Harvard, and the German Historical School: A Short Note on a Curious History." *Journal of Private Enterprise* 29.3 (2014): 43.

39. Recent examples include Mehrotra, Ajay K. *Making the Modern American Fiscal State: Law, Politics, and the Rise of Progressive Taxation, 1877–1929.* Cambridge University Press, 2013; Fink, Leon. *The Long Gilded Age: American Capitalism and the Lessons of a New World Order.* University of Pennsylvania Press, 2014.

40. Leonard, Thomas C. "'More Merciful and Not Less Effective': Eugenics and American Economics in the Progressive Era." *History of Political Economy* 35.4 (2003): 687–712; Leonard, Thomas C. *Illiberal Reformers: Race, Eugenics, and American Economics in the Progressive Era.* Princeton University Press, 2016.

41. Keynes, John Maynard. "Is Britain Overpopulated?" *New Republic,* October 31, 1923. Keynes, John Maynard. "The end of laissez-faire." *Essays in persuasion.* Palgrave Macmillan UK, 2010. 272–294; Magness, Phillip W. and Sean J. Hernandez, "The Economic Eugenicism of John Maynard Keynes," *Journal of Markets and Morality,* 2017.

42. Hofstadter, Richard. *Social Darwinism in American thought.* Beacon Press, 1944. For a critique of Hofstadter, arguing that he overstated and misinterpreted his evidence, see Zwolinski, Matt. "Social Darwinism and Social Justice: Herbert Spencer on Our Duties to the Poor." *Distributive Justice Debates in Social and Political Thought: Perspectives on Finding A Fair Share* (Routledge, 2015).

43. Ludwig von Mises, "Das Ende des Laissez-Faire, Ideen zur Verbindung von Privat und Gemeinwirtschaft." *Zeitschrift für die gesamte Staatswissenschaft.* 82 (1927): 190–191. Translation by Joseph Stromberg, https://mises.org/library/mises-keynes-1927

Chapter 3

The Historicity of Civil Liberties, a Challenge for Liberals

Anthony Gregory

Civil liberties are among the most underdeveloped themes in classical liberal historical writing. Liberals, which I use here as shorthand for classical liberals and modern libertarians, count civil liberties alongside international peace and the market economy as a core pillar of liberalism.[1] But the scholarship is thin and under-theorized. Liberals have punted on seeking rigorous understanding, allowing progressive and conservative theoretical frameworks to shape the scholarly discussion. This division of intellectual labor exposes tensions in liberal legal and political theory. Although liberal academic historians are few in number, liberal polemicists, journalists, think tanks, and second handlers also produce popular historical writings whose narrative premises perpetuate and exacerbate reductive assumptions. The problems identified here thus speak to an impoverished engagement with both the broader scholarly community and the broader liberal community.

When liberals do grapple with civil liberties as a historical subject, they often rely on one of two narrative approaches that seemingly reinforce liberal understandings of the present. One is to chronicle abuses by the modern state, the principal target of liberal animus. This type of story takes for granted the meaning and substance of civil liberties, a timeless human value that an expanding leviathan has crushed. The second approach highlights civil liberties' substance as a product of historical development, often amounting to a vindicatory genealogy of constitutional law or Western or American exceptionalism. According to this type of story, we should appreciate the liberties that were hard won and institutionalized by bulwarks like the Bill of Rights. Both types of stories can easily overlook history's messiness.

If insufficient appreciation of civil liberties compromises our general understanding of the past, the failure to appreciate civil liberties' history can reveal weaknesses in modern liberal political philosophy. Liberals do not

39

develop a sensitivity to the historicity of civil liberties, instead attempting to incorporate them into a reductive and mechanically legalistic appreciation of liberty. To maintain one's reductive liberalism, one must either adopt a reductive understanding of history or reject a more historically sensitive and subtle understanding of freedom itself. My own research experience, writing two books on civil liberties, awoke me to this problem.

Civil liberties are the pillar of liberalism least comprehensible without an open mind to historical change. Even in their most theoretical articulation, they are a product of contingency and culture, perhaps even more than the economic freedom to which liberals devote much of their attention. Economic liberalism finds reinforcement in the social science of economics, whereas the disciplines through which we appreciate civil liberties—history, law, and sociology—are less reducible into axiomatic formulation. There are no laws of history even in the way there are laws of economics.[2] Jurisprudence is nothing without change. Social norms and patterns turn heavily on cultural context. In law and civil liberty, theory and history must inform each other in dialectical reinforcement. Liberals who embrace historicity will be better equipped to tackle the literature. Considering how liberals today approach civil liberties history will reveal the fraught implications for modern liberal theory and point toward a research agenda that can enrich liberal theory and the wider scholarly world.

•••

Broadly speaking, liberals producing scholarship and popular writings tend to tell two kinds of civil liberties stories, both of which take the meaning and preferability of civil liberties for granted. In the first type of story, civil liberties are the subject of violence by the modern state, and in the second type civil liberties became a core, even immutable, fixture of modern liberty, and yet were discovered if not constructed over time, thanks to such venerable heritages as Anglo-American constitutionalism. There is a tension between these two approaches, although they can be reconciled under an overarching narrative that privileges some time in the past as the peak of civil liberties and laments the rise of the modern state for their decline.

The first type of narrative traces the structural war between big government and civil liberties, so as to condemn leviathan as inimical. It is a common trope for liberals to delegitimize the American government by pointing to its past crimes against civil liberty, particularly under great presidencies or during popular wars. In order to demystify Lincoln, Wilson, and Roosevelt, libertarians have long pointed to their due process violations, surveillance practices, or conscription, in part to question conventional wisdom of presidential greatness and more specifically to show the tensions between big government, often a cause célèbre of the left, and the violations of civil liberties, of which the left is presumably more enamored. There are stronger and weaker examples of this approach directed toward popular readers.[3]

Stellar historical works by academically trained scholars can also basically fit this description. Robert Higgs's *Crisis and Leviathan* traces the civil liberties casualties of World War I and World War II in the description of war's ratcheting threat to freedom.[4] Although an economic historian, Higgs makes a substantial theoretical point that questions of legal power are not easily legible to standard quantitative means of measuring "big government," and he grapples at length with the ideological antecedents to a free society. Jeffrey Rogers Hummel, another economic historian, carefully surveys the threats to civil liberties under the Union during the Civil War—and unlike all too many popular writers, takes good care to scrutinize Jefferson Davis's many depredations as well.[5] Both of these historians thus add some subtle understanding in showing the modern state emerging with collateral damage to due process rights, habeas corpus, and freedom of speech.

Such solid scholarship shows there is nothing inherently wrong with bracketing the historicity of civil liberties in telling a bigger story about American leviathan. But even the best scholarship in this vein cannot help but leave unanswered many questions that liberals have not had the resources to explore more deeply. And unfortunately, few liberal historians have engaged civil liberties with such sensitivity and nuance even when tracing the modern state's violence. We do not need to list the bibliography of books, many published by trade presses, that are much less nuanced, particularly on the Civil War.

Such formulations of the history of civil liberties can tempt liberals toward the "conservative" side of the spectrum in the history wars, against a dominant progressive paradigm, but other works do demonstrate that the state's war with purportedly ancient liberties stretches back to the early modern era. Murray N. Rothbard's four-volume series located the eternal war between liberty and power in the political contests of colonial America.[6] Even readers who stress *Conceived in Liberty*'s culmination in the rise of a modern British Empire against the freedom of medieval decentralism must confront Rothbard's due attention to slavery, feudalism, mercantilism, indentured servitude, and colonialist exploitation. Rothbard's emphasis on early modern oppression was consistent with his Whiggish assessments in "Left and Right: The Prospects of Liberty," which identifies the period before the age of revolutions for its ubiquitous depredations on freedom.[7] This approach nevertheless leaves civil liberties undefined, takes for granted their sacredness, and leaves it to the theorists, dominated by leftist thinkers, to explain what civil liberties are and why they are important in the first place.

The second approach sees civil liberties not as timeless but as historically constructed, albeit usually in the deep past. In principle, these works

are reconcilable in narrative arc if not in ideological assumptions to that in
Conceived in Liberty as well as works that target the late modern state. They
seek to uncover the ancient genealogy of a particular civil liberty, so as to
vindicate its transcending grandeur beyond the caprices of modernity. The
harkening back to the ancient origins of modern liberties is a common polem-
ical technique, with Burkean implications for the institutional development
of liberty as something we owe to efforts from a long gone era. Whereas historians employing the first narrative approach look to the past for violations
of civil liberties, these historians more often look to early America, England,
or Western civilization for principles predating the modern vagaries. Most
commonly we see this in defenses of such great constitutional principles as
habeas corpus, the right to bear arms, religious liberty, or federalism. William Watkins and Thomas Woods have written vindicatory genealogies of
nullification.[8] Some scholarship recognizes later advancements.[9] Stephen
Halbrook's work on the Second and Fourteenth Amendment acknowledges
the Reconstruction Era's contributions in arguing for an original individual
right to bear arms as understood by the Founders but made more universal a
century later.[10] One limitation, however, is the premise characterizing early
America or the old world as a more libertarian time, something Rothbard
sought to rebut in "Left and Right," or, in the most sophisticated examples,
seeing civil liberties as forged in a mostly libertarian cast in the founding
era with the only limitation remedied once all people became formally equal
under the law.

Libertarian vindicatory genealogies are particularly problematic as it concerns the common law. Overly romantic views of the common law are seen
among old legal culture's liberal admirers, very broadly defined. This is especially true of Straussian scholars, who extend their presentist interpretation
to American Constitutionalism.[11] Generally speaking, common law is upheld
for both its supposedly decentralized structure and its libertarian results, two
highly dubious reasons to unreservedly celebrate a system often promulgated
from the top-down by elites in furtherance of collectivist conceptions of
rights. Perhaps Hayek's influence continues to lure liberals into such roman-
ticization. Trenchant critiques of Hayek's account of the common law have
come from John Hasnas, who helps differentiate customary from common
law, as well as from Francis Fukuyama drawing on Harold Berman.[12] But
even if we narrow the question to the transmission of common law from
Britain to America, the subject is complicated, the lesson for liberals not
always so clear. Jeffersonians, whom liberals admire, opposed common
law, associated with royalism and elitism, except of course when they did
not, and used common law rights like jury trials to secure rights during and
after the revolution. Common law at times stood with business but against
free market principles. Common law standards of freedom of speech were

very restrictive. Historians who see American common law as a distinct late nineteenth-century phenomenon are also not entirely wrong.[13]

Personal experience made me wonder if liberals have overlooked the messiness of common law and constitutionalism, with broader ramifications for how liberals conceive of civil liberties. Scouring the literature as I wrote two books for the Independent Institute, the first on habeas corpus and the second on surveillance and the Fourth Amendment, I discovered the murky origins of two civil liberties libertarians tend to take for granted but whose histories few within the liberal tradition have studied closely. I came to believe that reductive libertarianism lacks a sophisticated theory of civil liberties, and that liberalism could use a more historicist approach.

My research on habeas corpus beginning in 2007 aimed to build a case against the Bush administration.[14] I planned a vindicatory genealogy of habeas corpus, much like Anthony Kennedy's ruling opinion in *Boumediene*, followed by a revisionist account of its time-honored status punctuated by depredations under such imperial executives as Lincoln, Roosevelt, and Bush.[15] What I found was much more interesting and complicated, but also somewhat unnerving. The secondary literature made me question the high esteem we placed on habeas corpus as a practical remedy. Habeas corpus's medieval origins were mysterious and ambiguous. At many times it served the central state at least as much as the individual detainee. In 2010, Paul Halliday's *Habeas Corpus: England and Empire* showed that Parliament violated suspects' rights as readily as the King, and used the writ to extend imperial power to its periphery.[16] Other works, like political scientist Justin Wert's *Habeas Corpus in America*, revealed its politicization over the years and its functionality in enforcing slavery.[17] The law literature revealed its limitations in protecting most defendants over time. In synthesizing all this scholarship, I had to forego my simplistic history but my libertarian theory of civil liberties remained essentially unscathed. Detention power was a clear-cut threat to bodily autonomy. Jurisdictional opportunism, despite posing problems for a kneejerk federalism, helped to reconcile habeas history to individualist theory.

More threatening to my theory of civil liberties was the research for a second Independent Institute book project.[18] Although the 2013 NSA scandal outraged liberals, I found it unfeasible to deduce modern conceptions of privacy from property rights and the non-aggression principle. Although in earlier times conservatives had a more capacious concept of privacy, in the late twentieth century libertarians often sided with legal conservatives in rejecting any "right to privacy," and it took progressive jurists and their rights revolution to cover warrantless wiretapping, which often does not invade physical private property, under Fourth Amendment protection. If the dreaded living Constitution and judicial activism seemed uncomfortably central to the development of habeas corpus, they appeared more fundamental to privacy rights. Moreover, the historical chapters in my surveillance work took me down another inconvenient road that could not sustain simplistic revisionist counterfactuals about a national security state that waged war without monitoring the public, or a policy prescription at once reformist, principled, and possible.

In attempting to criticize progressive and conservative statism, I found insufficient historical awareness in modern libertarian theory. My broader intellectual goal was originally to vindicate a liberal, propertarian conception of civil liberties, to defend the distinction between positive and negative rights and criticize progressives for wanting their cake and eating it too. Instead I discovered that both vindicatory genealogies and simplistic revisionism could not entirely reconcile civil liberties theory and practice. As a general matter, libertarian revisionism sometimes adopts a deformed mirror image of what Rothbard derided as a priori history.[19] Vindicatory genealogies tend to take the form of cherrypicking evidence and building a case for a particular conclusion, which is why all activist writing, not just liberal writing, tends toward it. It's why lawyers are good at it. This does not pose the same contradictions to conservative or progressive thought, however, because these belief systems are not as legalistic and mechanical as the libertarian affirmation of property rights and non-aggression as the defining elements of human liberty.[20]

Reflective of the more fundamental problem in liberal historical writing, liberals have under-theorized civil liberties, reducing them to corollaries of property rights and the non-aggression principle.[21] And at least much of this deficiency, in turn, is itself a product of insufficient historical thinking in the liberal tradition. Once we get through the methodological and theoretical problems, we can see our way to a revitalized research agenda.

•••

Libertarians, particularly ideologically driven polemicists, are reluctant to embrace historicism in contemplating the legal contours of a free society. An admission that liberty is conceptualized to mediate between social forces, and must be reconceptualized as those forces fundamentally change, smacks of the pragmatism and progressive positivism that liberals blame for the rise of the modern state.[22] If libertarians have a theory at all, it's that civil liberties, like all rights, are a transhistorical corollary of property rights and self-ownership. Thus the vindicatory genealogies track the fulfillment or discovery of a civil liberty protection somehow derivable from natural or property rights, and the revisionist histories contemplate how a secular institution has trampled over the timeless metaphysical rights of its subjects.

This approach is burdened by broad problems of history, theory, and application. An anachronistic conception of the separate spheres of property and state sovereignty that emerge more from later nineteenth-century origins than from eighteenth-century ideas is paradoxically used to vindicate common law and republicanism, and vice versa, despite the latter legal systems straying further from liberal individualism than most legal theorists of the twenty-first century do. In the abstract, libertarians enjoy the distinction between positive and negative liberties, cheering the latter and eschewing the former. Unfortunately, most civil liberties we value tend to straddle the divide. Some "civil liberties" guarantees, such as prohibitions on certain classes of legislation—prohibitions on disarming or conscripting—might seem to flow clearly enough from libertarian first principles, but most are not so simple. Aside from prohibitions on certain classes of statutes, civil liberties are rarely purely negative claims against aggression. Some civil liberties are not so different from civil rights. In applying the principles of private property mechanically, we find propertarianism would deride many cherished civil liberties as positive liberties because they entail claims on state action, advocacy for proportional remedy to rights violations, legal guarantees in tension with property rights, or protections over public space.

Among the most celebrated civil liberties are due process rights, and these often require the adjudication by a judge. To claim a right to due process is to make a positive claim on judicial mechanisms, and sometimes on conscripted third parties like witnesses and jurors. In any event, no libertarian has sufficiently demonstrated that a claim to financially expensive due process is superior to any other claim on tax-funded institutions. More fundamentally, it is not clear how due process flows inexorably from first principles. Assuming a person is guilty of a violent crime, we cannot very well argue for a metaphysical claim on due process. Assuming a person is innocent, no degree of due process could justify punishment.[23]

Questions of proportionality defy propertarian reductionism. Once someone commits a theft, there is simply no perfect answer as to the remedy. Perhaps if both perpetrator and victim agree on a resolution libertarians can be satisfied to stay out of it, but this transforms a tort into an agreement and such resolution is not always possible. Despite what some believe, there is no conflict between believing objective natural rights and subjective economic value, although a tension does seem to arise in remedies for theft. Some items of sentimental value are impossible to replace. For murder, punishment theory becomes even stickier. Some believe in detention or even forced labor for punishment but not for debt; others reverse this. Then there is torture, which most classical liberals oppose somewhat categorically, but which libertarianism itself seems to leave open. What is cruel and unusual is a historically contingent matter. Corporal punishment and tortures were more common than imprisonment when the 8th Amendment was ratified. Proportionality is not a simple propertarian principle.[24]

Liberals often wish to hand waive all this away and simply defend due process and other civil liberties as a prophylactic against government power. Better the guilty be freed than innocents be punished—that seems easy to defend. So does the notion that government spying, even when it doesn't violate property rights, is an exercise in government power, so why not oppose it for its own sake?[25] But this is an insufficient theorization. One could simply argue for an anarchist principle that the state should not do anything or at least not violate anyone. But it doesn't work for those who concede any role for the state. It fails to reckon with how the state should treat people captive in its grip, accept in the most abstract manner. It furthermore punts all questions on the blueprint for rules of order in a stateless society, if that is the goal. It also fails to reckon with the very difficult issues that arise when government forces civil liberties rights—which are not deductive negative liberties—to conflict, like the freedom from coerced speech and the right of defendants to have witnesses in their favor. When central states and local states clash over civil liberties questions, prophylactic arguments can often be made in both directions.

Then there is the tricky issue of public space. Freedom of speech in public is something that few uphold as an absolute. But classical liberals tend to defend the right to bear arms in public space. Civil liberties in public space must either be parasitic upon a theory of how first principles determine rules in public space—which seems impossible—or it must also be grounded in some sort of historicism. Mechanically imposing propertarian principles upon the problem of public space has unfortunately resulted in a contentious debate over immigration, in which some liberals have eschewed the classical liberal position of open borders and others refuse to acknowledge the real possibility that the policies of a free society could invite substantial social problems.[26] More generally, public space makes due process protections immune to reductive construction.

Because most civil liberties questions straddle the divide between positive and negative rights, lay claim to state action for remedy, or otherwise do not flow from property rights, reductive libertarianism is insufficiently dialectic and historicist to give satisfactory answers, which explains a weakness in liberal histories that touch on civil liberties. Non-reductive and historicist ideologies have a better time with civil liberties, which grew out of historical context and involve determinations that require historical awareness. The left and conservatives have dialectical tools to appreciate the contingency and cultural context behind the principles they hold dear. They have a theory of history at least implicit in their political ideology, whereas their normative commitments are not framed in as purely legalistic terms as liberals' tend to be. Despite the admirable efforts of theorists like Chris Matthew Sciabarra to affirm a dialectical libertarianism, most liberals and libertarians want to root their whole political philosophy in simple axioms of aggression and property, which conveniently reinforce their comparably reductive axiomatic understandings of economics.[27] In the main, liberals have not done as much as scholars of the left in even trying to define the law's contours outside of positivist interpretations of statute and precedent, instead repeating the older tendencies to see law as either autonomous or as a function of the ruling class, albeit with a different normative lens.[28]

Modern libertarianism should reclaim the historicism of nineteenth-century liberalism, which was more dialectically sensitive and appreciative of its historical context.[29] A historicist liberalism would better grapple with the history of civil liberties to both empirically appreciate the development of civil liberties and to enliven liberal theory. A research agenda shedding itself or at least more reflective of its reductive assumptions could analyze civil liberties violations under the modern state or the origins of civil liberties' construction to a much more fruitful end.

•••

A classical liberal historicism toward civil liberties issues could produce an exciting and fruitful research agenda, profiting both liberal second handlers and the greater scholarly world. We need bold and careful analysis of depredations, but without the common reductive assumptions. We need careful analysis of historical origins without debilitating assumptions that romanticize the past or privilege some periods as golden eras. Liberal scholars should consult the considerable relevant literature, despite temptations to discount work produced by ideological opponents. Denaturalizing contemporary liberal ideology would enrich its long-term dialectical development, and raise scholarly questions that those with other normative commitments might miss. Historicizing the origins of law and the collective social frameworks out of which individualist civil liberties arose in the modern liberal era would in turn better prepare scholars for a more sophisticated scrutiny of modern leviathan's depredations.

From American law's beginnings to the rise of liberalism and the modern state, the historiography provides a lot of fodder for appreciating the uneven trajectory of civil liberties. Tackling the origins of American legal order, particularly the legacies of colonialism, common law, constitutionalism, and republicanism, would deepen our knowledge about the construction of civil liberties. Liberals ought not neglect the work of recent legal historians in examining the dynamics of colonization as determining early American legal and political development. Christopher Tomlins has identified the imposition of a "rights-bearing individualism" in North America as understandably told as a partly emancipatory story in contrast to other imperial venues.[30] The question of unfree labor poses a theoretical challenge to those debating a doctrine of rights inalienability that would preclude indentured servitude. The jurisdictional multipluralism produced decentralist opportunities for liberty's protection but also marked a time when early modern European empires flouted due process rights according to geographical expedience.[31]

A less romantic assessment of the common law should keep in mind its troublingly anti-libertarian tendencies on freedom of speech and role as an engine of power and politics as demonstrated by historians from John Phillip Reid to Paul Halliday. As for Constitutional law, libertarians tend to adopt either the Spoonerite approach to damning the Founders or fall for Constitutional fetishism.[32] Those critical of the Constitution can consult a serious mainstream literature identifying its role in expansive government.[33] On Constitutional interpretation, Jack Rakove's account in *Original Meanings* does not sit well with those seeking unambiguous paper protections or who wish to identify twentieth-century libertarian strictures in an eighteenth-century document.[34] If there is an original meaning we can divine from the Constitution, it will only come after a degree of historical attention never given to anything but a small cross section of a language, and then its continuing relevance is still a question. Intellectual historians do such work, but the results can frustrate presentist civil libertarians.[35] The unmistakable rigor with which William Cuddihy made the best case possible for exactly what "unreasonable searches and seizures" meant to Americans in 1791 demonstrates that it meant something different in 1781 and could not possibly mean the same thing in 1801 let alone 2016.[36] The contingencies and ambiguities surrounding ratification have also inspired serious and provocative study.[37]

The United States' founding republicanism often neglected civil liberties, and not merely by omission but by its very structure. Studying this can teach us lessons about the expansive powers, both potential and actual, of supposedly constitutionally limited government. Hummel has provided a synthetic treatment of violations during the Revolutionary War, the Quasi-War with France, and the War of 1812, as well as taking on the other major wars through World War II.[38] Although in absolute terms executive power seems to have only grown in the long nineteenth century, its early illiberal tendencies are sometimes obscured by the proto-libertarian rhetoric. The republican foundations of early American law were hardly mechanically libertarian, and grappling with both the virtues and vices in this antiquated formulation of rights and obligations would contribute both to a demystification of the American founding and a more subtle rethinking of liberal conceptions of rights. A lot of the best work on republican obligations and law has focused on the intense stratification along gender and racial lines, subjects that liberals are far too reluctant to consider in their expositions of liberty's history.[39] Indeed, beyond republicanism, early America often resembled a caste hierarchy constructed around race and gender, categories that liberals today do not always confront with comfort. Such institutional collectivism defied liberal individualism in ways that persisted in weighing down the later conceptualizations of civil liberties along more libertarian lines.

Treatments of early America must reckon seriously with the legacies of slavery. Slavery's distortions of legal rights were hardly exceptions proving the rule. At times they deformed the entirety of the legal order. At other times slavery was constitutive of civil liberties structures like federalism in ways libertarians seem too uncomfortable to confront, or even helped produce the conceptualization of liberty for those not enslaved.[40] The historiography on American slavery is among the best in the field, and the legal historical literature alone is formidable. Ever since Genovese's *Roll, Jordan, Roll,* grappled with the "hegemonic function of the law," pitting a Weberian conception of the state against less positivist legal dynamics, slavery historians have been among the best at teasing out the difference between positive law and actual legal practice.[41] In fact, the rise of modern policing, incarceration, and surveillance out of the disciplinary mechanisms of slavery provides one of the most ripe areas of criticizing the modern state.[42] As a corollary to the lacuna in liberal scholarship on slavery, the Reconstruction Era has been a source of frustration, as libertarians are uncomfortable with the currently conventional narrative of a centralizing force at times violating strictures on power to combat white terror. Instead of understanding that even the most plausible of national emergencies can lead to unfortunate deprivations of civil liberties—of which most conservative-leaning libertarians seem more forgiving as it concerns the revolution—there is a denial of the very real predicament for human rights posed by decentralized forms of oppression worse than the imperial forms.

The racialized construction of national identity has animated a generation of legal historians. The civil liberties implications are deep, but as libertarians automatically question national power, and sometimes sheepish about emphasizing race as its own category of historical oppression, they have not taken the opportunity to contribute significantly to this. Exceptions like the Beitos' monographic biography of civil rights icon T. R. M. Howard, Jonathan Bean's document collection sponsored by the Independent Institute, and Andrew Napolitano's thoughtful trade volume *Dred Scott's Revenge,* almost serve to prove the rule.[43] Systematic degradation of racial minorities under both formal and informal laws, eventually tempered by the national state, makes the civil rights era tricky for today's liberals but they should confront the questions posed to propertarian reductionism and engage the literature exploring some of the greatest advances of modern freedom.

The construction of citizenship and subjecthood that blurs the line between positive and negative liberty poses a challenge to liberals who wish to keep the line impermeable, and engaging in the scholarship provides an opportunity to trace the sometimes neglected importance of freedom from state coercion while broadening one's appreciation of the importance of social inclusion in allowing freedom air to breathe. Kunal Parker offers a new synthetic overview of how formal legal categorization of the "other" shifted from a more multilayered effective caste system to a postwar system that more consistently affirms a federal binary between citizens and those deemed foreign. Parker's account of the rise of federal plenary immigration power alone informs our appreciation of the novelty of specific national threats to civil liberty without allowing refuge to those seeking the distant past for a libertarian era. More generally, the solidification of both federal authority and categories more consistent with liberal assumptions about rights offers fodder for liberal scholars seeking to understand the tradeoffs of different approaches to political inclusion. Even on immigration specifically, liberal economists have done some historically tinged work, but we need more engagement with the complex history of national, state, and local migration control. Looking to Parker and recent works like Maloney's *National Insecurities* and Mai Ngai's *Imposssible Subjects,* we see that racial construction was crucially constitutive in the formation of the modern state, and particularly its administrative arm. The unhappy coincidence that the national leviathan from the New Deal through the early Great Society emerged amid the most racially motivated immigration policy in U.S. history does not seem to have resonated enough with libertarians.[44]

Racial segregation and miscegenation laws are uncomfortable subjects for liberal historians.[45] Insofar as we acknowledge the significant progress on institutional racism, it seems we must give credit to the central state, and insofar as we don't want to credit the central state with solving it, the libertarian tool box offers few panaceas. This need not debilitate the honest historian, who can see the historical ubiquity of white supremacy as no more irreversibly damning to liberalism than it is to progressivism. Historians outside the liberal tradition have shown how lamentably the early 20th-century rational state handled racial segregation, from Vann Woodward's mid-century classic pinning modern Jim Crow as a deliberate policy unfolding decades after Reconstruction to Barbara Welke's *Recasting American Liberty,* whose important treatment of railroad car segregation provokes such questions as whether the move from common law to legal modernism was an unmitigated improvement.[46] Peggy Pascoe's *What Comes Naturally*, meanwhile, illustrates that miscegenation law well outside the deep south was often constructed through the discretion of mid-level administrators.[47] The bureaucratic state never looked so bad. Eugenics is another area where liberals and today's progressives seem to coincide in discomfort.[48]

Out of the collective institutionalism of the past both liberal individualism and the modern administrative state arose, a paradox that today's progressives might see as an indictment of that individualism, but whose work nevertheless can help guide a more sophisticated understanding of the progressive state. Historicizing civil liberties helps bring the progressive state under scrutiny. There are progressives who share liberal apprehensions about the fluidity of modern jurisprudence and see the virtue in exactly the pre-New Deal liberal categorizations of law that many libertarians favor.[49] On the other hand, progressive scholars have hinted at an appreciation of less formalistic means of making claims, decisively outside of the liberal rights paradigm, that could revitalize a new, if more nuanced, appreciation of customary law in the vindication of personal freedom.[50] And just as liberals can offer a critical lens to the regulatory state's civil liberties casualties, they can consult the mainstream historiography that has already identified classist criminalization as a feature of the administrative and conservationist progressive state.[51]

Of the under-theorized civil liberties issues, criminalization and punishment present some of the most unfortunate gaps in liberal scholarship. There are manifestos that envisage the broad outlines of stateless criminal justice, and few attempts to historicize law enforcement.[52] The traditional historiography has delved into the governing purposes of punishment in ways that shed light on the state. Drawing on Edward Ayers's cultural focus in *Vengeance and Justice* and Hindus's comparative *Prison and Plantation*, liberal historians can learn much from continuities between chattel slavery and the modern rational state they so disdain. Moving into the twentieth century, Rothman's *Discovery of the Asylum* long ago produced one of the more salient criticisms of Progressive ideology through the lens of punishment, although its core conception of the docility of prisoners was effectively challenged by Rebecca McLennan's focus on coerced labor in *Crisis of Imprisonment*. The latter work also depicts the subtle transformation through both privatized and more public-sector-oriented prison labor regimes, a theme with great importance today as reformers seek to privatize or socialize prisons instead of focusing on the core coercion of the institution regardless of the custodian.[53]

My own book on surveillance contains bibliographical suggestions on both spying and the right to privacy. Suffice it here to say that an entire research paradigm was opened up by McCoy's focus in *Policing America's Empire* of how the Progressive era wars abroad from the Philippines to World War I served as laboratories for surveillance at home. No recent work has better demonstrated that war is the health of the state. As for privacy rights, my work raised more questions than answers. I invite a more meticulous look at the theoretical history of privacy rights in America, perhaps starting with Brandeis and Warren's 1890 formulation of the idea and culminating with its adoption in the 1960s cases on wiretapping and reproductive right, which make conservative libertarians squeamish, and so liberals have often agreed on détente here.[54] It's unfortunate, because nothing better demonstrates how something can seem so primordially fundamental and so historically contingent at the same time. The last generation of scholarship on sex, gender, and marriage history demonstrates the troublingly fluid line between civil liberty and more positive claims.[55]

In the early twenty-first century, one civil liberties question that often divides the more and less conservative wings of libertarian scholarship concerns policing.[56] Journalist Radley Balko's *Rise of the Warrior Cop* invites more academic historians to the problem.[57] Some of the best criticism of the Progressive Era's marriage of social science to social policy helps us understand the deep roots of racialization in 20th-century criminal justice.[58]At a time when mainstream scholars are more than ever willing to attribute the rise of modern crime to 20th-century social statism, liberals, scholarly or not, should not neglect policing.[59]

There was no golden era and historicizing civil liberties, far from flattening our historical appreciation, would inform the different ways civil liberties were constructed, violated, and transformed at different times. Liberals can continue to highlight the central role of physical coercion in the modern state's violations of civil liberty while recognizing the nuances that defy simplistic ideology. This sensitivity to historicity and contingency would improve our accounts of the development of a core pillar of the liberal program, enrich the theoretical assumptions undergirding liberalism, and help produce better histories of state building that would serve the contemporary liberal movement and the wider scholarly world.

NOTES

1. I use "liberal" to describe libertarians and classical liberals; "libertarian" to describe more narrowly the radical market individualism that arose in the late twentieth century and tends toward deontological adherence to Rothbardian, Randian, or similar conceptions of private property and the non-aggression principle; and "progressive" very broadly to mark modern left-of-center egalitarian thinkers.

2. And yet many economics controversies provoke animated debates among liberals.

3. Two books exemplify this work when aimed at popular consumption: Gene Healy, *The Cult of the Presidency: America's Dangerous Devotion to Executive Power* (Cato Institute, 2008); Ivan Eland, *Recarving Rushmore: Ranking the Presidents on Peace, Prosperity, and Liberty* (Independent Institute, 2014). Both books take civil liberties as important and consider fraught questions like charismatic authority and civil rights that defy legalistic reductionism simplistic narrative arc. Many works in this tradition are less rigorous.

4. Robert Higgs, *Crisis and Leviathan: Critical Episodes in the Growth of American Government* (New York: Oxford University Press, 1987). See especially chapters 6 through 9.

5. Jeffrey Rogers Hummel, *Emancipating Slaves, Enslaving Free Men: A History of the American Civil War* (Open Court, 1996).

6. Murray N. Rothbard, *Conceived in Liberty* (New Rochelle, NY: Arlington House Publishers, 1975, 1976, and 1979).

7. Rothbard, "Left and Right: The Prospects for Liberty," *Left and Right* (Spring 1965), 4–22.

8. William J. Watkins, *Reclaiming the American Revolution: The Kentucky and Virginia Resolutions and Their Legacy* (Palgrave, 2004); Thomas E. Woods, Jr., *Nullification: How to Resist Federal Tyranny in the 21st Century* (Regnery Publishing, 2010).

9. Jim Powell's *Greatest Emancipations: How the West Abolished Slavery* (St. Martin's Press, 2008) frames slavery as an ancient evil only eventually vanquished by the liberal state.

10. Stephen P. Halbrook, *Freedmen, the Fourteenth Amendment, and the Right to Bear Arms, 1866–1876* (Praeger, 1998).

11. See, for example, Alan Bloom, ed.m *Confronting the Constitution: The Challenge to Locke, Montesquieu, Jefferson, and the Federalists from Utilitarianism, Historicism, Marxism, Freudianism, Pragmatism, Existentialism … .* (Washington, DC: AEI Press, 1990); Harry V. Jaffa with Bruce Ledewitz, Robert L. Stone, George Anastaplo, *Original Intent and the Framers of the Constitution: A Disputed Question.* Foreword by Lewis E. Lehrman *Washington, DC: Regnery Gateway, 1994); Thomas F. Pangle, *The Spirit of Modern Republicanism: The Moral Vision of the American Founders and the Philosophy of Locke* (Chicago: University of Chicago Press, 1988).

12. John Hasnas, "Hayek, the Common Law, and Fluid Drive," *New York University Journal of Law & Liberty* 1, (2004); Francis Fukuyama, *The Origins of Political Order: From Prehuman Times to the French Revolution* (Farrar, Straus and Giroux, 2011).

13. On Jeffersonian opponents of the common law, see Richard E. Ellis, *The Jeffersonian Crisis: Courts and Politics in the Young Republic* (New York: W.W. Norton and Company, 1974 [1971]). On the common law's use against the British Empire, see John Phillip Reid, *In a Defiant Stance: The Conditions of Law in Massachusetts Bay, the Irish Comparison; and the Coming of the American Revolution* (University Park, PA: Pennsylvania State University Press, 1977). On common law as a producer of (not necessarily libertarian) capitalism, see William E. Nelson, *Americanization of the Common Law: The Impact of Legal Change on Massachusetts Society, 1760–1830* (Athens, GA: University of Georgia Press, 1994) and Howard Schweber, *The Creation of American Common Law, 1850–1880: Technology, Politics, and the Construction of Citizenship* (Cambridge: Cambridge University Press, 2004). On common laws on historicism, see Kunal M. Parker, *Common Law, History, and Democracy in America, 1790–1900* (Cambridge: Cambridge University Press, 2013).

14. The final work is Anthony Gregory, *The Power of Habeas Corpus in America: From the King's Prerogative to the War on Terror* (New York: Cambridge University Press, 2013).

15. *Boumediene v. Bush,* 553 U.S. 723 (2008).

16. Paul D. Halliday, *Habeas Corpus: From England to Empire* (Harvard University Press, 2010).

17. See especially chapter 2 of Justin Wert, *Habeas Corpus in America: The Politics of Individual Rights* (University of Kansas Press, 2011).

18. Gregory, *American Surveillance: Intelligence, Privacy, and the Fourth Amendment* (Madison: University of Wisconsin Press, 2016).

19. See Rothbard, "Revisionism and Libertarianism," *The Libertarian Forum*, February 1976. Although different methods tend to come into play, vindicatory genealogies and sloppy revisionist stories are in another respect two side of the same coin, what Rothbard, drawing on Mises, derided as priori history. But whereas Rothbard was pushing back against Cold War patriotism that cast liberal empires as always good, rose-colored a priori history also afflicts libertarians in the way they discuss the Founding, the common law, the nineteenth century, and the past generally. Different factions of liberals tend to look admirably at different episodes and actors. Depending on who's doing it, the British Empire, the Confederacy, the Axis Powers, the Soviet Union, Saddam Hussein, or Islamic radicals are seen not only as an excuse for the liberal empire to commit questionable acts, but as not as nefarious as often depicted. The a priori revisionist tendency picks up on war propaganda but is usually always holistically wrong. A corollary of this problem is a priori revisionism, toward which radical libertarians tend. And so instead of downplaying the evils of the liberal empire, there is a tendency, as is also seen in the paleo-right and the radical left, to downplay the evils of the liberal empire's enemies. The implication for civil liberties is to downplay the complexity of the policy tradeoff between civil liberties and security priorities. Even if one's anarchism or radicalism leads to absolutist conclusions on civil liberties, it is intellectually dishonest to suggest there has never been a real social cost to preserving them.

20. An alternative is to value liberty as a broader question of human freedom and agency. This thicker conception of liberty could more easily accommodate the fraught historical development of civil liberties, although its major proponents still advocate the non-aggression principle as a baseline stricture against state power. See Charles Johnson, "Libertarianism Through Thick and Thin," Foundation for Economic Education, 1 July 2008.

21. Along such lines Rothbard argues that the only protection of privacy can be a corollary of property protection in chapter 16 of *The Ethics of Liberty* (Atlantic Highlands, NJ: Humanities Press, 1982). The non-aggression principle was also the core commitment of the other champion of 20th-century deontological libertarianism, Ayn Rand. See "Man's Rights" in the *Virtue of Selfishness* (1961). Less deontological leaders of libertarianism, such as Mises, Hayek, and Friedman, tended toward economics as a discipline, which reinforced their consequentialist case for liberty but nevertheless encouraged thinking about social principles in terms of axioms and less in terms of historicism. At the same time, the three authors, perhaps because of their reluctance toward reductionist liberalism, often engaged history sensitive to counterintuitive complexities.

22. John Dewey's, *Liberalism and Social Action* (1935) is a classic exposition on liberty's historicism, one most liberals will contest.

23. See Part III of Gregory, *Power of Habeas Corpus in America*.

24. See Chapter 12 of Rothbard, *The Ethics of Liberty*. for a treatment of proportionality.

25. See chapters 7, 8, and 9 in Gregory, *American Surveillance*.

26. For one criticism of the restrictionist view, see Gregory and Walter Block, "On Immigration: Reply to Hoppe," *Journal of Libertarian Studies* 21, (3) (2007).

27. Chris Matthew Sciabarra, *Total Freedom: Toward a Dialectical Libertarianism* (Penn State Press, 2000).

28. See Robert Gordon, "Critical Legal Histories" 36 *Stanford Law Review* 57 (1984), for a discussion of law's "relative autonomy." A classic work of legal history that privileges context over formalism is Hendrik Hartog, "Pigs and Positivism."

29. Ralph Raico explains the affinity between European liberalism's more contextualist belief system and axiomatic economics in the title essay of *Classical Liberalism and the Austrian School* (Auburn, AL: Ludwig von Mises Institute, 2012).

30. Christopher Tomlins, "Introduction: The Many Legalities of Colonization," in Tomlins and Bruce H. Mann, ed., *The Many Legalities of Early America* (University of North Carolina Press, 2001), 18.

31. Lauren Benton, *A Search for Sovereignty: Law and Geography in European Empires, 1400–1900* (Cambridge University Press, 2009).

32. For one of the most serious libertarian critical engagements of the Constitution compared to the Articles of Confederation, see Sheldon Richman, *America's Counter-Revolution: The Constitution Revisited* (Griffin & Lash, 2016).

33. See Max M. Edling, *A Revolution in Favor of Government: Origins of the U.S. Constitution and the Making of the American State* (Oxford University Press, 1998).

34. Jack Rakove, *Original Meanings: Politics and Ideas in the Making of the Constitution* (Vintage, 1997).

35. Liberal legal theorists make arguments for libertarian Constitutional interpretation, which we might welcome in the courtroom but still question as dispassionate legal history. See Randy E. Barnett, *Restoring the Lost Constitution: The Presumption of Liberty* (Princeton University Press, 2004).

36. William J. Cuddihy, *The Fourth Amendment: Origins and Original Meaning 602—1791* (Oxford University Press, 2011).

37. On the state-level ratification process, Pauline Maier, *Ratification: The People Debate the Constitution, 1787–1788* (Simon & Schuster, 2011), is indispensable. On the unreliability of Madison's notes on the national convention, see Mary Sarah Bilder, *Madison's Hand: Revising the Constitutional Convention* (Harvard University Press, 2013).

38. Hummel, *War Is the Health of the State: The Impact of Military Defense on the History of the United States*. San Jose State, 2012, https://papers.ssrn.com/sol3/papers.cfm?abstract_id=2151041.

39. Kerber, Linda. *No Constitutional Right To Be Ladies; Welke, Belonging*.

40. Christopher Tomlins, *Freedom Bound: Law, Labor, and Civic Identity in Colonizing English America, 1580–1865* (Cambridge University Press, 2010).

41. Eugene Genovese, *Roll, Jordan, Roll: The World the Slaves Made* (New York: Vintage, 1972), 25–49. Thomas Morris discusses the duality of slaves as persons and property in *Southern Slavery and the Law: 1619–1860* (Chapel Hill and London: University of North Carolina Press, 1996). More recent monographic work has

identified this duality in the courtroom. See *Double Character: Slavery and Mastery in the Antebellum Southern Courtroom* (Princeton University Press, 2000). "Liberals can learn from the customary law's maintenance of slaves' property, despite the shifting vagaries of formal law," in *The Claims of Kinfolk: African American Property and Community in the Nineteenth-Century South* (University of North Carolina Press, 2003). The difficulties presented to anti-slavery jurists and legal theorists, including libertarian icons William Lloyd Garrison and Lysander Spooner, are explored in Robert Cover, *Justice Accused: Antislavery and the Judicial Process* (Yale University Press, 1984).

42. See Gregory, *American Surveillance*, 18–19; Michael S. Hindus, *Prison and Plantation: Crime, Justice, and Authority in Massachusetts and South Carolina, 1767–1878* (University of North Carolina Press, 2012), and, on post–Civil War carceral forced labor, David M. Oshinsky, *Worse than Slavery: Parchman Farm and the Ordeal of Jim Crow Justice* (Free Press, 1997).

43. David T. Beito and Linda Royster Beito, *Black Maverick: T. R. M. Howard's Fight for Civil Rights and Economic Power* (University of Illinois Press, 2009); Jonathan Bean, *Race and Liberty in America: The Essential Reader* (University Press of Kentucky, 2009); Andrew P. Napolitano, *Dred Scott's Revenge: A Legal History of Race and Freedom in America* (Thomas Nelson, 2009).

44. Kunal Parker, *Making Foreigners: Immigration and Citizenship Law in America, 1600–2000* (Cambridge University Press, 2015); Deirdre M. Moloney, *National Insecurities: Immigrants and U.S. Deportation Policy since 1882* (University of North Carolina Press, 2012); Mae M. Ngai, *Impossible Subjects: Illegal Aliens and the Making of Modern America* (Princeton University Press, 2004); Lucy E. Salyer, *Laws Harsh as Tigers: Chinese Immigrants and the Shaping of Modern Immigration Law* (University of North Carolina Press, 1995).

45. Some exceptions arise in the economic history written in the liberal tradition, such as Jennifer Roback's "The Political Economy of Segregation: The Case of Segregated Streetcars," *The Journal of Economic History* 46, (4) (Dec., 1986), 893–917.

46. Barbara Welke, *Recasting American Liberty: Gender, Race, Law, and the Railroad Revolution, 1865–1920* (Cambridge: Cambridge University Press, 2001).

47. Peggy Pascoe, *What Comes Naturally: Miscegenation Law and the Making of Race in America* (New York: Oxford University Press, 2009).

48. See Thomas C. Leonard, *Illiberal Reformers: Race, Eugenics, and American Economics in the Progressive Era* (Princeton University Press, 2016).

49. Duncan Kennedy, *The Rise and Fall of Classical Legal Thought.* On the other hand, Horwitz, in *The Transformation of American Law, 1870–1960: The Crisis of Legal Orthodoxy* (New York: Oxford University Press, 1992), laments the "static fundamentalism" and "unhistorical and abstract universalisms" that came to define postwar progressive jurisprudence, as opposed to building on the progressive legal realism that had replaced classical legal thought (271–272).

50. Laura F. Edwards, *The People and Their Peace: Legal Culture and the Transformation of Inequality in the Post-Revolutionary South* (University of North Carolina Press, 2009).

51. William J. Novak makes a persuasive case for an extensive nineteenth-century regulatory regime at the state and local levels in *The People's Welfare: Law and*

Regulation in Nineteenth Century America (University of North Carolina Press, 1996). Progressives can see this as a defense of the modern state against accusations of novelty, but liberals can see such examples as the local law of nuisance as an example of reactionary regulation. Karl Jacoby's *Crimes against Nature: Squatters, Poachers, Thieves, and the Hidden History of American Conservation* (University of California Press, 2014) invites further study of the intersection of modern administration, conservationism, and criminalization.

52. For distinctly historical works, see Allen Steinberg, "'The Spirit of Litigation': Private Prosecution and Criminal Justice in Nineteenth Century Philadelphia," *Journal of Social History* 20, (2) (Winter, 1986): 231–249; and Stephen Davies, "The Private Provision of Police during the Eighteenth and Nineteenth Century," chapter 7 in *The Voluntary City: Choice, Community, and Civil Society* (Oakland: Independent Institute, 2002).

53. Edward L. Ayers, *Vengeance and Justice: Crime and Punishment in the Nineteenth-Century American South* (Oxford University Press, 1985); Michael S. Hindus, *Crime, Justice, and Authority in Massachusetts and South Carolina, 1767–1878* (University of North Carolina Press, 2012); David Rothman, *The Discovery of the Asylum* (Transaction Publishers, 1971); Rebecca M. McLennan, *The Crisis of Imprisonment: Protest, Politics, and the Making of the American Penal State, 1776–1941* (Cambridge University Press, 2008).

54. Samuel D. Warren and Louis D. Brandeis, "The Right to Privacy," *Harvard Law Review* 4, (5) (1890): 193–220.

55. Leigh Ann Wheeler, *How Sex Became a Civil Liberty* (Oxford University Press, 2014); Hendrik Hartog, *Man and Wife in America, A History* (Harvard University Press, 2002); Nancy F. Cott, *Public Vows: A History of Marriage and the Nation* (Harvard University Press, 2002). Some of the best works on the modern progressive state's assaults on civil liberty arise at the intersection of sex, gender, and policy. On homosexuality and modern leviathan, see Margot Canaday, *The Straight State: Sexuality and Citizenship in Twentieth-Century America* (Princeton University Press, 2011). On the criminalization of abortion and the role of the modern medical establishment, see Leslie J. Reagan, *When Abortion Was a Crime: Women, Medicine, and Law in the United States, 1867–1973* (University of California Press, 1997). Wendy McElroy's *Freedom, Feminism, and the State* (Independent Institute, 1991), remains one important historically tinged work by a feminist libertarian.

56. Richard Epstein is critical of the description of police abuse as "institutional racism." See "Hasty Judgment On 'Institutional Racism,'" Hoover Institution, July 11, http://www.hoover.org/research/hasty-judgment-institutional-racism.

57. Radley Balko, *Rise of the Warrior Cop: The Militarization of America's Police Forces* (PublicAffairs, 2013).

58. Khalil Gibran Muhammad, *The Condemnation of Blackness: Race, Crime, and the Making of Modern Urban America* (Cambridge, MA: Harvard University Press, 2010).

59. Naomi Murakawa, *The First Civil Right: How Liberals Built Prison America* (Oxford University Press, 2014); Elizabeth Hinton, *From the War on Poverty to the War on Crime: The Making of Mass Incarceration in America* (Harvard University Press, 2016).

Chapter 4

Lost in *Methodenstreit*

Reflections on Theory, History, and the Quest for a Science of Association

Lenore T. Ealy

I fell back on what still seems to me the fact rather than the argument that historical inquiry is anti-paradigmatic, in the sense that it multiplies without theoretical limitation the problem-situations, contingencies and contexts in which any historical occurrence may have been situated, and therefore performs the liberal-conservative function of warning the ruler on the one hand, and the revolutionary on the other, that there is always more going on than either can understand or control.

J. G. A. Pocock, *Political Thought and History: Essays on Theory and Method*[1]

To act "in contradiction to all past historical experience" is to render human beings helpless. We cannot know the Truth. We can, however, attempt to develop a critical awareness of the relationships of the languages we use to thought, the relationships of thought to the actions we take, and the relationships of communicating, associating, and working with others to what is achieved. The institution of languages is the fundament of order in all human societies.

Vincent Ostrom, *The Meaning of Democracy and the Vulnerability of Democracies*[2]

INTRODUCTION

The purpose of this book is to reflect on the goals, aims, progress, and future prospects of classical liberal history. At once, the concept "classical liberal history" poses challenging questions. Is classical liberal history merely that

history written by historians who embrace an ordinal preference for liberty
among the varieties of competing normative values? Is classical liberal history primarily the historiography of a political theory or of a framework of
political economy known as classical liberalism? Or does classical liberal
history represent a more robust and ongoing normative tradition of historiography itself, one that employs a distinct epistemological approach to historical understanding and that embrace conceptual presuppositions—such as
methodological individualism and/or methodological subjectivism?

This chapter seeks to contribute to this discussion by exploring the challenges presented to classical liberal scholarship both by the methodological
contests in which it has been engaged and by complications surrounding the
concepts of progress and social change that are entangled in modern thought.
The attempt to define and delineate a "classical liberal" approach to scholarship arises at in part in reaction to the modern preoccupation with progressive
reform and its scholarly foundations. More recent problems of post-modernity
have further precipitated the current desire among classical liberal scholars to
narrate their own history. Whether these autonomous narratives of the classical liberal tradition can succeed in holding at bay the radical deconstruc-
tive tendencies of postmodern historiography, which "assumes the political
purpose of breaking down historical identities and continuities where they
may have been asserted,"[3] will largely depend upon whether classical liberal
scholars can better explain and garner assent for three essential foundations:
(1) the anthropological postulate that human beings purposefully act; (2) the
epistemological premise that human knowledge of human action is irreducibly
subjective but that this does not condemn us to relativism; and (3) the analytical principle that social harmony and prosperity among free individuals in civil
society is an emergent property of human action rather than human design.

Classical liberalism is an intellectual tradition oriented around a constellation of ideas linked by their rational complementarity. It is also a historical,
rhetorical, and political enterprise sustained by actors who seek to promote
these ideas as guides to human and social action.[4] Ludwig von Mises, one of
the foremost expositors of the classical liberal tradition in the 20th century
(though he still uses the original term *liberalism*), cautioned that should one
want "to know what liberalism is and what it aims at, one cannot simply turn
to history for the information and inquire what the liberal politicians stood for
and what they accomplished. For liberalism nowhere succeeded in carrying out
its program as it had intended." Nor, Mises, added, "does it any longer suffice
today to form one's idea of liberalism from a study of the writings of its great
founders. Liberalism is not a completed doctrine or a fixed dogma. On the contrary, it is the application of the teachings of science to the social life of man."[5]

Mises' caution that classical liberalism cannot be understood only historically, however, neither relieves us of the responsibility to understand the

history of the classical liberal tradition nor allows us to dismiss the ongo-ing influence of the classical liberal tradition in inspiring both theoretical frameworks and aesthetic visions of a free, prosperous, and peaceful society. Historical inquiry is essential to properly understand how some features of the classical liberal idea-language complex emerged from logical ratiocina-tion and how others features were forged in the context of specific intellec-tual and political debates. As a phenomenon of "modern" history, classical liberalism took shape during an age of scientific, religious, and political revolutions. Classical liberalism invokes "science"—rather than faith or power—as its authoritative appeal, but any history of classical liberalism will have to account for our new understanding that even science is irreduc-ibly a social endeavor that can generate authority only under conditions of consensus about what is warrantable as "truth."[6] Arguing about what counts as truth and why is the central task of epistemology. Understanding the processes by which epistemic agreements are worked out is one function of historical inquiry. While theory seeks to present the logical coherence of idea complexes, history seeks to understand ideas in the context of the problem situations confronted by the specific human beings who do things with them. Nevertheless, neither theory nor history can be conducted without the other.

One purpose of this chapter is to propose that the continuing analytical reappraisal and normative renewal of the classical liberal tradition requires a reconsideration of the purposes of history, a deeper reflection on epistemo-logical and methodological problems in historiography, and an intentional effort to reintegrate historical research with other research programs that seek to understand the sciences of human and social action. There have been recent efforts by scholars working in classical liberal traditions of social science, such as Austrian economics, constitutional political economy, and some aspects of sociology, to restore historical study to their methodological tool kit.[7] It is my contention that there is much more of this work to be done, and that fruitful collaborations will require scholars across the disciplines to explore the long history of *methodenstreit*, the methodological contests over and about the authority of the sciences conducted by their various institu-tional representatives, independent practitioners, and publicists.

After identifying some possible paths for deeper methodological inquiry that might reunite history and theory as partners in advancing the sciences of human action, I will suggest that a key arena for increased collaboration among historians and social theorists will be to take up more intentionally Alexis de Tocqueville's call for the development of a "science" of voluntary association. In *Democracy in America*, published in two volumes in 1835 and 1840, Tocqueville famously observed that "In democratic countries the science of association is the mother science; the progress of all the others depends on the progress of that one."[8] Almost two centuries later, however, we are still far from having a sound picture—historically or theoretically—of the way that people utilize associations in pursuing their plans. We need to pay more attention to the roles that voluntary, and especially non-political, associations play in shaping human action and thereby understand how these contribute to the development and institutional dynamics of the patterns of order we call a society.

Steven Scalet and David Schmidtz argue that classical liberals have grounded their policy prescriptions precisely on the imperative to "Nurture voluntary associations."[9] Notwithstanding, I want to suggest that this "grounding" has been more lip service than critical analysis. There remains much serious work to do to develop credible answers to the questions Tocqueville was posing, and which we should pose, about the uses people make of associations and the way associations contribute to the generation of social order. Moreover, I want to propose that it has been this comparative lacuna in classical liberal social thought that has left us ill equipped to address the radical dissolution of history and theory and traditional social institutions that has been a goal of postmodern critical theory. Libertarian activist Richard Cornuelle made the astute observation many years ago that the classical liberal specialization in economics, while suited to its early battles with socialism, was not yet equipped to contend with social democracy. Economic specialization, Cornuelle argued, "has become a kind of disability. Social democracy is a *social* program, built on contentions about the shortcomings of free societies we are not yet well equipped to confront."[10]

METHODOLOGICAL BABEL?

In *The Meaning of Democracy and the Vulnerability of Democracies*—leadingly subtitled "A Response to Tocqueville's Challenge"—Vincent Ostrom explores the difficulties of understanding the relationships between ideas and deeds. The "essential relationship of 'ideas' to 'deeds,'" he writes, "depends on discrete individuals in discrete language communities achieving complementarities in their uses of language." The diversity of human purposes generates plural languages that yield ongoing challenges to mutual understanding and action. Our bounded rationality and fallibility further complicate the possibilities of living well together. Nevertheless, if we are to exist without being isolated and helpless individuals, that is, if we are to coexist in civil society, our challenge, as Ostrom frames it, is "how to take languages that run the risk of profuse babbling and use them in ways that enhance the responsible use of human knowledge, skills, and intelligibility within the meaningful expressions of artisanship in the processes of being and becoming."[11]

European (and later American) colleges and universities emerged as specialized social institutions where scholars have negotiated the boundaries of definition and authority among the diverse languages of human intellection and action. Even a brief look at the waxing and waning of disciplines through the centuries offers us a window into these processes. Theology, for instance, reigned for almost a millennium as the queen of the sciences and began to be displaced only during the Enlightenment era. Gradually, the empirical sciences distinguished themselves from philosophy, and later new "social sciences" differentiated themselves from the natural sciences. This process of differentiation, however, has not been linear and irreversible; rather it has been a dynamic process full of progressions, recursions, and recombinations. Theology and science have been very separate endeavors for centuries now, but contests between them still occur as do efforts to find *rapprochements*.

The social sciences also never fully broke away from the natural sciences. Social scientists continue to recur, even if only metaphorically, to the vocabularies and models of the natural sciences. Scientism, the more problematic effort to apply natural science methodologies directly in the social sciences, remains a sort of strange attractor for some social scientists.[12] From the positivism of early sociology to the behavioralism of psychology in the 20th century to the ongoing importation of evolutionary conceptions across all domains of human thought, the epistemic goals of the natural sciences have complicated the development of a general consensus about the proper methodology for the sciences of human action.

There has also been an ongoing tension between theory and history that has complicated collaboration between historians and social scientists in exploring the presuppositions, methodologies, and general orientations most appropriate to the study of human action. In describing the differentiation of the social sciences—principally economics, sociology, and political science—as distinct scholarly disciplines in the United States during the 19th century, Dorothy Ross proposes that the "effort to create social sciences was bound up with the discovery that history was a realm of human construction, propelled ever forward in time by the cumulative effects of human action ... ."[13] These continuing tensions between the social sciences and history require further investigation, as does Ross' suggestion that the social sciences emerged as a response to a new historical awakening, a new understanding of human action in time.

In the 14th and 15th centuries the recovery of classical texts previously lost to Western European scholars began to foster a new historical awareness of discontinuities between past and present that helped give shape to Renaissance humanism. With the age of European exploration and empire came another awareness of discontinuity that was more spatial than temporal. The discovery of "primitive" cultures on other continents sharpened an awareness of the diverse possibilities of social organization, which critical observers would soon come to recognize in the differences between the cultures of Western European nations themselves. Vernacular languages began to compete with scholarly Latin, and by the 15th century scholars were not only increasingly studying the Bible in the old Hebrew and Greek but also stepping up the production of vernacular translations.

Advances in linguistic scholarship as well as the growing recognition of discontinuity between the early Christian church and the perceived institutional corruptions of the Roman Catholic Church helped to fuel calls for doctrinal refinement and ecclesiastical reform. The Reformation thus generated its own pluralisms, as new church institutions took shape in both nationalist and dissenting forms. Gradually, more secular and plural conceptions of history began to compete with Christian-oriented understandings of history as a singular realm of providential operation. It became increasingly possible for scholars to inquire into the influence of human action on historical change as well as to conceive of social institutions as contingent products of human choices rather than providential authorship. What was more difficult to work out, however, was just how human action influenced the development (or decline) of social and political institutions and to what extent human action could advance (or constrain) the processes of historical change.

Such changing paradigms of history helped give rise to modern social thought, which was also influenced by new conceptions of nature. In *Social Change and History*, Robert Nisbet discusses the turn made by 18th-century thinkers as diverse as "the physiocrats, Rousseau, Adam Smith, Diderot, Adam Ferguson, and others" to what was called "natural history" or "conjectural history." These new natural histories described unfolding stages of institutional development. But these thinkers often sought to discern the essential principle of development "that *will manifest itself* provided only that corrupting, deflecting, or interfering circumstances of one kind or other do not intrude."[14] Nisbet observes that both Smith and Rousseau used the techniques of conjectural history, although they came to very different assessments of the value of the growing division of labor and the resultant interdependence of men. For Rousseau, the happiest civilization was one in which people "undertook only what a single person could accomplish, and confined themselves to such arts as did not require the joint labor of several hands." For Smith, by contrast, the drive to the division of labor, to associative forms of production, and to commerce was a natural expression of the human instinct to "truck, barter, and exchange" which was too often obstructed by the burden of misguided mercantilist policies.[15]

In his important work on *Theory and History* (1957)—subtitled *An Interpretation of Social and Economic Evolution*—Mises describes the contest that arose between mercantilists and classical liberals in the late 18th century as an argument over whether there could be a harmony of interests in society, as the classical economists proposed, or whether "there is an irreconcilable conflict of interests among men and among groups of men." The belief that society was fundamentally a place of conflict that required sustained intervention by government was, Mises argues, "the essence of the teachings of Mercantilism and the main target of the Classical economists' critique of Mercantilism, to which they opposed their doctrine of the harmony of the rightly understood or long-run interests of all members of a market society."[16] Nature for the classical liberals, in other words, did not really resemble the "state of nature" earlier described by Thomas Hobbes as a war of all against all requiring the steadying hand of a sovereign Leviathan. Instead, nature (and, for some, natural laws,) were less matters of positive social contract than "spontaneous" developments from the very nature of things. Drawn voluntarily to engage in acts of association and exchange, people would discover the "laws" of comparative advantage and the division of labor, and thus as the result of human action but not human design productive patterns of social order would arise and along with the possibility of peaceful commerce and civil society.

Such disputes have long been part and parcel of the Western intellectual tradition, which holds space open for contestation as a means of sifting the ideas worthy of addition to the canons of "scientific" knowledge. Moreover, the pursuit of mutual understanding among scholars has also given rise to an extended "republic of letters" working to expand the sphere of possibility for sharing knowledge. We might even hazard the suggestion that the associative practices of trucking, bartering, and exchanging ideas through the republic of letters resembles similar practices in the commercial sphere and that histories and social analyses of the scholarly enterprise and institutions through which it is conducted should form an important chapter in the story of the emergence of a conception of a spontaneously developing civil society.

Ostrom notes the fundamentally social character of the quest for knowledge, which not only depends on the existence of external objects and phenomena to be understood, but is also relational, turning on "the character and degree of common knowledge, mutual understanding, social accountability, and trust."[17] The pursuit of understanding in the scholarly enterprise thus depends upon mutual respect for the pragmatic and scientific rather than the political use of language. Adapting George Orwell's concept of "Newspeak," Ostrom introduces us to the problems that arise when the "language of political discourse" exerts dominance over the "languages of everyday life" and the "languages of science and technologies." When the language of partisan politics claims authority to define social reality, the habits of mind and methods important to solving both scientific problems and the problems of everyday life become truncated. Thought is forced into political channels, and partisan purposes can even encourage the misinterpretation and reinterpretation of evidence. Before long, Ostrom notes, "citizens experience themselves as spectators in political processes rather than as participants in something called 'democracy.'"[18] The result is a confusion of thought that conduces to revolutionary schemes for political and social change.

What is especially relevant to our narrative here is that in the modern era scholarly disputes began increasingly to spill out of the schools and into public contests about political, social, and economic *policy*. This is not to imply that there were ever "Chinese walls" between the spheres of politics and science. Nevertheless, the discernment of discontinuity, whether great or small, is one of the tasks of the historian and is often even the starting point of historical inquiry.[19] The term *policy*, derived from the classical Greek πολιτεία (politeia), increasingly appeared in English usage after the 14th century, and the story of the modern social sciences might best be told in terms of the history of the concept and its applications. Those authors to whom we look in the canons of early modern political thought, such as Machiavelli, Hobbes, and Locke, just to mention the most familiar names, sought not only to present conceptual models of polity but also to influence the arenas of ecclesiastical and civil policy.[20] Likewise, as Mises notes, early classical liberal authors such as Adam Smith made explicit the policy implications of their scholarly analyses. In the first half of the modern era scholars had gradually worked the standards for the warrantability of scientific knowledge free from theological doctrine and ecclesiastical authority, opening the scientific processes to wider exploration, contestation, and refinement within a community of practitioners. By the early 19th century, however, an international brotherhood of revolutionaries began to elevate a more radically political (and politically radical) use of language that shook the community standards of warrantability that had been the hallmark of early liberalism. Addressing the revolutionary program developed by Marx and Engels, in particular, Ostrom explains how these intellectuals turned political reformers associated themselves with a political discourse of historical determinism and effectively disassociated themselves "from individual moral responsibility for the ideas they profess and the actions that they propose."[21]

The condition of our contemporary culture almost two centuries later reflects the steady elevation of political discourse in culture and scholarship. The scholarly enterprise, though never free of internal *methodenstreit*, had largely worked for over a millennium to advance the language and methods of the sciences as a complement to and check on prevailing ecclesiastical, social, and political powers. The revolutionary vanguard of history, by contrast, has ushered in a world where increasing numbers of scholars are engaged less in pursuits of advancing warrantable scientific knowledge than in the promulgation of political languages, the production of political theater, and the pursuit of power itself. From its inception the classical liberal tradition developed more on the model of the early modern republic of letters. Classical liberal scholars were strongly tethered to the pragmatics of everyday language (or common sense) and to the common aspirations and community standards of scientific inquiry. Nevertheless, classical liberalism has also evolved into a language of political discourse, with its own orientations to scholarship and history and policy. The political discourse of classical liberalism gained its current shape at the intersection of two fields of substantial tension: the internal methodological tensions of the sciences and the external epistemic tensions that arose as the politics of the rising revolutionary vanguard of progress began to act as a caustic agent on the very possibility of politically neutral thought and action.

SOCIAL CHANGE AND THE ASSAULT ON HISTORY

The development of modern historical awareness helped to give rise to new conceptions of human action in historical development, and early classical liberals understood historical change as the (unintended and unpredictable) result of human beings doing what comes naturally to them. Historical change could be re-narrated as something that was the result neither of divine direction nor of the cunning wisdom of princes, and classical liberal scholars began to probe these possibilities. The techniques of comparative historical and cultural analysis further fueled the development of classical liberal political economy, especially in the hands of Smith, Hume, and, later, Tocqueville.[22] These thinkers sought to commend policy, but also began to raise the possibility that ideal policy would entail fostering a permissive space for human action within a general framework of procedural rules rather than constructing a comprehensive code of prescriptive legislation. The insights of these scholars likely drew as well upon resources available to them in the tradition of permissive natural law that scholars of legal history are only now beginning to explicate.[23] There were others in the modern era who grew impatient of the pace and/or perceived direction of time's arrow and sought a more energetic role for men in effecting social change through more prescriptive policy or outright revolution. This impetus to revolutionary change rather than waiting for slower-evolving reforms was a form of assault on history and tradition, and, as Ostrom observes, would eventually come to challenge the standards for warranting the authority of ideas as guides for action.

The early modern wars of religion had set the tone for this assault. A few French Huguenot writers of the 16th century developed justifications of monarchomachy, king-killing. By the mid-17th century there had been an English regicide and the replacement of monarchy by a short-lived Republic (1649–1660). In the end, the English proved to have little stomach for such radicalism and restored the throne and the Stuart-line of royal succession. Such conservatism in England was to a great extent a comparion of Common Law jurisprudence, which engendered a distinct historical awareness. English political discourse has thus long been conducted as a unique form of historical debate. The "Glorious Revolution" in 1688 was not only a triumph for Parliament (and Protestantism) but could also be seen as a conservation of the "ancient constitution" and "rule of law."[24]

By the mid-18th century, nevertheless, more radical and rationalist assaults on the "natural" course of history were increasingly discernible. In *The Theory of Moral Sentiments*, the first edition of which was published in 1759, Adam Smith noted a distinction between the "man of humanity" and the "man of system" that still resonates. The man of humanity, says Smith, "will respect the established powers and privileges even of individuals, and still more those of the great orders and societies, into which the state is divided." He will not use force to subdue the people, and he will seek to accommodate policy to "the confirmed habits and prejudices of the people." By contrast, the man of system "is apt to be very wise in his own conceit; and is often so enamoured with the supposed beauty of his own ideal plan of government, that he cannot suffer the smallest deviation from any part of it." Whether he goes against nature or custom, the man of system seeks to establish his policies completely, imagining, as Smith puts it, "that he can arrange the different members of a great society with as much ease as the hand arranges the different pieces upon a chess-board." The rationalist man of system "does not consider that the pieces upon the chess-board have no other principle of motion besides that which the hand impresses upon them; but that, in the great chess-board of human society, every single piece has a principle of motion of its own, altogether different from that which the legislature might chuse to impress upon it."[25]

Smith's discussion of the "man of system" pinpointed a critical mistake that would come to mark the radical revolutionary imperative unleashed during the French Revolution, which was to forget that human beings have autonomous powers of acting and that society cannot be modeled or governed in merely mechanical terms. In L'Ancien Régime et la Révolution, published in 1856, Tocqueville likewise diagnosed a problem of the systematizing spirit, noting the anti-historical prejudice of the radical revolutionaries. Tocqueville believed that the revolutionaries of 1789 had made:

> the greatest effort that has ever been made by any people to sever their history into two parts, so to speak, and to tear open a gulf between their past and their future. In this design, they took the greatest care to leave every trace of their past condition behind them; they imposed all kinds of restraints upon themselves

in order to be different from their ancestry; they omitted nothing which could disguise them.[26]

While the effort to understand social changes had formerly been an aid to historical understanding as well as political and economic thought, by the time Tocqueville published L'Ancien Régime, theories of change were becoming instrumentalities of policy making, of social reform, and even of social revolution. Whether as means to human betterment through liberal reform (as in the utilitarian meliorism of Bentham) or to the revolutionary translation of society to a new evolutionary stage of development (as in the Marxist vision of the ultimate transition of the capitalist economy into socialism), theories of social change became levers to be used to change the world in the direction of some desired *telos* of social progress.

The idea of progress has been a principle driver of social and political action in modern Western societies. Formal utopianism presents only the most extreme end of the widespread belief in the idea of progress, however, which has appeared in social theories as diverse as those that call for radical revolution, those that caution prudent reform, and even those that are fundamentally conservative. The quest to describe, explain, and theorize social change as a means to promoting progress has been one of the key signatures of the modern intellectual enterprise. With the emergence of the fields of inquiry of political economy and sociology and, later, more differentiated studies of economics and political science,[27] the imperative to develop a universal theory of change continued to gain strength.[28] By the 20th century, the business of the social sciences had increasingly become that of offering theories of social change as guides for policy development and social action. Increasingly, modern intellectuals and social activists, have seen institutional traditions and continuities not as integral and vital parts of the social order but rather as structural obstacles to be overcome, or vehicles to be harnessed, for the accomplishment of directed social change.

Such has been the trend now for long enough that the dominant (and exceedingly ironic) feature of "postmodern" society, with its emphasis on narrating and re-narrating our personal identities, is that increasing numbers of people "identify" less with their society's received cultural traditions and institutions (which are fair game for deconstruction) and subsume themselves in the latest popular "memes" and collective aspirations for progress, whether expressed as the attainment of expanding liberty or the realization of social justice, or sometimes both together. Such is the phenomenon of Jacobinism, which is depicted in classic works of literature such as Anatole France's dark exploration of the Reign of Terror in *The Gods Will Have Blood* (*Les dieux ont soif*, 1912) and in the exploits of the character Marius Pontmercy in

Victor Hugo's *Les Miserables* (1862) (which most of us today know through the stirring Broadway musical numbers "ABC Café/Red and Black" and "Do You Hear The People Sing?").

A recent book by Micah White, a leading figure in the Occupy Wall Street protests—one of the most recent imitative acts of manning (should we say "peopling"?) the barricades—exemplifies the belief that the end of human progress (and history?) is liberation: "The contemporary activist is the culmination of several thousand years of human experimentation in the social techniques of collective liberation. The role of the activist is to secure greater freedom for humanity."[29] Whites explanation of the importance of having a theory of change, and of getting one's theory of change right, however, suggests that the ongoing purpose of "liberation" is less freedom than revolution itself.

I call Occupy Wall Street a constructive failure because the moment revealed the underlying flaws in dominant, and still prevalent, theories of how to achieve social change through collective action. Occupy set out to "get money out of politics," and we succeeded in catalyzing a global social movement that tested all of our hypotheses. The failure of our efforts reveals a truth that will hasten the next successful revolution; the assumptions underlying contemporary protest are false. Change won't happen through the old models of activism. Western democracies will not be swayed by public spectacles and mass media frenzy. Protests have become an accepted, and therefore ignored, by-produce of politics-as-usual. Western governments are not susceptible to international pressure to heed the protests of their citizens. Occupy's failure was constructive because it demonstrated the limitations of contemporary ideas of Protest. I capitalize *p* to emphasize that the limitation was not in a particular tactic but rather in our concept of Protest, or our theory of social change, which determined the overall script. Occupy revealed that activists need to revolutionize their approach to revolution.[30]

Such appeal to theories and models of change is altogether typical today among American social scientists, progressive policymakers, and even philanthropists. In the last two decades or so, even "conservative" and "classical liberal" social thinkers and philanthropists are increasingly invoking theories of social change as guides for action, and herein we can see the subtle and pervasive influence of the progressive orientation in modern social and political thought. When deployed instrumentally, whether as guides for governance, policy administration, philanthropy, or outright revolution, theories of change can prove powerful solvents of the traditional institutions that undergird a free society. As even a comparatively peaceful revolutionary such as White concludes, "Justice to the activist is a question of how far to go in pursuing revolution."[31]

The idea of progress combined with the belief that an intelligentsia sufficiently schooled in the processes of social change can manage social, political, and economic processes toward greater human welfare generated the three great anti-classical liberal frameworks of the modern age: socialism, communism, and progressivism. Classical liberalism itself, however, has co-evolved in the crucible of modern history with its chief antagonists, and has not been impervious to the enthusiasms of progress. Careful attention is needed to discern the complex interplay of ideas and issues that shaped the development of classical liberalism and to uncover the relationship of history to classical liberalism's epistemic, constitutional, and institutional commitments.

A cautionary guide to whom we might turn on this journey is the work of the sociologist Robert Nisbet, who reminds us of the fundamental struggles for the authority of vocabularies, conceptions, and methodologies that are underway. Nisbet seeks to demonstrate "through historical as well as analytical arguments ... the frailties in reigning theories of change—chiefly functionalism, developmentalism, and evolutionism—in the contemporary social sciences."[32] Nisbet describes the way that the terms growth, progress, development, and evolution have become substitutable for one another in Western thought and traces their various uses in classical, Christian, and modern theories of social development. As tempting as it has been for centuries, however, the organic metaphor of growth, suggesting "the inexorability" and "intrinsically teleological character" of change is inappropriately applied to the analysis of social change. "Social change, unlike biological," writes Nisbet, "is not the product of immanent, endogenous forces. It is not natural, not native to social institutions and other structures, as growth so plainly is to organisms."[33]

We cannot live without metaphor, Nisbet acknowledges, but the metaphor of growth or development is only useful, he proposes, in proportion to "the cognitive distance of the object to which the metaphor is applied." "The larger, the more general, abstract, and distant in experience the object of our interest," Nisbet writes, "the greater the utility of the metaphor." The Western mind, he observes, seems to have a fascination with great, abstract wholes— *"Civilization, Mankind, Society, and Culture"*—and to the extent we can ask what has happened, is happening, or will happen with such wholes, constituted as they are by a vast and unmanageable field of human knowledge and action across time, we cannot dispense with metaphor.[34] When we turn to "the smaller, more concrete, finite and empirical," however, Nisbet believes we are more likely to abuse metaphor or find it irrelevant to our investigation.

Insisting on the autonomy of the social from the natural sciences, Nisbet draws a sharp methodological line and cautions against problematic methodological appropriations. The use of the techniques of sociobiology to try "to predict the actual variety and diversity of social behavior in the world ... is fatuous. All that the human brain gives in this wise is its inexhaustible capacity for generating and assimilating an endless variety of behavior. From that point on, only history can explain the social."[35] Nisbet asserts that most useful work of contemporary social sciences has been that which has made a historical turn, taking as its subject matter "the social behavior of human beings in specific areas and within finite limits of time." Nisbet draws "one cardinal conclusion":

> the theory of change embodied in both the classical theory of social evolution and the contemporary theories of neo-evolutionism and functionalism is singularly without merit when it comes to our understanding of the nature of change, the conditions under which change takes place, and the effects of change on social behavior.[36]

"We turn to history and only to history," Nisbet concludes, "if what we are seeking are the actual causes, sources and conditions of overt change of patterns and structure in society."[37] For Nisbet then, the study of social change must not take on teleological assumptions. Whether social change marks "decline" or "progress" can only be assessed against a teleological direction that itself cannot be known. The historian's role in understanding change becomes essential, for it is "impossible to understand the nature of change apart from the impact of events upon people's lives." On Nisbet's account, "fixity, conventionalization, and habit" are the "natural state of man"; people's allegiances to patterns of thought and traditional institutions tend *not* to change unless change is necessary, which happens "only when they perceive some kind of problem, which is a form of crisis." The historian's task is thus in part to evaluate what events are significant enough to provoke men to think differently about their institutions and to change their behaviors. Seeking to understand the thought and action of particular historical actors is indispensable.

CLASSICAL LIBERALISM AND HISTORY

As will be clearer below, Nisbet's focus on human action resonates with the classical liberal perspective, but before we can explore this more deeply we must first point out the tensions that can arise for classical liberalism because of the influence of developmentalism. The search for organic patterns of growth in its various forms in modern social thought poses a particular historico-political problem for contemporary classical liberal scholars. Since its inception, classical liberal thought has been challenged by a Janus-faced relationship to history. Facing the past, classical liberalism, especially in its English expressions, received, refined, and developed many of the traditional languages and conceptions of Western political thought. Facing the future, however, classical liberalism has embraced the pursuit of material, moral, and social progress that has been the ascendant feature of modernity. Practically, classical liberalism has thus come to exist in an uneasy relationship with both the drogues of conservative traditions and the strong winds of progressive change. While classical liberals do not tend to embrace the business of deliberately steering the "ship of state" through history, they are nevertheless often eager to create optimum conditions for progress. These tensions present us with trenchant questions about grounds of intersection between classical liberalism and history in theory and practice.

In a paper delivered at the Tokyo Meeting of the Mont Pelerin Society in September 1966, F. A. Hayek summarized "The Principles of a Liberal Social Order." In contrast to Mises, who defined liberalism as "the application of the teachings of science to the social life of man,"[38] Hayek begins his account with a historically anchored definition of "liberalism":

> By "liberalism" I shall understand here the conception of a desirable political order which in the first instance was developed in England from the time of the Old Whigs in the later part of the seventeenth century to that of Gladstone at the end of the nineteenth. David Hume, Adam Smith, Edmund Burke, T. B. Macaulay and Lord Acton may be regarded as its typical representatives in England. It was this conception of individual liberty under the law which in the first instance inspired the liberal movements on the Continent and which became the basis of the American political tradition.[39]

Hayek continued by distinguishing this conception from a contending view that had also taken up the mantle of liberalism:

> The first [classical liberalism] is based on an evolutionary interpretation of all phenomena of culture and mind and on an insight into the limits of the power of human reason. The second [modern liberalism] rests on what I have called "constructivist" rationalism, a conception which leads to the treatment of all cultural phenomena as the product of deliberate design, and on the belief that it is both possible and desirable to reconstruct all grown institutions in accordance with a preconceived plan. The first kind is consequently reverent of tradition and recognizes that all knowledge and all civilization rests on tradition, while the second type is contemptuous of tradition because it regards an independently existing reason as capable of designing civilization.[40]

In contrast to Mises' definition of liberalism as something of a neutral procedure, Hayek offers both a substantive conceptual definition of liberalism as an order of "individual liberty under the law" and an historical definition of liberalism as a phenomenon arising in place (England) and time ("from the time of the Old Whigs in the later part of the 17th century to that of Gladstone at the end of the nineteenth"). Among the "typical representatives" of liberalism identified by Hayek we find several authors known to us today as preeminent British historians. Hayek also notes the historical legacy of liberalism, both on a handful of Continental thinkers and as the foundation for the American political tradition.

Hayek clearly acknowledges the importance of attending to the historical development of liberalism, yet his treatment of our relationship in the present to the historical artifacts of spontaneous order raises important questions. If liberal establishments are the products of historical evolution (or even accident), to what extent are we to seek to bring about ongoing evolutionary developments, and to what extent are we to conserve their previous outcomes? Should classical liberal scholars declare the institutions that emerged in the late 18th century to be a "high water mark" of historical development and thus, as William F. Buckley commended, stand athwart history yelling, "Stop"? Or, could they choose different conditions of historical optimality; for instance, might they look with Francis Fukuyama upon liberal democracy circa 1990 as "the end of history"? Should they seek to *arrest* decline (by institutional conservation) where commercial civil society is flourishing and wealth is growing? Should they seek to *design* development through nation-building interventions, for example, where the processes of the "great enrichment" have not yet taken off? The classical liberal actor in history seems to have to steer a delicate path between social conservatism, on the one hand, and social change, on the other, either of which course of action might compromise the very principles of spontaneous order in which he professes belief.[41]

Thus far, we have a threefold definition of liberalism—methodological, substantive, and historical—that complicates our approach to discerning the relative contributions to be made to our understanding by historical modes of analysis and by other methodologies of the social sciences. In seeking to identify, describe, and anchor itself to an intellectual conception of social order that emerged in a particular historical time and place, classical liberalism seems to dwell in a paradox. Classical liberalism as a political language began to take shape when its earliest theorists recognized that they were the beneficiaries of a remarkable social order that was, in the words of Adam Ferguson, "the result of human action, but not the execution of any human design."[42]

Classical liberalism was born as its progenitors, embracing a new understanding of the historical condition, sought to better understand the social traditions and institutions they had received. Then, having made the astonishing—and largely non-intuitive—recognition that invisible hands might be more successful than deliberating minds in fostering conditions in which people might flourish, these same observers felt compelled to commend principles to guide economic, political, and social policy. As Hayek put it in a quite curious locution, early classical liberals desired, "to make as full use of these powerful spontaneous ordering forces as possible."[43]

To reiterate: classical liberalism arose in part in response to a new historical awareness that generated opportunities for the development of new modes of investigating patterns of social relationships and the orders that emerged from them. These investigations produced a new "science" and a new imperative to commend policies that would *conserve* and *sustain* the spontaneous ordering forces but also at times *employ* them in the practice of commercial and political arts. This still does not fully explain what makes it possible for Hayek to acknowledge the historically contingent emergence of classical liberal political thought in the discourse of the Old Whigs while simultaneously looking with anticipation to evolutionary development of classical liberal principles in "the unknown civilization that is growing in America," to which he dedicated *The Constitution of Liberty.*

While both Mises and Hayek attend to a certain extent to the historical conditions of liberal origins, there remained a tension in the relationship of their economics with the approach of the German Historical School. The "*Methodenstreit*" that helped to give Austrian economics its name and to shape its founding methodological commitments and institutional manifestations, seemed *prima facie* to pit economics against history. In fact, the *Methodenstreit*, was an important chapter in the effort of the social sciences to fully differentiate, first from the faculties of theology and law and moral philosophy (and more rarely the natural sciences), and later from one another. These differentiations occurred in both international and national contexts and have significantly advanced our understanding of what Mises calls "the sciences of human action." But questions remain as to whether we can achieve the sort of robust and productive relationship between economics and history that Nisbet believes was necessary between sociology and history.

Mises' *Human Action* is a magisterial methodological statement of the principles of economics, "the youngest of all sciences,"[44] that seeks to situate it in a coherent epistemological and methodological framework. In this exercise Mises developed a new vocabulary that has subsequently been a source of continuing confusion. Mises describes economics (which he later calls *catallactics*) as one branch of a broader general theory of human action, which he calls *praxeology*. Praxeology, the general theory of human action, however, is only one part of the sciences of human action. The other main branch is *history*, "the collection and systematic arrangement of all the data of experience concerning human action."[45] The data of history, unlike the

data derived from the observation of the natural world, do not provide praxeologists "with facts in the sense in which the natural sciences employ this
term to signify isolated events in tested experiments." Because the sciences
of human action are undertaken by humans, they are complex phenomena,
they are not amenable to simple measurement and experimental methods, and
their theoretical statements are not induced from facts but are rather deduced
from a priori theorems. These a priori statements arise from "reflection about
the essence of human action," which Mises takes to have universal logical
structure.[46]

In the context of his debate with the German Historical School, Mises
was threading a needle between the conservative policy interventionism of
the Historical School and the radical revolutionary principles of early 20th-
century socialists and Marxists. Mises argued that in trying to avoid the errors
of positivism (a goal he shared), proponents of the Historical School had
resorted to a hyper-historicism in which economic laws could only be derived
from and operative in the historical conditions in which they originated. This
orientation introduced relativism into economics and foreclosed the possibility of an economic science that could discern economic laws that would be
universally valid. If economics could only recommend policies based on
contingent historical conditions rather than policies based on regularities
described by such "laws" as those of comparative of advantage, diminishing
returns, and the patterned relationships between supply and demand, economics would be little more than exercise in discerning how history would
determine the future. This meant that historicism was primarily an exercise
in mapping a teleological philosophy of history onto events. In contrast to
the earlier "natural histories" that looked for similar human responses that
would logically be chosen in response to similar problems, Mises charges the
German Historical School with periodalism, holding that institutional development in every society had to proceed through the same stages, regardless
of how purposive individuals conceived of their situations and chose to act.
An abstract conception of social development rather than the study of human
action was what guided the historicists' policy recommendations.[47]

By contrast, the proper "meaning and use of the study of history," Mises
argued, had much in common with fundamental premise of the praxeology
being developed by Austrian economists, which was that purposeful human
action is the starting point of any study of society and social institutions. In
Human Action, Mises summarized this fundamental premise:

> Society is concerted action, cooperation. Society is the outcome of conscious
> and purposeful behavior. This does not mean that individuals have concluded
> contracts by virtue of which they have founded human society. The actions
> which have brought about social cooperation and daily bring it about anew do

not aim at anything else than cooperation and coadjuvancy with others for the attainment of definite singular ends. The total complex of the mutual relations created by such concerted actions is called society. It substitutes collaboration for the—at least conceivable—isolated life of individuals. Society is division of labor and combination of labor. In his capacity as an acting animal man becomes a social animal.[48]

Society, in other words, could better be described in terms of the probability of similar patterns of interactions and institutions emerging from similar human problem situations rather than in terms of a "genetic" or internally determined process of development.

Mises' criticism of historicism is important to distinguish from his insights into the importance of history, properly understood, but these distinctions can be hard to tease out, because his interlocutors in the *Methodenstreit* seem ever present in even his most analytical writings. To understand his work deeply thus requires both theoretical and historical attention, the one to evaluate the credibility of his logic and the other to sift statements that are directed at specific contextual debates in which he was engaged. In other words, we face the daunting intellectual task of being as careful theorists as we are historians, and vice versa. There are many moments at which understanding may require a careful theorist and a careful historian to engage in a mutual exploration, and what follows in the remainder of this essay are the beginning reflections of a historian who invites conversation with theorists and other historians.

In *Theory and History*, Mises' clarifies his conception of history as an essential part of the sciences of human action. "Acting man," he writes, "is faced with a definite situation. His action is a response to the challenge offered by this situation; it is his reaction. He appraises the effects the situation may have upon himself, i.e., he tries to establish what it means to him. Then he chooses and acts in order to attain the end chosen."[49] Epistemologically, to understand the conditions in which he has to act, man can have either descriptive knowledge of the situation supplied by applied natural science (there is a leak in the pipe) or interpretive knowledge supplied by historical inquiry (the pipe broke due to freezing). The present is always moving into the past, and knowledge of future is yet inaccessible. The historian's work is therefore "of the utmost practical importance." "Actually," Mises writes, "the understanding of the past is in perpetual flux. A historian's achievement consists in presenting the past in a new perspective of understanding. The process of historical change is actuated by, or rather consists in, the ceaseless transformation of the ideas determining action."[50]

Ludwig Lachmann further elucidates the role of such dynamism in the praxeological theory of institutions in which "the existence of certain institutions is explained as the unintended result of the pursuit of individual plans by large numbers of actors—as a 'resultant of social forces,' not a product of social design."[51] Lachmann's conception of a "kaleidic world" establishes a more complex and non-linear backdrop for understanding social change and evocatively presents the understanding of social institutions as slowly developing from the concatenation and harmonization of innumerable human actions.[52] Adapting the term from G. L. S. Shackle, Lachmann uses the kaleidic image to evoke the dynamics of an ever-changing world. "Shackle's *kaleidic society*," he writes, is "a society in which sooner or later unexpected change is bound to upset existing patterns, a society 'interspersing its moments or intervals of order, assurance and beauty with sudden disintegration and a cascade into a new pattern.'"[53] Similarly, Nisbet describes history in terms of the occurrence of "a great many phenomena which may reflect adjustment, readjustment, bustle, alternation of techniques and habits, and other instances of mere movement of motion," but notes that this mere motion may "not reflect outright change or transformation." Social change can be observed only when there are widespread shifts (cascades?) in the overall patterns of behaviors and institutions, such as the rising importance of the conjugal over the extended family or the shift from agrarianism to industrialism.[54]

If Mises makes room for historical understanding of human action, the insights added to praxeology by Lachmann and Shackle offer additional incentive for grappling with the understanding of historical/social change. The epigraph of Shackle's 1972 book, *Epistemics and Economics: A Critique of Economic Doctrines*, cites a 1959 work by Lachmann that emphasizes the importance of bringing considerations of time fully into the economists' considerations:

> *Time* and *Knowledge* belong together. The creative acts of the mind need not be reflected in changing preferences, but they cannot but be reflected in acts grasping experience and constituting objects of knowledge and plans of action. All such acts bear the stamp of the individuality of the actor.
>
> The impossibility of prediction in economics follows from the facts that economic change is linked to change in knowledge, and future knowledge cannot be gained before its time.
>
> As soon as we permit time to elapse we must permit knowledge to change, and knowledge cannot be regarded as a function of anything else.[55]

Lachmann and Shackle seem to make more clear than Mises that while we can at best anticipate rather than predict the future, even our best expectations are always subject to the possibility of surprise. Unlike the predictions of natural science, which, at least until the development of quantum physics, were largely based on observed patterns of regularity of "objective" phenomena, the expectations of praxeology must always take into account the "subjective" interpretive processes of purposive human beings. The self-motive character of human action and the possibility for surprise and novelty—the pluripotentiality of human action, in other words—suggests the value of a strong symbiosis between praxeology and history as complementary tools for understanding and choosing. In their shared focus on the meaning of purposive human action, their efforts to address the dimension of time, and their openness to being surprised, the economist and the historian may find common ground.

If we flip the coin, and approach the meaning of history through the eyes of a historian, we can find many points of resonance with the writings of economists we have been examining. Each historian, in seeking to bring to light new understanding of the past, can be thought of as an intellectual entrepreneur, delving through the archives with alertness for the unexpected and surprising.[56] The writing of history, as J. G. A. Pocock intimates, can arise both from the recognition of radical discontinuities between the present and the past and from the effort to ascribe continuity (and often legitimacy) to a particular social tradition. Explaining continuities is less dramatically imagined than Gibbon's Capitoline moment, but it is the bread and butter of historical scholarship, seeking to document and understand the past and its relationships to—that is, its continuities with and continuing influences on—the present.[57] Pocock observes that this form of historical inquiry "is a form of thought occasioned by the awareness of society's structure and processes" and that the "past" in question represents "a state of affairs of some social complexity existing over a period long enough to make it intelligible, a period now gone by but remembered."[58]

Historical study is an activity that helps to delineate and describe the persisting traditions that give shape to the identity of a society. Such inquiry often serves the social function of preserving and transmitting these traditions. At some inflection point, however, intellectual conservation of tradition can give way to engagement in a form of historical inquiry that assumes critical distance from and a stance of critique of traditional ways of understanding a society's past. This form of historiography becomes a possibility when there is recognition that historical problems exist for which traditional explanations do not provide adequate answers. Such problems may originate when some critical event takes place or some new pattern attracts the attention of the historian. The historian, for example, may try to explain the significance of some artifact, the use of which is no longer known, or he may note the persistence of traditional institutions that seem to have waned in their relevance to new social relationships. More fundamentally, though, the historian seeks to understand some past human action in the context in which the actor(s) perceived himself (themselves) to be acting.[59]

The stuff of history is primarily the actions of human beings, and at times we can surmise that the results of these actions indicate that a significant social change has occurred. Social change, as well as individual action, is part of the landscape of the past from which historical problem-situations present themselves to the historian, and attention to social change is an intrinsic component of the motive to historical inquiry. Nevertheless, describing social change often requires abstraction to collective wholes (states, civilization, society, culture, etc.) which may be thought of as thinking and acting only in specific conditions where corporate consensus or authority can be determined to exist, so epistemological problems immediately arise. Hypotheses about how social changes occur may in turn become part and parcel of the historian's explanatory framework (and should be differentiated from theories of how to *cause* social change, though the latter may draw upon the former). In any case, not all explanations of social change will turn out to be historical explanations. What will distinguish a *historical* explanation will be the historian's attempt at explaining what actually happened through the use of particular empirical evidence available in the historical record.

Pocock states that historical study requires three preconditions:

> First, it is necessary that evidence about the past should be available in such detail and organization as to make a measure of consistent and self-validating description possible; second, it is necessary that the problem-situation should have arisen in such a way as to compel recognition that the past cannot be studied in traditional terms or as a simple extension of present continuities; third, it is necessary that concepts should have been or become available to the historian in which one can describe, not only the past which existed, but the process of its becoming the present.[60]

The historian will thus study not only the traditional, inherited narratives but must also have access to a body of historical artifacts, including "documents that reveal the character of the past in laws, churches, languages, and other phenomena of social life."[61]

While the historian may in his capacity as a citizen put his analysis to use later in the form of a political argument where he makes a value judgment about the outcome of a historical event or the merit or demerit of an intellectual position,[62] his work as a historian is to try to describe (and imaginatively recreate) the event or argument for his reader. This requires a form of intellectual sympathy and a suspension of value judgment.

This understanding of the historian's craft is quite compatible with Mises' observation that "[i]t is not the task of the historian qua historian to pass judgments of value on the individuals whose conduct is the theme of his inquiries. As a branch of knowledge history utters existential propositions only. But these existential propositions often refer to the presence or absence of definite judgments of value in the minds of the acting individuals. It is one of the tasks of the specific understanding of the historical sciences to establish what content the value judgments of the acting individuals had."[63]

PURSUING THE SCIENCE OF ASSOCIATION

Having explored the fundamentally epistemic foundations of civil society, the attack on history made in the name of social change, the tensions between classical liberalism and history, and the potential methodological resonance between praxeology and history, we can return to the question raised in the introduction of this chapter. Namely, can we supply a rationale for and a methodological approach suited to answering Tocqueville's call for a new science of association? The pronoun "we" means to signal that understanding our present institutional environment and its history, and forming a vision of the future of civil society is a necessarily social activity. But how do we best engage in such social inquiries and reflections? And why have the investigations of scholars—even those who positively value classical liberal understandings of liberty—left us largely without a persuasive analytical and historical account of the role of voluntary associations in modern civil society?

It should be clear at this point that any such "science" of association must overcome the epistemic incoherence that has been generated by the embrace of inappropriate methodological presuppositions in the sciences of human action. This means that, ultimately, what we are seeking is an account of associational practices based on the *praxeological* premise that, among the other things people may do, they act purposefully, both individually and collectively. Such a science will also need to resist the domination of the languages of political discourse, for as Tocqueville perceived them, the most important associations of the Americans in resisting the onset of despotism were not their political associations but the associations they formed to fulfill the purposes of everyday living. Can the science of association Tocqueville sought thus provide a means of combating Newspeak?

Despite Tocqueville's clear delineation of the distinction between "political" associations and "intellectual and moral" associations, and his emphasis on understanding the latter, scholars who have generated most of the literature on associations and civil society over the last century have been primarily preoccupied with exploring the *political* uses of associations and their functional roles in democratic political structures. In discussing scholarly interpretations of associationalism in the 19th century Jason Kaufman presents three representative views that seem to persist in current scholarship: (1) a *neo-Tocquevillian perspective* that sees voluntary association as an alternative to government action, (2) *a social movements/pluralist perspective* in which associations can be seen as interest groups promoting government action for their favored projects, and (3) *a social capital perspective* that sees associational activity as a pathway to broader and more meaningful political participation.[64] Looking at more recent scholarship, Michael Goodheart has explored how the intersections of democratic theory and civil society studies have been taken up in the study of global democratization. "Many scholars and activists," Goodheart explains, "have begun to conceive of an emergent 'global civil society' as a model or strategy for global democracy and democratization. These theorists and practitioners increasingly adopt global civil society (GCS) as a conceptual framework for supranational democracy and as a concrete political project."[65] Again, the context is primarily shaped by political concerns.

Tocqueville, of course, was concerned with such questions about the relationship between democratic political institutions and associational activities, but he took care to emphasize that attention needed to be paid especially to understand modes of human action that were not oriented in the first place to political purposes. Nevertheless, even classical liberal scholars whose attractions to the principles of limited government bias them against excessive state agency in most fields of human endeavor have largely neglected to explore in history or theory the broad array of ways in which people make use of associational activity. This neglect of association is unfortunate, both because it leaves gaps in our understanding of our own institutional history and because freedom of association is plausibly the third leg of a classical liberal framework without which the legs of property and contract cannot hold the weight of a free society. Why have classical liberals in particular failed to venture farther into these investigations?

Tocqueville's call for the development of a new science of association was a challenge to his contemporaries to grapple with the discontinuities unleashed by the American and French revolutions, each of which had advanced hopes for "popular" government (though with many different understandings of what that meant). In their revolutionary fervor against the royal and aristocratic powers, the French had resorted to such violence that their experiments with republican government had proven exceedingly unstable. Looking back on both revolutions, Tocqueville's efforts to understand the character of American self-governance thus sought to address "a sort of religious terror in the author's soul," and to help him discern whether democracy would inevitably usher in men's savage instincts. Like the French, the Americans had repudiated monarchy and the trappings of aristocracy, but they had conserved much of their legal and political tradition and had settled on constitutional arrangements that constrained popular majoritarianism. It seemed possible, at least by the time of Tocqueville's travels in North

America, that conditions in America would signal to the rest of the world the ultimate possibilities for freedom.

Central to Tocqueville's analysis was his observation of the role of associations in American life. Tocqueville observed that because Americans were exposed to equality of conditions in eking out a living, they necessarily depended on voluntary associations: "if they did not acquire the practice of associating with each other in ordinary life, civilization itself would be in peril."[66] As equality of conditions expand, people tend to become more individualistic. Nevertheless, the American colonists, having eked civilizations out of wildernesses, had found a way to confederate that made room for existing arrangements of decentralized responsibility and interfered very little with the habits of its citizens to cooperate on "small affairs." The resulting variety of interactions among people cultivated the habits of the heart that at every moment attuned them to a sense of living in society, and thus effectively counteracted the centrifugal forces of individualism.

In many ways, the American experience of equality exemplified what could be the expected outcome of the operation of the division of labor described earlier by Adam Smith. As Tocqueville observed: "It is easy to foresee that the time is approaching when a man by himself alone will be less and less in a state to produce the things that are the most common and the most necessary to his life."[67] Whether originating from necessities of geographic conditions or from industrial developments, such as those produced by the expansion of the division of labor, the future that seemed to be irresistibly arriving would leave individual men comparatively weak in their economic capacity. Society would thus seem to be possible only under two conditions: either a public administration must arise to "direct all the industries for which an isolated citizen cannot suffice" or the people must themselves associate and take upon themselves the administration of industry, benevolence, and political affairs. Tocqueville's call for a new science of association, then, was necessary to avert the evolution of democratic government into "an insupportable tyranny."

Can a more intentional partnership between praxeology and history help us, after 200 years, take up Tocqueville's questions anew?

That a reassessment of the relationship between praxeology and history is of some urgency is revealed by the historical problem-situation confronting classical liberals that we may now restate: *Why, despite the demonstrated beneficial outcomes of the "system of natural liberty" in the forms of economic growth and expanding personal liberties, do people continue to embrace ideals (such as social justice) and social arrangements (such as centralized administrative government) that are ultimately destructive of the principles and institutions of a classical liberal social order?*

This was a question that continued to nag both Hayek and Mises, and it remains a key challenge for classical liberal scholars today. In the opening pages of *The Constitution of Liberty* (1960), for example, Hayek proposed to offer a restatement of the essential principles of classical liberal thought in order to strengthen the position of classical liberals against their contemporary intellectual and political rivals:

> It has been a long time since that ideal of freedom which inspired modern Western civilization and whose partial realization made possible the achievements of that civilization was effectively restated. In fact, for almost a century the basic principles on which this civilization was built have been falling into increasing disregard and oblivion. Men have sought for alternative social orders more often than they have tried to improve their understanding or use of the underlying principles of our civilization. It is only since we were confronted with an altogether different system that we have discovered that we have lost any clear conception of our aims and possess no firm principles which we can hold up against the dogmatic ideology of our antagonists.[68]

This essay has been moving toward the contention that classical liberalism is less troubled by the lack of "firm principles" than by a dearth of historical accounts and analytical narratives of the ways in which people form purposes and develop means—often working together—to achieve their plans. It is in this context where the neglect to explore the history of voluntary associations dampens the potential power of classical liberalism as a viable language of political discourse. Voluntary associations such as those that Tocqueville described as flourishing in 19th-century America are nothing more nor less than the informal and formal institutions people develop when they realize their dependence upon one another for the fulfillment of their plans. People in the modern world are often preoccupied with the making of authentic selves. What more powerful persuasion, then, of the importance of individual human persons in history than to provide narratives that show what problems our forbearers have confronted in their own historical settings, what plans and associations they developed to address these problems, and how in fulfilling their plans they needed both to engage with existing institutional constraints and to exercise creativity?

The historian of political thought seeks to examine the language complexes people develop as they work out the reasons for and meaning of their actions. This requires coming to terms with the conceptual languages in common use by a people to describe their political, economic, and social affairs.[69] In America, a prevailing conception has been those habits of associating Tocqueville observed, and this vision we hold of being an associating people continues to resonate with Americans because they continue to feel the experience of associating "in their hips."[70] Nevertheless, without historical, analytical, and normative reference points that will help us retain clear ideas of the value of associating, the principles of voluntary governance, and the limits of legitimate associational action (with respect both to majority coercion of minorities or excessive deference to government), our traditions of association may begin to fade away. Elsewhere I have explored the "intellectual crisis of civil society" we are experiencing, suggesting that we increasingly mistake the ends of association as influencing government and public policy rather than cultivating the artisanship of citizenship essential to securing limits of governmental power.[71] The remedy for this crisis is a more intensive intellectual effort to recount the rich, nuanced history of associational life and to use these new historical interpretations as the basis for a new science of association and a renewed art of associating.

In their shared frame of reference in exploring *purposeful* human action, historians and praxeologists are equally engaged in describing and evaluating the success or failure of human action. But an account (or general theory) of human action needs to be complemented by an account (or general theory) of institutions, and this is largely a discursive exercise meaningless outside of— or even possibly in inevitable tension with—a broader understanding of the pragmatic patterns of human association and the full architecture of choice. As Vincent Ostrom has cogently argued:

> The choices that are made with regard to production, exchange, and the use of goods and services as they are available in the competitive market economies and open diversely organized public economies are different than the choices that are to be made with regard to the rules of a fair game used in constituting the patterns of order in human societies. These, in turn, are different than the choices that apply to the warrantability of knowledge, which needs to be taken into account if we are to anticipate the consequences that follow from the ideas or conceptions being put into practice. Choices in human societies are not simply, straightforward, linear computations but multiple strands of interdependent computations that need to be considered as complements to one another.[72]

There is much complementarity between the methodologies of historians of thought such as Pocock and economists of the Austrian school such as Mises and Lachmann, especially where they turn their attention to understanding the concatenation of human efforts to make meaning of and in their social worlds.[73] Pocock's concept of "languages," for example, can be brought fruitfully alongside the view of Deirdre McCloskey of social institutions as sites for the creation of human meaning. In contrasting the Austrian and old institutionalist view with that of the new institutionalists, for whom institutions are given constraints on human action, McCloskey invokes Lachmann's concept of institutions as "certain superindividual schemes of thought . . . to which

schemes of thought of the first order [notice that to the Austrians the economy
is in fact thought, all the way down], the plans, must be oriented, and which
serve therefore, to some extent, the coordination of individual plans." For
McCloskey, "a language is a scheme of thought, backed by social approval
and conversational implicatures."[74]

There is much in Lachmann, besides, that can resonate with Pocock's
methodological reflections on history. In *The Legacy of Max Weber* (1971),
Lachmann rejects Carl Menger's needs theory ("no institution can exist
for long unless it satisfies some need") as the basis for a general theory of
institutions in favor of his "praxeological theory of the origin of undesigned
('organic') institutions." Here, notes Lachmann,

> we have a theory which explains the origin of such institutions in the same way
> as other innovations. Some men realize that it is possible to pursue their interests
> more effectively than they have done so far and that an existing situation offers
> opportunities not so far exploited. In concert with others they do exploit them.
> If they are successful their example will find ready imitators, at first a few, later
> on many.
>
> Successful plans thus gradually crystallize into institutions. Within the sphere
> of freedom of action new institutions arise as additional orientation points,
> which may take the place of older institutions that became obsolete . ... Institu-
> tions are the relics of the pioneering efforts of former generations from which
> we are still drawing benefit.[75]

To the beginnings of this theory of institutions, Lachmann adds an important consideration: "The coherence and permanence of the institutional order
are of paramount importance to those engaged as we are, in tracing all the
major conditions of rational action. In reducing the uncertainty of the future
which enshrouds all human action, and helping us overcome the limits of
our ignorance of the present, such coherence and permanence are indeed of
primary importance."[76]

Such attention to the necessity of coherence and permanence become, in
Pocock's estimation, essential to our ability to reflect and "re-narrate" our
traditions:

> I take it to be an exercise of the sovereignty, autonomy or self-command of
> a civil society that it can narrate, re-narrate and interpret its history, with the
> consequence that it recognizes sovereignty even in this sense to be contest-
> able, conditional and in short historical; and I oppose my argument to the
> impulse, inherent in the ideology of globalized post-modernity, to assert that
> because the autonomous society, and the autonomous self, exist in more rela-
> tionships than they can define or control, they do not and should not have the
> ability to relate their pasts and enact their futures. I incline to see having a

history as more important than having an identity, the ability to criticize and re-narrate one's history as a means of navigating Oakeshott's bottomless and boundless sea.[77]

All of this is to intimate that somewhere along the way, in navigating numerous methodological disputes—including those with materialist determinism, with positivism, with historicism, and with a host of other revolutionary assaults on the sphere of free human action out of which our traditions/institutions take shape—scholars defending the classical liberal tradition developed a robust political economy but often failed to pursue the necessary historical research that would have enabled them to see, and much more to analyze in depth, the vast activity of voluntary associations outside of the market and the state that have been the most important source of norms, rules, and institutions that order human societies. By the mid-20th century Robert Nisbet and Richard Cornuelle had begun to call attention to this mislaid "sector" of human enterprise. Cornuelle believed that human beings were still wired for voluntary association, and that such associating was still happening, but that the methodological and historical lenses people had chosen to wear had made these activities largely invisible to social scientists and policy planners.[78]

Even Hayek, for example, seemed genuinely shocked, if also intrigued, by Cornuelle's belief that there once was and again could be a vibrant landscape of voluntary human action such as Tocqueville had observed in the 19th century. It is worth reproducing at length the text of the footnote Hayek provides, which suggests that Cornuelle has gotten his attention:

Cornuelle concludes (p. 40): "If fully mobilized the independent sector could, I believe: (1) Put to work everyone who is willing and able to work. (2) Wipe out poverty. (3) Find and solve the farm problem. (4) Give everyone good medical care. (5) Stop juvenile crime. (6) Renew our towns and cities, and turn anonymous slums into human communities. (7) Pay reasonable retirement benefits to all. (8) Replace hundreds of governmental regulations with more effective codes of conduct, vigorously enforced by each profession and an alert press. (9) Handle the nation's total research effort. (10) Turn our foreign policy into a world crusade for human welfare and personal dignity. (11) Lever a wider distribution of stock ownership. (12) Stop air and water pollution. (13) Give every person the education he needs, wants, and can profit by. (14) Provide cultural and educational outlets for everyone who wants them. (15) Wipe out racial segregation. The independent sector has power to do these formidable things. But, curiously, as its strength has increased we have given it less and less to do, and assigned more and more common tasks to government." *I reproduce this remarkable claim to tempt as many readers as possible to consult this unduly neglected book.*[79]

By the late 20th century, a host of scholars (including Cornuelle, Nisbet, Peter Berger, Robert Putnam, Amitai Etzioni, and others) had begun to explore whether some form of social science could make room to explore the role of associations in American public life, and in other cultures. In most cases, however, these thinkers were yet unable to set men's association for political purposes alongside rather than above other forms of human action, such as commercial activity, religious worship, family formation, charitable endeavors, mutual aid, and "clubbing" for a wide variety of shared purposes. Voluntary associations of the sort Tocqueville believed we must better understand—the intellectual, moral (and we may add beneficent) associations that shaped the habits of the heart—were almost lost in *methodenstreit*, their visibility clouded by the Manichean-like contest between capitalism and communism, market and state.

Cornuelle proposed that voluntary association should be considered as an *independent sector* of entities that people formed with motives distinct from their economic and political motives. Ironically, at the time he wrote this he was engaged in a political movement focused on getting the White House to create an administrative office to nurture a renaissance of American voluntarism.[80] A decade later Peter Berger and Richard John Neuhaus proposed that voluntary association should be considered as a *mediating sector* that could serve to mitigate the alienating impact of social life in modernity as the continuing growth of megastructures left individuals increasingly alone to pursue meaning and identity.[81] Neither approach consistently is holding well against the prevailing view that civil society is essentially comprised of public-private partnerships that work as the extended arms and hands of the modern state.[82] The administrative state has grown Leviathan-like and now consumes individuals and their associations alike into atoms of the political rather than the social body. Rule of law, once understood as a fractal replication of patterns of voluntary governance through associational bylaws that were complementary to the laws of the state, has increasingly been absorbed into the central directive authority of the national bureaucracy.

Where we might go from here, I think, depends on whether we can begin to use history to excite people's imagination about what might be possible if they reclaim their agency in public affairs. We need to take a look at the vast evidence in the historical record that shows how the business of human living has gotten done when people simply got together to do things in word and deed, not merely to truck, barter, and exchange, not merely to labor, produce, and consume, not merely to agitate, vote, and govern, but also to care for one another, to share resources, to make meaning together, to play and create, to help one another withstand the short-term shocks of creative destruction and natural disasters, to pursue truth, beauty, and goodness, to live, in other words, not in History, but in history and, as Robert Penn Warren put it, "the awful responsibility of Time."

In reflecting on the libertarian task in the first half of the 21st century, Richard Cornuelle pointed out the significance and scope of the work ahead:

> The world is waiting for the application of liberal methodology to other forms of human action. The civil society we are again talking about is blindingly complex. It consists of several million commercial undertakings of various shapes and sizes which hit moving economic targets without conscious coordination thanks to a guidance system we understand pretty well. Running in and among and around and through these commercial entities like glue is (probably) an equal number of non-commercial, but still voluntary organizations that we understand hardly at all. But there is gathering evidence that these half-forgotten, potentially powerful, largely dormant social forces might, in time, become an accepted alternative to state action. This dimension of society is practically begging to be rediscovered, explored and understood."[83]

It is largely in the hands of classical liberal scholars, with the praxeological and historical tools of the sciences of human action at their hands, to finally give proper voice to the nature and potential of the Tocquevillean Moment.

NOTES

1. J. G .A. Pocock, *Political Thought and History: Essays on Theory and Method* (Cambridge University Press, 2009).

2. Vincent Ostrom, *The Meaning of Democracy and the Vulnerabilities of Democracies: A Response to Tocqueville's Challenge* (University of Michigan Press, 1997).

3. J. G. A. Pocock, "Historiography and political thought," *Ideas in History*, Vol. III, no. 3 (2008), 97.

4. A rich resource for exploring the breadth of thinkers and ideas that can be encompassed in the classical liberal tradition is the website of David M. Hart, http://davidmhart.com/liberty/ClassicalLiberalism/index.html.

5. Ludwig von Mises, *Liberalism: The Classical Tradition* (Indianapolis: Liberty Fund, Inc., 2005), xviii–xix.

6. See especially Michael Polanyi, *Science, Faith and Society* (Chicago: University of Chicago Press, 1946); Michael Polanyi and Harry Prosch, *Meaning* (Chicago: University of Chicago Press, 1975); and Thomas Kuhn, *The Structure of Scientific Revolutions* (Chicago: University of Chicago Press, 1962).

7. See for instance, Peter J. Boettke, Christopher J. Coyne, and Peter T. Leeson, "Comparative historical political economy," *Journal of Institutional Economics* 9, no. 3 (2013), 285–301, as well as the discussions of Robert Nisbet below.

8. Alexis de Tocqueville, *Democracy in America*. Translated, edited, and with an Introduction by Harvey Mansfield and Delba Winthrop (Chicago: University of Chicago Press, 2000), 492.

9. The full statement reads: "The heart of classical liberalism is a simple policy prescription: Nurture voluntary associations. Limit the size, and more importantly, the scope of government. So long as the state provides a basic rule of law that steers people away from destructive or parasitic ways of life and in the direction of productive ways of life, society runs itself. If you want people to flourish, let them run their own lives." Steven Scalet and David Schmidtz, "State, Civil Society, and Classical Liberalism," in Nancy L. Rosenblum and Robert C. Post, eds. *Civil Society and Government* (Princeton: Princeton University Press, 2002), 26. This text provides a good introduction to a variety of perspectives and literature shaping civil society studies.

10. Richard Cornuelle, "The Libertarian Task in the Next Half Century," *Remarks at the Annual Dinner of the Institute for Humane Studies*, Ritz-Carlton Hotel, McLean, Virginia, November 4, 1993 (Fairfax, Virginia: Institute for Humane Studies, 1993), 6.

11. Vincent Ostrom, *The Meaning of Democracy and the Vulnerability of Democracies* (Ann Arbor: University of Michigan Press, 1997), 169, 167.

12. See, for instance, F. A. Hayek, *The Counter-Revolution of Science: Studies in the Abuse of Reason* (Glencoe, IL: The Free Press, 1979).

13. Dorothy Ross, *The Origins of American Social Science* (Cambridge: Cambridge University Press, 1991), 3.

14. Robert A. Nisbet, *Social Change and History: Aspects of the Western History of Development* (London: Oxford University Press, 1969), 142. F. A. Hayek observed that evolutionary thought in the social sciences actually preceded and influenced the development of theories of evolution in the natural sciences. See, F. A. Hayek, *The Fatal Conceit: The Errors of Socialism*, ed. W.W. Bartley, III, published as Volume 1 of *The Collected Works of F. A. Hayek* (London: Routledge, 1988), 24.

15. Nisbet, *Social Change and History*, 143–155.

16. Mises, *Theory and History*, 30.

17. Ostrom, *The Meaning of Democracy*, 66.

18. Ostrom, *The Meaning of Democracy*, 67.

19. One can imagine oneself, for example, in the shoes of Edward Gibbon as he experienced the "surprise" of his "Capitoline vision" while gazing at the ruins of ancient Rome and conceived the unprecedented project of telling the tale of the rise and fall of that classical empire.

20. One is tempted to invoke a "Machiavellian moment" as a critical inflection point in the awakening attention of European scholars to their relationships to political sovereigns, and subsequently their efforts to re-define sovereignty itself. See J. G. A. Pocock, *The Machiavellian Moment* (Princeton: Princeton University Press, 1975).

21. Ostrom, *The Meaning of Democracy*, 69.

22. See Boettke, Coyne and Leeson, "Comparative historical political economy." For a broader overview and bibliography, see James Mahoney and Dietrich Rueschemeyer, *Comparative Historical Analysis in the Social Sciences* (Cambridge: Cambridge University Press, 2003).

23. See Brian Tierney, *Liberty and Law: The Idea of Permissive Natural Law, 1100–1800* (Washington: Catholic University of America Press, 2014). The corpus of Harold J. Berman, especially *Law and Revolution: The Formation of the Western*

Legal Tradition (Cambridge, Massachusetts: Harvard University Press, 1983), is also important in this context.

24. For extended discussions of the English "ancient constitution" and "rule of law" see especially J. G. A. Pocock, *The Ancient Constitution and the Feudal Law: A Study of English Historical Thought in the Seventeenth Century*, 2nd ed. (Cambridge: Cambridge University Press, 1987) and John Phillip Reid, *Rule of Law: The Jurisprudence of Liberty in the Seventeenth and Eighteenth Centuries* (Dekalb: Northern Illinois University Press, 2004).

25. Adam Smith, *The Theory of Moral Sentiments*, ed. D. D. Raphael and A. L. Macfie (Oxford: Oxford University Press, 1976; reprinted Indianapolis, Liberty Fund, 1982), 233–234.

26. Alexis de Tocqueville, *The Old Regime and the Revolution*. Translated by John Bonner (New York: Harper & Brothers, 1856), i.

27. Political and social *philosophy*, as distinct from positive political and social *science*, of course, has much deeper roots in classical and medieval thought.

28. For a helpful survey on the centrality to the social sciences of the need to explain social change, see Trevor Noble, *Social Theory and Social Change* (New York: St. Martin's Press, 2000).

29. Micah White, *The End of Protest: A New Playbook for Revolution* (Toronto: Alfred A. Knopf Canada, 2016), 52.

30. White, 27.

31. White, 212.

32. The author's description of his purpose is in Robert Nisbet, *History of the Idea of Progress* (New Brunswick: Transaction Publishers, 1994), xvii. Originally published by Basic Books, 1980. See also Robert Nisbet, *Social Change and History: Aspects of the Western Theory of Development* (1969).

33. Robert Nisbet, "Social Change" in *Prejudices: A Philosophical Dictionary* (Cambridge: Harvard University Press, 1982), 274–275.

34. Nisbet, *Social Change and History*, 240.

35. Nisbet, *Prejudices*, 275.

36. Nisbet, *Social Change and History*, 270. The history of methodology Nisbet traces out here is complex. He notes that functionalism arose in part as a criticism of classical evolutionists such as Comte, Spencer, Morgan, and Tylor, but that later functionalists found no way forward in developing theories of change than to return to the earlier premises of the classical evolutionists that social change arose from endogenous sources—"immanence, genetic continuity, differentiation, directionality, and uniformitarianism" (235). Theories of change had come full circle: "Professor Parsons may be said to be the first of the contemporary functionalists (I am referring here solely to sociology) to lead the way back to thoroughgoing, classical, large-scale evolutionism—from which, of course, functionalism was derived in the first place" (239).

37. Nisbet, *Social Change and History*, 302.

38. See n.1 above.

39. F. A. Hayek, "The Principles of a Liberal Social Order," in *Studies in Philosophy, Politics and Economics* (London: Routledge and Kegan Paul, 1967), 160.

40. Hayek, "The Principles of a Liberal Social Order," 161.

41. Such questions have been taken up recently in Paul Dragos Aligica and Peter Boettke, "Institutional Design and Ideas-Driven Social Change: Notes from an Ostromian Perspective," *The Good Society* 20, no. 1 (2011): 50–66.

42. Adam Ferguson, *An Essay on The History of Civil Society* (1767), Part III, Section 2.

43. Hayek, "The Principles of a Liberal Social Order," 162.

44. Ludwig von Mises, *Human Action: A Treatise on Economics*, 3rd revised ed. (New York: Regnery, 1966; first published by Yale University Press, 1949), 1.

45. Mises, *Human Action*, 30–41.

46. This, of course, resonates with the key insight (noted above) that Adam Smith made when he observed that "in the great chess-board of human society, every single piece has a principle of motion of its own."

47. Ludwig von Mises, *Theory and History: An Interpretation of Social and Economic Evolution* (New Rochelle, New York, Arlington House, 1969. Originally published by Yale University Press, 1957), 198–204.

48. Mises, *Human Action*, 143.

49. Mises, *Theory and History*, 286.

50. Mises, *Theory and History*, 290–91.

51. L. M. Lachmann, *The Legacy of Max Weber* (Auburn: Ludwig von Mises Institute, 2007), 57. Lachmann adds that "In Menger's terminology, they are the institutions of *organic*, not *pragmatic* origin."

52. In using "concatenation" and "harmonization" here I am not making a direct correlation to concatenate and mutual coordination as discussed by Klein and Orsborn, though connections might be explored. See Daniel Klein and Aaron Orsborn, "Coordination in the History of Economics," working paper accessed May 22, 2016 at http://econfaculty.gmu.edu/pboettke/workshop/spring08/Klein-Orsborn_Coordination_in_Economics3%20_3_.pdf. On the kaleidic world, see Ludwig M. Lachmann, *The Market as an Economic Process* (New York: Basil Blackwell, 1986).

53. Ludwig M. Lachmann, "From Mises to Shackle: An essay on Austrian economics and the kaleidic society," in Don Lavoie, ed., *Expectations and the Meaning of Institutions*: Essays in Economics by Ludwig Lachmann (London: Routledge, 1994), 224.

54. Nisbet, *Prejudices*, 275–276.

55. Ludwig M. Lachmann, *Metroeconomica*, Vol. XI (1959), cited in G. L. S. Shackle, *Epistemics and Economics: A Critique of Economic Doctrines* (New Brunswick, New Jersey: Transaction Publishers, 2009; originally published by Cambridge University Press, 1972).

56. Many historians will attest that one of the chief delights of archival work is that moment when our subject surprises us.

57. If Nisbet's analysis is correct that people don't change unless change is necessary, this work of documenting continuities takes on even greater significance, since change can only become visible against the backdrop of continuity.

58. J. G. A. Pocock, "The Origins of the Study of the Past," in *Political Thought and History: Essays on Theory and Method* (Cambridge: Cambridge University Press, 2009), 147–148.

59. The work of R. G. Collingwood becomes important here, but I will not take it up in this essay for sake of space.

60. J. G. A. Pocock, "The Origins of Study of the Past," in *Political Thought and History: Essays on Theory and Method* (Cambridge: Cambridge University Press), 155.

61. Pocock, "The Origins of Study of the Past," 152.

62. And here we are not equating value judgment with evaluations of progress or decline against a teleological philosophy of history; among other things, value judgments may be consequentialist (the actor achieved or failed to achieve what he intended) or may be morally normative (the actor's behavior was good or evil).

63. Mises, *Theory and History*, 19–20. What we might be arriving at is a normative theory of historical judgment: A historian may appropriately make a consequentialist judgment (the actor achieved or failed to achieve what he intended). He should refrain qua historian from making a normative moral judgment—the actor's behavior was good or evil—unless he is assessing what the actor's contemporaries thought of the behavior. Finally, the historian has little business evaluating Progress or Decline against a teleological philosophy of history, though he may observe that certain actions lead to more or less complex forms of social order (in which cases he may need to borrow theoretical frameworks from the sociologist, the economist, or the political theorist).

64. Jason Kaufman, "Three Views of Associationalism in 19th Century America: An Empirical Examination," *American Journal of Sociology* 104, no. 5 (1999): 1296–1345.

65. Michael Goodheart, "Civil Society and the Problem of Global Democracy," *Democratization* 12, no. 1 (2005): 1–21.

66. Tocqueville, *Democracy in America*, 490.

67. Tocqueville, *Democracy in America*, 491.

68. F. A. Hayek, *The Constitution of Liberty*, republished in The Collected Works of F. A. Hayek, Volume XVII (Chicago, University of Chicago Press, 2011), 48.

69. As Pocock describes things: "Any stable and articulate society possesses concepts with which to discuss its political affairs and, and, associates these to form groups or languages. There is no reason to suppose that a society will have only one such language; we may rather expect to find several, differing in the departments of social activity from which they originate, the uses to which they are put and the modifications which they undergo. Some originate in the technical vocabulary of one of society's institutionalized modes of regulating public affairs. ... A society's political thought is built up largely in this way, by the adoption of technical vocabularies from different aspects of its social and cultural traditions and by the development of specialized languages in which to explain and defend the use of the former as means of discussing politics." J. G. A. Pocock, "The History of Political Thought," in *Political Thought and History*, 14–15.

70. The memorable phrase "in their hips" is one often used by the late M. Stanton Evans, but it originated with Willmoore Kendall.

71. Lenore T. Ealy, "The Intellectual Crisis in Civil Society," presented at The Annual Meeting of The Association for Private Enterprise Education (April 2015).

72. Ostrom, *The Meaning of Democracy*, 32.

73. For a deeper investigation of the Austrian understanding of historical science, see Roderick T. Long, "R. G. Collingwood: Historicist or Praxeologist?" Author's working paper accessed May 19, 2016 at http://praxeology.net/asc9long.pdf.

74. Deirdre Nansen McCloskey, "Max U *versus* Humanomics: a critique of neo-institutionalism," *Journal of Institutional Economics* 12 (March 2016): 1–27 doi:10.1017/S1744137415000053, 22. McCloskey is quoting Lachmann's *Capital, Expectations, and the Market Process* (1977).

75. Ludwig Lachmann, *The Legacy of Max Weber* (Auburn: Ludwig von Mises Institute, 2007), 67–68.

76. Lachmann, 70.

77. Pocock, "Preface," *Political Thought and History*, x. The phrase attributed to Oakeshott appears in Michael Oakeshott, "Rationalism in Politics," in *Rationalism in Politics and Other Essays*, with a foreword by Timothy Fuller (Indianapolis: Liberty Fund, 1991; originally published London: Methuen & Co. Ltd, 1962), 60. The full passage reads: "In political activity, then, men sail a boundless and bottomless sea; there is neither harbour for shelter nor floor for anchorage, neither starting-place nor appointed destination. The enterprise is to keep afloat on an even keel; the sea is both friend and enemy; and the seamanship consists in using the resources of a traditional manner of behaviour in order to make a friend of every hostile occasion."

78. We should note that Cornuelle was a graduate student of Mises at NYU for a time, but left academia and later became a prototype "social entrepreneur." He had been very influenced by the journalists of the "Old Right," such as Garet Garrett, Frank Chodorov, Rose Wilder Lane, and others who had tried to combat the expansion of the administrative welfare state in the early 20th century.

79. Hayek, *Law, Legislation, and Liberty*, Vol. 3, 186, n. 8 (emphasis added). Hayek here references Richard C. Cornuelle, *Reclaiming the American Dream* (New York: Random House, 1965).

80. Libertarian philosopher Murray Rothbard made a scathing critique of his old friend's new political aspirations in a 1969 essay entitled "The Nixon Administration: Creeping Cornuellism." "Here is what the Washington Post now reports: a 'central theme' of the new Administration will be a nationwide drive to stimulate 'voluntary action' against social ills. It adds that Secretary George Romney is 'in charge of planning the voluntary action effort.' This concept needs to be savored: government, the quintessence of coercion, is going to plan a nationwide 'voluntary' effort. George Orwell, where art thou now? War is Peace, Freedom is Slavery, Voluntary Action is Government Planning." Murray N. Rothbard, "The Nixon Administration: Creeping Cornuellism," *The Libertarian*, March 1, 1969, in *The Complete Libertarian Forum 1969–1984* (e-book), ed. Murray N. Rothbard (Auburn: Ludwig von Mises Institute, 2012), 63.

81. Peter Berger and Richard John Neuhaus, *To Empower People: The Role of Mediating Structures in Public Policy* (Washington: American Enterprise Institute, 1977).

82. See Lenore T. Ealy, "The Intellectual Crisis in Philanthropy," *Society* 51, no.1 (2014): 87–96.

Chapter 5

Some Roads Taken, and Not Taken, from the Progressive Era to the New Deal

David T. Beito

It can be taken for granted that left-of-center historians dominate discourse on the Progressive Era and the New Deal periods and have for generations. One of the consequences is a tendency to *also* take for granted that the rise of the welfare-regulatory state was long overdue and that Franklin D. Roosevelt deserves plaudits for helping to make it possible. While no other president since Lincoln comes close to getting the same praise as Roosevelt, these historians also show high regard for the two other main architects of bigger government during this period: Theodore Roosevelt and Woodrow Wilson. A survey in 2009 of sixty-five presidential historians and other scholars named all three in the top ten of "greats." Wilson may well slip in future rankings, but primarily because of his racism not for his other policies. This consensus is powerful but, at the same time, few periods present more leeway for scholarship informed by classical liberal perspectives. These opportunities span a wide range of fields including political, economic history, the history of race, and social history.[1]

High on the list of promising topics for further exploration is the clash between two of the major ideological paradigms in the late nineteenth century: classical liberalism and progressivism. Because each category (in the context of the period) encompassed widely diverse, and sometimes contradictory, perspectives, only broad definitions are possible. A good rule of thumb is that classical liberals were more likely to support governmental restraint including balanced budgets, a gold standard, lower tariffs, individual rights, and a less interventionist foreign policy. To varying degrees, progressives stood for greater governmental involvement in economics and personal morality and most (though not all) favored a more activist foreign policy. What were the reasons for the relatively abrupt decline of classical liberalism as a mainstream political philosophy and the subsequent rise, and

95

eventual dominance, of progressivism? A good place to start is to delve more deeply into the internal dynamics of each of these ideological traditions in the decades after the Civil War.

One conclusion can safely be stated. During the Gilded Age, classical liberalism remained a formidable force among policymakers and the public. This can be credited in no small measure to its vibrant ideological vanguard: the Mugwumps. That term, originally an epithet, derived from an Algonquian word meaning "important person." The Mugwumps were political independents, centered in New England, who crusaded against political corruption and in favor of free trade and the gold standard. A shared intellectual influence was a now little-known figure: economist and philosopher Francis Wayland who weaved together an emphasis on free-market economic ideas and moral virtue. According to historian David Tucker, "Wayland's Moral Philosophy was the most common source of Mugwump moral thought." Wayland's ideas, in turn, drew from Adam Smith. During the late nineteenth century, Mugwumps, like publicist and economist Edward Atkinson and publisher R. R. Bowker found inspiration in the efforts of the famous free traders, Richard Cobden and John Bright. They created a network of free-market and sound money organizations, such as the Free Trade Alliance, the Free Trade Club, and the Society for Political Education. From its founding in 1865 until just after the turn of the twentieth century, the *Nation* was a key outlet for their views. Originally Republicans, many of them had left the party during the 1870s because of cronyism and corruption.[2]

The Mugwumps (when getting any attention at all) have not fared well from historians. The first major scholarly account, John Sproat's "The Best Men": Liberal Reformers in the Gild Age, depicted them as sanctimonious elitists, who gradually became more conservative over time. Challenging this view, David Tucker emphasizes the multiple ways that the Mugwumps defended marginalized groups. Most of them never forgot their backgrounds as abolitionists or children of abolitionists and took part in virtually every movement for human rights in the late nineteenth and (sometimes) early twentieth centuries. Atkinson and Horace White (the editor-in-chief of the Nation for a time) both smuggled Sharps rifles to John Brown's army, and they, as well as U.S. Senator Carl Schurz and E. L. Godkin, the Mugwump founder of, and frequent writer for, the Nation, continued to speak out against segregation and disfranchisement for their entire lives. "The Mugwumps were a movement of hope rather than fear," writes Tucker. "They were essentially optimistic about the poor and the immigrants. They believed all peoples responded favorably to liberty, education, and free markets."[3]

When Grover Cleveland, a champion of the small-government causes favored by the Mugwumps, finished his second term in 1897, classical liberalism was spent as an electoral force and progressivism was making inroads, especially at the local level. By 1912, the transition was complete. Three of the major candidates, Woodrow Wilson, Theodore Roosevelt, and William Howard Taft, were progressives and the fourth, Eugene Debs, was a socialist. The progressives left behind an indelible mark of big-government policies including deeper controls on economic behavior, restrictions on personal morality via anti-drug and prostitution laws, and an increasingly interventionist foreign policy.[4]

A CLASH OF TWO IDEOLOGICAL VANGUARDS

The progressives, like the Mugwumps, had their own ideological vanguard: the Social Gospel. Sidney Fine's Laissez-Faire and the General-Welfare State sheds much light on it. Social Gospelites were crucial in influencing elite attitudes to the detriment of classical liberalism and to the benefit of progressivism. Led by theologians, such as Josiah Strong, Walter Rauschenbusch, and Washington Gladden, they were making great headway in the mainline Protestant churches by the 1870s. Social Gospelites promoted an interventionist middle ground, or "golden mean," between laissez-faire and socialism. Like earlier Protestants, they set out to quash sinful behavior but, unlike them, had an unusually expansive definition of the meaning of sin that included poverty, business exploitation, and poor housing.[5]

Because they regarded human nature as malleable, the Social Gospelites were optimistic about the potential of human action, including the force of government, to create a sin-free "Kingdom of God on Earth." Rauschenbusch looked forward to a world characterized by cooperation and solidarity rather than competition. Agreeing, Gladden rejected the conception of government as only concerned with protecting property, enforcing contracts, and upholding personal freedom. He declared that "the State is something far higher and more godlike than this, and that if we could only invest it in our thought with its true divine character, we should need no other agency for the unification of society."[6]

In the battle of the two ideological vanguards, the Social Gospelites had a clear edge in prestigious academic credentials. Beginning in the 1870s, they had flocked to study in German universities, at a time when relatively few Americans even completed high school. Highly influential in the faculty of the German Universities were the so-called "professorial socialists" or "socialists of the chair." This group advanced several theories that later appeared in the thought of the progressives and put them starkly at odds with the classical liberal paradigm. Like the Social Gospelites, the German professors sought a middle ground (or golden mean) between what they called the "anarchism" of laissez-faire and the total state control of communism. Both Fine and

Daniel T. Rodgers in Atlantic Crossings Social Politics in a Progressive Age document the instrumental role of the German-trained students as progressive torchbearers in such causes as social insurance, urban planning, and expansion of higher education. Richard Ely and John R. Commons (in economics), and Albion Small (in sociology) were among then. All three were influenced by Social Gospel views. As Rodgers puts it: "Those in the cohort of American students whom the German assault on laissez-faire had taken most by surprise came back in the late 1870s and early 1880s with not only massive doubts about laissez-faire but also sweeping, still inchoate visions of radical change. Albion Small taught students his 'abomination of laissez-faire.'"[7]

A combined accomplishment of the German university alumni and Social Gospelites was the founding of the American Economic Association (AEA) in 1885. Ely intended the group to embody the "field of practical Christianity." The AEA's initial prospectus, which he authored, characterized the "state as an educational and ethical agency whose positive aid is essential to human progress" and dismissed laissez-faire doctrine as "unsafe in politics in unsound in morals." Five out of the six of the AEA's first officers had studied in Germany as well as twenty out of its first twenty-six presidents. This German experience, though crucial, was part of a broader international trend. Incipient intellectual progressivism also drew on sources from other countries, such as British Fabian socialism.[8]

By the late 1890s, the ideas first nurtured by the Social Gospel and the German alumni were starting to trickle down from intellectual elites to political leaders and voters in both parties. The Republicans proved the most receptive to the progressive agenda, at least initially. This is not too surprising. During the Cleveland era, Republicans were generally more inclined than Democrats to support protectionism, business subsidies, Civil War pensions, foreign-policy intervention, bigger military budgets, and immigration restriction. The Republican progressives built upon and extended the range of this interventionist agenda.[9]

Classical liberals were unable to mount an effective response to the rise of progressivism. The reasons are not entirely clear. While Tucker does much to correct the older depiction of the Mugwumps as insular elitists, he also identifies one of their key vulnerabilities: an aging membership. He writes that "the battle over imperialism waged mainly in the East between generations, seventy-year old Mugwumps versus forty-year-old imperialists." Unfortunately, Tucker never really explores this inability to infuse new blood into the ranks.[10]

A Mugwump weak point was also one of the movement's defining features: the preoccupation with civil service reform. As the power of political machines eroded and governments replaced patronage with merit-based appointments, an unintended result for many was to bolster the case for government intervention. Especially skilled in turning the old Mugwump suspicion of politics to progressive advantage was the German-educated Lester Frank Ward, soon to become the first president of the American Sociological Association. Thomas C. Leonard, in *Illiberal Reformers: Race, Eugenics, and American Economics in the Progressive Era*, aptly described him as "the intellectual spearhead of the assault on laissez-faire."[11]

Ward agreed with the classical liberals that the suspicion of big government was salutary in the eighteenth century but, unlike them, emphasized that recent reforms in governmental structure had made this stance outmoded. A Democratic government shorn of tyranny, corruption, and backed by science, Ward asserted, had almost limitless potential to accomplish positive goals because it was finally shedding the taint of patronage, amateurism, and corruption. Ward did much to popularize a conception of government as an essential cooperative tool representing the "public will" rather than an alien force or "necessary evil."[12]

Also rattling classical liberal faith in free markets was a perception that big business had become an unaccountable force shielded from competition. Anxiety only heightened during the merger wave beginning in the late 1890s. If big and distant corporations now dominated the economy, many liberals concluded, the only resort was the countervailing force of a Democratic, and more efficient government. To some extent, it was the business community itself that fostered the impression that this consolidation had rendered the free-market obsolete. This was, in part, according to Martin J. Sklar, because business leadership had shifted from the "entrepreneur-debtor" to the "administrator-investor." The latter group sought to empower "government bureaucracies, like those of the better-managed corporations, based solely on merit." In retrospect, the popular and elite perception of all-powerful big business immune from market forces was mostly just that, a perception. It had scant basis in reality. As Gabriel Kolko and others find, the merger wave was largely a bust, and competition, if anything, became more intense.[13]

Broader social, cultural, and political trends dealt additional blows to believers in a classical liberal worldview. The inclination of so many more Americans to view individuals through the lens of class and race directly clashed with older theories that posited a separation of state and society. As Leonard documents, this transformed environment proved fertile for an emerging generation of progressives who championed eugenics and immigration restriction as means to combat "race suicide" and embraced a doctrine of imperialism laced with white supremacy. Older movements for human rights that originally had a classical liberal cast reformulated themselves along more progressive lives.[14]

One of the areas where this transformation was most apparent was feminism. Aileen Kraditor in her provocative Ideas of the Woman Suffrage

Movement, traces a shift in the 1890s away from the ideals of the Seneca Falls Conference which emphasized that women were individuals and thus deserved the same rights as men, no more or less. Elizabeth Cady Stanton restated this idea in 1892 proclaiming that in "discussing the rights of woman are to consider, first, what belongs to her as an individual, in a world of her own."[15]

As more Americans lost enthusiasm for theories of universal natural rights and individualism, feminists adapted by embracing, and then modifying to their own purposes, older stereotypes used their opponents. They relied increasingly on arguments based on "expediency" that championed suffrage not so much as a matter of rights but as a means to implement "feminine" values such as altruism and maternalism. Progressive advocates of this reformulated feminism, such as Jane Addams and Carrie Chapman Catt, said that the vote gave women a unique opportunity to apply their special feminine traits to government. "May we not say," wrote Addams, "that city housekeeping has failed partly because women, the traditional housekeepers, have not been consulted as to its multiform activities."[16]

GOLD DEMOCRATS AND ANTI-IMPERIALISTS

A good case study for tracing not only the decline of classical liberalism during this era but also the transition to progressivism is the story of the National Democratic Party (NDP) of 1896. The party's ranks constituted a veritable who's who of classical liberals. Cleveland Democrats launched it in reaction to William Jennings Bryan's takeover of the Democratic Party. After nominating two former governors, John Palmer and Simon Bolivar Buckner, the NDP adopted a pro-gold standard platform which also rejected protectionism and government paternalism. It represented a diverse coalition. The NDP included such respected former Democratic Party "regulars" as Senators William Vilas of Wisconsin, former Mayor John P. Hopkins of Chicago, former U.S. Representatives William D. Bynum of Illinois, and William C.P. Breckinridge of Kentucky. Some others in the NDP's leadership were Henry Watterson, the editor of the *Louisville Courier-Journal*, as well such pro-gold/pro-free trade Mugwumps as Edward Atkinson and Oswald Garrison Villard, the grandson of abolitionist William Lloyd Garrison, and Thomas Mott Osborne, the grandnephew of Lucretia Mott, the abolitionist organizer of the first women's rights conference at Seneca Falls.[17]

Despite netting some major newspaper endorsements, the NDP failed miserably (receiving only 1 percent of the vote), in part because many Americans saw it as a "wasted vote" which would end up helping to elect McKinley. During the campaign, the NDP leadership had compounded this vulnerability by depicting their cause as a temporary refuge for pro-Gold Democrats rather than as effort to build a third party to challenge both Democrats and Republicans.[18]

For many classical liberals, the NDP was a jumping off point to the American Anti-Imperialist League. Formed in 1898, it represented a kind of last hurrah to classical liberals, who were prominent in the League's leadership. The most notable name on that list was former president Grover Cleveland who was one of the League's forty-one vice presidents. A fellow vice president was William Graham Sumner, a Yale anthropologist, sociologist, and economist and the best known American exponent of laissez-faire. Few have more forcefully depicted the corrupting influence of empire on society. In his seminal speech in 1899, "The Conquest of the United States by Spain," Sumner declared that "My patriotism is of the kind which is outraged by the notion that the United States never was a great nation until in a petty three months' campaign it knocked to pieces a poor, decrepit, bankrupt old state like Spain. To hold such an opinion as that is to abandon all American standards, to put shame and scorn on all that our ancestors tried to build up here, and to go over to the standards of which Spain is a representative."[19]

Another NDP veteran, Moorfield Storey, was a key officer in the League and later its president. His career began just after the Civil War as secretary to the legendary Senator Charles Sumner of Massachusetts and was capped off by his election as president of the American Bar Association in 1896. American imperialists, Storey charged, had recklessly thrown aside "that wise policy of non-intervention" for the European model of large navies and big standing armies. Under imperialism, he predicted, "taxation must increase, our currency become disordered, and worse than all the corruption which threatens us cannot fail to spread." Despite some initial successes, the League began a steep decline after the U.S. defeated the insurgency in the Philippines.[20]

FROM CLASSICAL LIBERALISM TO PROGRESSIVISM

The presidential nomination of Alton Parker in 1904 gave a victory of sorts to pro-gold Democrats, but it was a fleeting one. By World War I, the key elder statesman in the movement had died. Never again did classical liberal ideas have such sway over a major political party. Although many of the younger key NDP activists and voters had long careers ahead of them, few remained on the same ideological path. By the turn of the century, Sklar writes, "no significant segment of organized opinion advocated a return to the old competitive market or the preservation of laissez-faire prohibitions on regulatory intervention ... Cleveland Democracy, and Republican mugwumpery were already antiquities."[21]

For many, the classical liberalism of the National Democratic Party gradually morphed into the big-government liberalism of the twentieth-century Democratic Party. It is remarkable that a party which garnered only 1 percent of the vote left such a lasting legacy, albeit more often than not a progressive one. In some cases, the transition away from classical liberalism took time. Villard continued to defend free trade, the gold standard, and generally support small government even though he voted for Wilson in 1912. Part of this attraction might have stemmed from Wilson's rhetoric about empowering the entrepreneurial "man on the make." But Woodrow Wilson, who also voted for Palmer and Buckner, was clearly a progressive declaring in 1908: "No one now advocates the old *laissez faire* ... no one questions the necessity for a firm and comprehensive regulation of business operations." By 1920, Villard was advocating positions he once had vigorously condemned, such as nationalization of the railways, but he remained a committed civil libertarian and free trader and, on occasion, expressed skepticism about economic intervention. For closer to Wilson was fellow NDP backer George Peabody, who sponsored the publication of The New Freedom, a 1913 collection of Wilson's essays. Peabody later defended the New Deal and the nationalization of railroads, and Thomas Mott Osborne helped secure Wilson's nomination in 1912.[22]

Supporters of Palmer and Buckner in 1896 also had key roles in the wartime bureaucracy and Democratic leadership under Wilson. All of the following had belonged to the NDP national executive committee: the special counsel to the Railroad Administration in World War I, two members of the Democratic National Committee, the assistant secretary of the Navy, the director of the War Finance Corporation, and the deputy chairman of the Federal Reserve Board of New York. Bernard Baruch, the famous "wizard of Wall Street" and director of the War Industries Board later recalled that he had "probably voted for John M. Palmer, the gold Democrat."[23]

Most strikingly, all three of Wilson's appointments to the Supreme Court—Louis Brandeis, James C. McReynolds, and John H. Clarke—had campaigned for the NDP in 1896. The tenure of each on the Court, however, did not reveal a common thread. Brandeis generally voted to sustain expanded governmental intervention. Clarke, the chairman of the NDP convention in Ohio in 1896, ended his career as a vocal public defender of the New Deal and of FDR's court-packing plan. McReynolds, an NDP candidate for the U.S. House in Tennessee, moved in the opposite direction. As a leader of the conservative "four horsemen," he repeatedly voted to strike down New Deal legislation.[24]

Although civil rights was not a concern of the NDP itself, several former members were in the vanguard of that movement. With the exception of some prominent NDP supporters, who expressed bigoted opinions, such as former Secretary of the Agriculture Sterling Morton and Senator Donnelson Caffery of Louisiana, the general pattern was an advanced perspective on race. Breckinridge and Watterson were both Kentucky Democrats but they favored suffrage and the right of blacks to testify in Court. Although all of them were white, Villard, Horace White, Osborne, and Storey were founders of the National Association for the Advancement of Colored People in 1910. Storey became the president, Villard was the disbursing treasurer and chairman of the board, and Osborne sat on the general committee. Unlike Villard and other old allies, Storey held on to many of his earlier anti-statist beliefs, including opposition to federal prohibition of child labor. According to a biographer, his views "included pacifism, anti-imperialism, and racial egalitarianism fully as much as it did laissez-faire and moral tone in government." Storey and Villard aggressively defended civil liberties during World War I and the subsequent Red Scare thus providing a bridge between classical liberalism and modern civil libertarianism. Historian Mark A. Graber asserts that they, along with Godkin and Atkinson, advocated a "conservative libertarian" perspective that upheld both civil liberties and property rights.[25]

TONTINES, MUTUAL AID, AND THE WELFARE STATE

The period from the Progressive Era to the end of the New Deal brought a great transformation in the relationship between Americans and the state. For example, governments at all levels launched wars against drugs (Harrison Act of 1915, Marijuana Tax Act 1937), prostitution (the Mann Act, numerous state abatement and injunction laws), cigarettes, and, of course, alcohol (prohibition).

These years also witnessed a clash between the expanding American welfare-regulatory state and older institutions of self-help and mutual aid. An illustration was legislation which banned an early example of individual retirement accounts: semi-tontine insurance. At the turn of the century, it was the leading form of commercial life insurance in the United States adding up to nine million policies. The purchaser paid a portion of the premium for a standard life insurance policy but, unlike regular life insurance, the dividends (or surplus over the reserve) flowed into a common fund which usually expired after twenty years. If the insured died before the end of the term, the beneficiaries collected on the face of the policy. If the insured survived, he or she, along with other members of the fund, divided the accumulated proceeds plus interest. Semi-tontines earned higher returns than savings accounts in banks. "In addition to securing conventional life insurance," write Ransom and Sutch, "the purchaser ... was creating a retirement fund for old age."[26]

At the height of its popularity, however, semi-tontine insurance became one of the most prominent victims of Progressive Era muckraking. In 1905, it came under fire from the Armstrong Committee of the New York legislature. The committee and other critics charged that it had fostered a "gambling instinct" and lavish salaries for insurance executives. It found no evidence, however, that it was actuarially unsound or otherwise fraudulent. Upon recommendation of the Armstrong Committee, New York banned further sales. Other states soon followed suit. The result was to stop dead in its tracks a promising experiment in individually purchased retirement savings. The ban on semi-tontine insurance also speeded a trend to centralize social welfare in either employers or government.[27]

This increased employer and governmental provision often worked at cross purposes with social welfare provision via mutual aid. The pinnacle of organized mutual aid was the fraternal society. Fraternal societies took several forms including the secret societies (which featured more informal mutual aid) such as the Masons, sick-benefit societies such as the Odd Fellows (which offered early forms of health insurance) and life insurance societies such as the Modern Woodmen of the World. A conservative estimate is that after the turn of the century about one-third of American men belonged to these organizations. Fraternal societies were particularly well represented among immigrants and blacks. This also made inroads among women (who preferred the term fraternal, rather than sororal), particularly from those two groups. Membership growth had leveled off by the 1920s as the life insurance societies completed a difficult transition to more sustainable actuarial practices.[28]

Few topics of such clear historical importance have received so little attention from historians as the role of lodges in American society and as dispensers of social welfare. This is particularly true for black history. With the possible exception of churches, more blacks belonged to fraternals than any other kind of organization. This did not escape the notice of contemporaries. In 1905, Fannie Barrier Williams, later one of the founders of the NAACP, observed that in "nothing does the colored man live such a strenuous life as he does as a lodge man. The lodge, more than any other merely social organization, is a permanent and ever-increasing force." One indication of just how much historians have neglected this topic is the lack of any academic study of the Grand United Order of Odd Fellows and the Household of Ruth. In 1916, they were respectively the largest black organizations for black men and women. The Grand Order had over 300,000 members and the Household just shy of 200,000 members (that's out of a total black population of about 10 million).[29]

Lizabeth Cohen's much cited book, *Making a New Deal*, brought new attention to the role of mutual aid during the 1920s and 1930s. During the 1920s, she writes, ethnic communities in Chicago, including fraternal societies, "provided more assistance than other institutions, public or private, which were only viewed as a last resort." Her depiction of the fraternal response to the Great Depression is much harsher. She contends that these societies only survived by shedding expensive benefits other than standard life insurance. Pointing to the record of the Slovene National Benefit Society, she concludes that fraternals "failed" ethnic workers.[30]

The evidence presented by Cohen does not support this assessment. The actions of the group she highlights, the Slovene National Benefit Society, were not a typical of societies during the period. Taken as a whole, societies did not fail members during the Great Depression and, in fact, responded with resourcefulness and redoubled commitment to social welfare. One indicator of that was that a higher percentage of societies offered sickness, disability, and old-age benefits in 1935 compared to 1930. That year, they boasted a ratio of assets to liabilities of nearly two to one. Moreover, in 1939, the number of residents in fraternal orphanages and homes for the elderly was higher than ever before. These organizations did not use hard times as a pretext to reduce benefits. Not until the 1940s did societies significantly scale back social welfare benefits. While fraternal memberships sagged during the 1930s, the main reason was not because they were unable or unwilling to pay benefits but because of the impossible burden of continuing to carry members on the rolls in arrears during a full decade of double-digit unemployment. It makes more sense to blame this membership drop off on the misfired Republican and Democratic policies which created and worsened the depression than on any intrinsic shortcomings of mutual aid per se.[31]

DEPRESSION, NEW DEAL, AND ROADS NOT TAKEN

While an adequate examination of key theories on the Great Depression's cause (or causes) is impossible in a short survey, one conclusion is clear: underconsumptionist explanations still predominate in the history texts. These hold, in broad outlines, that unequal distribution of wealth in the 1920s left consumers unable to purchase the goods produced by industry. Robert A. Divine, T. H. Breen, George M. Frederickson and R. Hal Williams in their popular text, The American Story, frame it this way: "U.S. factories produced more goods than the American people could consume ... . Too much money had gone into profits, dividends, and industrial expansion, and not enough had gone into the hands of the workers, who were also consumers."[32]

Divine et al., and the authors of most other survey texts, devote little space to competing theories on the causes of the Great Depression. Although some give a slight nod to Milton Friedman and Anna Schwartz's Monetarist perspective that the Federal Reserve worsened matters by letting the money supply contract, mention of the Austrian theory is almost entirely absent. Unlike the Monetarists, advocates of this view identify central bank credit expansion as a leading culprit. Specifically, Austrian economists, such as F. A. Hayek, Ludwig Von Mises, Murray Rothbard, blame the Federal Reserve's policy of low discount rates for creating unsustainable malinvestments in the capital goods sector during the 1920s. These malinvestments collapsed after the Fed raised rates in 1928 and 1929. A point in favor of the Austrian explanation, and one that underconsumptionists slight, was that capital goods prices fell much more steeply than those of consumer goods at the outset of the downturn. If the underconsumptionists are right, would not the converse be true?[33]

Identifying the cause (or causes) of the depression, however, seems less important than explaining its long duration. It started as a garden variety recession. Only in 1931 did it become apparent that this would be something on a much greater scale. Since the 1980s, Robert Higgs and other historians have explored why this recession morphed into a decade-long Great Depression. Higgs stresses the impact of repeated shocks to the system, such as the Smoot-Hawley Tariff and Roosevelt's high marginal tax rates and class warfare rhetoric. The cumulative effect of these shocks was to create a kind of "regime uncertainty" which discouraged business investment. Similarly, Burton Folsom attributes the persistence of the depression not only to these factors but also the misguided cartelization policies of the Agricultural Adjustment Administration and the National Recovery Administration. Most historians agree that the New Deal did not produce full recovery; however, unlike the Austrians, Higgs, and Folsom, they generally blame the federal government for doing too little, not too much.[34]

For related reasons, these historians overwhelmingly agree that ultimate recovery was the by-product of stimulus caused by a vastly ramped up governmental spending during World War II. The authors of the *American Story* declare that "Four years of fighting brought about industrial recovery and unparalleled prosperity. The old pattern of unregulated free enterprise was as much a victim of the war as of the New Deal." Agreeing, their counterparts in *Of the People: A History of the United States* proclaim that "Big government and corporations made possible the 'miracle of production' that was winning the war and raising living standards ... . The economy boomed."[35]

In a trail-blazing article in the *Journal of Economic History*, Higgs vigorously challenges this consensus. He raises serious questions about the official GDP figures by examining distortions caused by the wartime command economy. Instead of enhanced prosperity, Higgs concludes, that the "duration" brought great deprivation in the form of higher accident rates, shoddy goods, shortages, and rationing. Private investment continued to sag. The much heralded achievement of full employment was largely a matter of shifting Americans from the unemployment lines into jobs that "entailed substantial risks of death, dismemberment, and other physical and psychological injuries."[36]

In trying to explain the slowness of recovery from depression, Richard K. Vedder and Lowell E. Gallaway underscore the failure of real wages to smoothly adjust downward. Along with James Grant in *The Forgotten Depression*, they highlight the contrast to previous downturns, such the depression of 1921, when real wages, along with profits and prices, fell rapidly in the initial stages. By contrast, as Vedder and Galloway emphasize, real wages were substantially higher in 1933 (the worst year of the crisis) than in 1929 (at the height of the boom). Meanwhile, employers saved on payrolls by laying off workers as unemployment spiked to an all-time record of 25 percent. Wages stayed high for a combination of complicated reasons including exhortations by President Hoover and business allies, such as Henry Ford, at a series of White House conferences as well as such policies as the Smoot-Hawley tariff and Davis-Bacon Act. Vedder and Galloway assert that genuine recovery only occurred after World War II when the wartime command economy was dismantled and real wages finally fell to sustainable levels.[37]

While some economic historians comment on it, the persistence of high wages under Hoover has largely escaped scrutiny from non-economic historians. To the contrary, the overall impression they leave is that Hoover, despite trying mightily, was unable to prop up real wages. In a generally measured survey, The New Deal: The Depression Years, 1933–1940, Anthony J. Badger, stresses "Hoover's vain exhortations to keep wages up" and the failure of his business conferences to achieve that goal. Writing on the Hoover years, Eric Rauchway flatly declares "unemployment rose and overall wages dropped even in cases where the nominal rate of pay remained the same."[38]

Perhaps because of a tendency to look backward from the New Deal, historians have discounted the possibility that Americans prior to 1933 might have made another choice, other than the "big three" of fascism, socialism, or the modern welfare-regulatory state. While a clear ideological shift more favorable to statism was underway by 1933 (due in no small measure to Roosevelt's unusual leadership skills and charisma), the years immediately prior to that are harder to classify. The years 1929–1933 can best be characterized as an interlude of ideological flux and uncertainty, when few options could be entirely ruled out.

Sometimes in treatments of Roosevelt's 1932 election victory, historians leave the impression, perhaps unintentionally, that voters had somehow endorsed the welfare-regulatory policies of the New Deal or something like

it. But before his election, Roosevelt gave at best only a glimmer of his eventual destination in 1933. Campaign statements that seemed to foreshadow elements of the New Deal appeared alongside contradictory pledges to carry out
the Democratic platform's pledge to cut government spending by 25 percent.
More than once during the campaign, Roosevelt accused Hoover of presiding
over the "greatest spending administration in peace times in all our history."[39]

There is undeniable evidence that popular support for anti-big-government
attitudes during the Hoover years not only remained strong but, arguably,
enjoyed a renaissance. Americans may have wanted change in 1932 but it
does not perforce follow that they desired more government intervention.
To voters during these years, change entailed a wide range of possibilities. In the state houses, it included the policies of progressives, such as
Governor Phillip La Follette of Wisconsin, as well as those of economizers
such as Harry G. Leslie of Indiana. Badger's approach to this issue is fairly
typical of historians. While he chronicles the popularity of state and local
budget cutters during the Hoover era, he is ultimately dismissive of them.
"State governments," he laments, "responded to the Depression first with
complacency, then bewilderment, but above all with conventional policies
of retrenchment, balanced budgets, and regressive taxation, notably sales
taxes."[40]

The most radical species of this economizing tendency from 1929 to
1933 was tax resistance. In 1932, *New York Times* journalist Anne O'Hare
McCormick described this movement at its height. She stated that the
"nearest thing to a political revolution in the country is the tax revolt. ...
taxpayers are wrought up to the point of willingness to give up public services. 'We'll do without county agents,' they say. 'We'll give up the public
health service.'" From another perspective, the head of the International
City Managers Association bemoaned that, "There seems to be no game
laws of any kind to protect public officers and the establishment we call
government. Taxes have been assailed as economic waste and those who
spend tax money have been pictured as wastrels." The background to the
tax revolt was a local and state fiscal crisis. Property tax delinquency rose
to a still-standing record of 26.3 percent in 1933, from 10.1 percent in 1930.
In many areas, the tax system broke down and payment became almost
voluntary. Throughout the country, Americans formed "taxpayers' leagues"
to demand spending cuts, arguing that since they had tightened their belts,
politicians should too. The *National Municipal Review* reported that at least
3,000 such groups had emerged by 1933 compared to only forty-seven in
1927. Because of tax league pressure, nineteen states and numerous locali-
ties brought property levies under control by capping mill rates or limiting
overall property taxes to a percentage of assessed value. A few tax leagues
pressed more radical approaches. The best known was the Association of

Real Estate Taxpayers in Chicago, which led one of the largest tax strikes in American history. At its height in 1933, it had 30,000 paid members, a budget of $600,000, and a weekly radio show.[41]

The failure to appreciate the unpredictable flux of 1929 to 1933 has fostered a rather "whiggish" assumption, often unstated, that something akin to a New Deal was almost inevitable. An illustration is the constricted historical debate on whether the New Deal represented true reform or merely a ploy to "save capitalism." On one side of this binary, Paul Conkin highlights a "supreme irony." The "enemies of the New Deal were wrong. They should have been friends." He wondered why the critics on the right did not realize that FDR's policies served as an insurance policy for preserving capitalism. More recently, Rauchway cites the "overriding evidence" that "in both word and deed that the Roosevelt administration came time after time to rescue American capitalism and had no intention of replacing it." This view, albeit in modified form, serves as a basis of Ira Katznelson's deservedly hailed *Fear Itself: The New Deal and the Origins of Our Time.* The New Deal, he argues, preserved the system by "reshaping liberal democracy" and thus made possible a compelling alternative to dictatorships.[42]

Pronouncements that Roosevelt "rescued" capitalism or preserved democracy, of course, include the unstated assumption, or counterfactual, that capitalism or democracy needed "saving" via more statism. The assumption becomes more problematic given a wealth of historical counterexamples, most recently of Warren G. Harding in 1921, of presidents who responded to depressions through spending retrenchment and, in doing so, did not incite a revolution, coup, or a significant expansion in the welfare-regulatory state. To be sure, the Great Depression lasted much longer than these other crises but, as of 1932, despite much discontent, there was no ideological groundswell in the United States to implement radical political change. Fascist movements were almost non-existent and the Socialist and Communist presidential candidates received less than 3 percent of the vote between them.[43]

Assuming a counterfactual, if Roosevelt had attempted to implement a policy of scaled-back government and free markets, on what basis can it be assumed that he would have automatically failed? To any critics who charged that Roosevelt was making a radical break from past experience in doing this, he could cite ample historical precedent as well as his own campaign vows to cut spending and avoid reliance on bureaucratic solutions. The famed Roosevelt charisma worked wonders in selling the New Deal. Why could it not have worked similar wonders in advancing such an agenda?

International comparisons (so popular today among historians in other contexts) can also reveal possible free-market roads not taken. An obvious example is the differing response of the United States and Canada to the banking response. Canada did not have a central bank during the early years of the Great Depression, yet it did not suffer a single banking failure. The United States had over ten thousand. Most economic historians credit Canada's success to laws permitting private banks to branch, and thus spread risk, in contrast to the United States where unit banking laws impeded these practices. At the federal level, the McFadden Act of 1927 reinforced many of these regulations. Also, in contrast to the United States, banks in Canada had much greater leeway to form clearinghouses to monitor members as well as act as lenders of last resort.[44]

While economic historians, such as Michael D. Bordo, Angela Redish, and Hugh Rockoff have documented the Canadian story, the standard history texts and overviews rarely allude to it. Two notable exceptions are Badger and Rauchway. Badger briefly notes that because "neighboring Canada with extensive branch banking had avoided bank failures, while suffering much the same economic problems as the United States, there was also some powerful backing for the extension of branch banking." Badger leaves it pretty much at that. He then goes on, somewhat in contradiction, to stress as a general proposition the impotency of "private initiative" and "business self-regulation" to deal with problems created by the depression. Rauchway even more explicitly acknowledges the success of the Canadian system but, like Badger, shows no inkling of it as a possible free-market alternative. Like Badger, however, he stresses the lack of "action" by Hoover and other political leaders as the main culprit in the financial crisis. A historian sympathetic to a classical liberal perspective, by contrast, would take the opportunity to explore whether a similar free-market policy toward banks in the United States might have eliminated the need for increased regulation, banking holidays, or even federal deposit insurance.[45]

The failure of historians to imagine free-market "roads not taken" in banking applies to many other historical topics from the late nineteenth century to the New Deal period and beyond. The only counterfactuals considered, or even hinted at, assume that progressive or New Deal policies "had" to happen to prevent something far worse. Such assumptions have served as the basis for endless historiography and created an unjustified sense of inevitability. Explicit or implicit claims that key episodes from the Progressive Era to New Deal, such the rise of the welfare-regulatory state, as well as business cycle interventionism, were pretty much fated to play out as the only means to stave off more radical lurch to the left or fascist right, need to be re-examined. If they accomplish nothing else, historians informed by classical liberal perspectives can make a valuable contribution if they get their colleagues to openly acknowledge their counterfactuals, which are now often assumed and unstated.

NOTES

1. "2209 C-Span Poll Presidential Rankings by Historians, http://www.teacherweb.com/MO/BSHS/APGov/C-Span-Best-Pres-2009.pdf, accessed October 23, 2016.

2. David M. Tucker, *Mugwumps: Public Moralists of the Gilded Age* (Columbia: University of Missouri Press, 1998), 7, 77, 83.

3. John G. Sproat, *"The Best Men": Liberal Reformers in the Gilded Age* (New York: Oxford University Press, 1968), 271, 273–281; Tucker, 6, 48–49, 123; and David T. Beito and Linda Royster Beito, "Gold Democrats and the Decline of Classical Liberalism, 1896–1900," *Independent Review* 4, no. 4 (Spring 2000), 558.

4. Robert H. Wiebe, *The Search for Order, 1877–1920* (New York: Hill and Wang, 1967), 217.

5. Sidney Fine, *Laissez Faire and the General-Welfare State: A Study of Conflict in American Thought, 1865–1901* (Ann Arbor: University of Michigan Press, 1956), 3–7, 10, 36–37, 73, 170–197.

6. Fine, 172–189; and Washington Gladden, *Social Facts and Forces* (New York: G.P. Putnam's Sons, 1897), 203.

7. Daniel T. Rodgers, *Atlantic Crossings Social Politics in a Progressive Age* (Cambridge: Belknap Press of Harvard University Press, 1998), 98–103, 529; and Fine, 199–200, 213.

8. Fine 216–218; Rodgers, 86, 106–107; and James T. Kloppenberg, *Uncertain Victory: Social Democracy and Progressivism in European and American Thought, 1870–1920* (New York: Oxford University Press, 1986), 207–212.

9. Paul Kleppner, *The Cross of Culture: A Social Analysis of Midwestern Politics, 1850–1900* (New York: Free Press, 1970), 142–156; Theda Skocpol, *Protecting Soldiers and Mothers: The Political Origins of Social Policy in the United States* (Cambridge: The Belknap Press of Harvard University Press, 1992), 124–130; and Richard Franklin Bensel, *The Political Economy of American Industrialization, 1877–1900* (Cambridge: Cambridge University Press 2000), 151–204.

10. Tucker, 115.

11. Thomas C. Leonard, *Illiberal Reforms: Race, Eugenics, and American Economics in the Progressive Era* (Princeton: Princeton University Press, 2016), 23.

12. Gerald W. McFarland, *Mugwumps, Morals and Politcs, 1884–1920* (Amherst: University of Massachusetts Press, 1975), 127–128; Lester Frank Ward, "False Notions of Government," [1887] in Henry Steele Commager, ed., *Lester Ward and the Welfare State* (New York: Bobbs-Merrill, 1967), 106–116.

13. Fine, 373–377; Martin J. Sklar, *The Corporate Reconstruction of American Capitalism, 1890–1916* (Cambridge: Cambridge University Press, 1988), 30; McFarland, 128–148; Robert Higgs, *Crisis and Leviathan: Critical Episodes in the Growth of American Government* (New York: Oxford University Press, 1987), 106–114; and Gabriel Kolko, *The Triumph of Conservatism: A Reinterpretation of American History, 1900–1916* (New York: The Free Press, 1963), 27–30.

14. Leonard, 122–124, 141–152.

15. Aileen S. Kraditor, *The Ideas of the Woman Suffrage Movement, 1890–1920* (Garden City, NY: Anchor Books, 1965), 40–42.

16. Kraditor, 54–55, 157–159.

17. Beito and Beito, 557–562.

18. Beito and Beito, 556–562, 564–567.

19. Michael Patrick Cullinane, *Liberty and American Anti-Imperialism: 1898–1909* (New York: Palgrave Macmillan, 2012), 22–24; and William Graham Sumner, "The Conquest of the United States by Spain," [1898] in Robert C. Bannister, editor, *On Liberty, Society, and Politics: The Essential Essays of William Graham Sumner* (Indianapolis: Liberty Fund, 1992), 297.

20. Cullinane, 146, 149–158, 163; "View of Prominent Men on the Policy of 'Imperialism,'" *Literary Digest* 17 (July 13, 1898), 6; and Moorfield Storey, "The 'Imperial' Folly," *Friends Intelligencer and Journal*, Seventh Month 2, 1898, 475.

21. Beito and Beito, 568–569; Cullinane, 163; and Sklar, 180.

22. Michael Wreszin, *Oswald Garrison Villard: Pacifist at War* (Bloomington, Indiana University Press, 1965), 28–33, 144–147; John Milton Cooper Jr., *Woodrow Wilson: A Biography* (New York: Alfred A. Knopf, 2009), 392; Sklar, 392, 406; and Beito and Beito, 569.

23. Beito and Beito, 569; Bernard M. Baruch, *Baruch: My Own Story* (New York: Henry Holt and Company, 1957), 307.

24. Beito and Beito, 569.

25. William B. Hixson, Jr., *Moorefield Story and the Abolitionist Tradition* (New York: Oxford University Press, 1972), 39, 123–126, 154–158; Beito and Beito, 569–570; and Mark A. Graber, *Transforming Free Speech: The Ambiguous Legacy of Civil Libertarianism* (Berkeley: University of California Press, 1991), 22–23, 238–240.

26. Roger L. Ransom and Richard Sutch, "Tontine Insurance and the Armstrong Investigation, 1868–1905," *Journal of Economic History* 47 (June 1987), 381–382, 385.

27. Ransom and Sutch, 388–390.

28. David T. Beito, *From Mutual Aid to Welfare State: Fraternal Societies and Social Services, 1890–1967* (Chapel Hill: University of North Carolina Press, 2000), 14, 36–43, 140–142.

29. Beito, *From Mutual Aid to the Welfare State*, 20–21, 50–51.

30. Lizabeth Cohen, *Making a New Deal: Industrial Workers in Chicago, 1919–1939* (New York: Cambridge University Press, 1990), 219, 227–229.

31. Beito, 223–225, 227–232; and Cohen, 224.

32. Robert A. Divine, T.H. Breen, George M. Frederickson, and R. Hal Williams, *The American Story* (New York: Longman, 2002), 837.

33. Gene Smiley, *Rethinking the Great Depression* (Chicago: Ivan R. Dee, 2002), 56–58; and Murray Rothbard, *America's Great Depression* (Kansas City: Sheed and Ward, 1963), 58, 81.

34. Robert Higgs, *Depression, War, and Cold War: Challenging the Myths of Conflict and Prosperity* (Oakland: The Independent Institute, 2006), 1–32; and Burton Folsom, *New Deal or Raw Deal? How FDR's Economic Legacy Has Damaged America* (New York: Simon and Schuster, 2008), 43–75, 122–145.

35. Divine, Breen, Frederickson, and Williams, 900; James Oakes, Michael McGerr, Jan Ellen Lewis, Nick Cullather, and Jeanne Boydston, *Of the People: A History of the United States* (New York: Oxford University Press, 2011), 713.

36. Robert Higgs, "Wartime Prosperity? A Reassessment of the U.S. Economy in the 1940s," *Journal of Economic History* 52 (March 1992): 41–60.

37. Richard K. Vedder and Lowell E. Gallaway, *Out of Work: Unemployment and Government in Twentieth Century America* (New York: New York University Press, 1993, 1997), 91–103; and James Grant, *The Forgotten Depression: 1921: the Crash that Cured Itself* (New York: Simon and Schuster, 2011), 212–218.

38. Anthony J. Badger, *The New Deal: The Depression Years, 1933–1940* (New York: Ivan R. Dee, 1989), 49, 300; and Eric Rauchway, *The Great Depression and the New Deal: A Very Short Introduction* (New York: Oxford University Press, 2008, 26.

39. Beito, *Taxpayers in Revolt: Tax Resistance during the Great Depression* (Chapel Hill: University of North Carolina Press, 1989), 163.

40. Beito, *Taxpayers in Revolt*, 163; and Badger, 56.

41. David T. Beito, *Taxpayers in Revolt*, 6–19, 60–100.

42. Beito, *Taxpayers in Revolt*, 163–164; Rauchway, 106; and Ira Katznelson, *Fear Itself: The New Deal and the Origins of Our Time* (New York: W.W. Norton, 2013), 24–35.

43. On the forgotten depression of 1921, Harding's response, and how it differed from Hoover's in the Great Depression, see Grant, 202–218.

44. Marcus Witcher and Joseph Horton, "From Prosperity to Poverty: The Story of American Economic Decline during the 1920s," *Journal of Applied Business and Economics* 14 no. 4 (2013), 80.

45. Badger, 43, 72, 75; Rauchway, 26, 30–31; and Michael D. Bordo, Angela Redish, and Hugh Rockoff, "Why Didn't Canada Have a Banking Crisis in 2008 (Or In 1930, Or 1907, Or ...)?" *National Bureau of Economic Research*, Working Paper, No. 17312, August 2011, http://www.nber.org/papers/w17312.pdf, accessed November 16, 2016.

Chapter 6

A Manifesto for Liberty

Toward a New History of Civil Rights in U.S. History

Jonathan Bean

INTRODUCTION

To say that left-liberals and leftists dominate the study and teaching of American history, particularly civil rights, is an understatement.[1] The academic Left *utterly* dominates this field. Classical liberal and conservative views in U.S. history are not systematically taught in American universities. If classical liberalism is discussed at all, it is often in the context of critiques of "neoliberalism" and globalization.[2] The situation is arguably worse at the research universities producing the next generation of historians.

This chapter makes a case for studying the classical liberal tradition of civil rights, with its emphasis on natural rights, individual freedom, color-blind law, and the embrace of market capitalism as a liberating force for minorities in U.S. history. Part I examines recent scholarly trends merging left-wing activism with race history. Marxists and postmodernists have searched for a past with political uses for the present. This has led to the study of neglected figures on the Left, yet rarely have such scholars shown interest in figures who were not on the Left. Part II outlines my interpretive framework for understanding the classical liberal tradition of civil rights (drawn from my *Race and Liberty in America: The Essential Reader*, which is a good place for researchers to begin building a classical liberal literature).[3] Part III offers original topics for further research.

In short, most American historians studying civil rights are ignorant of traditions outside the orbit of left-wing ideologies. The historians who dominate this field write with a political agenda seeking a "usable past." This is not objectionable per se but it is limiting, and there is room for competing perspectives that may contribute a deeper/more nuanced view. As it stands, "Who controls the past controls the future; who controls the

present controls the past." And the Left controls the teaching and presentation of the past.

I. CURRENT TRENDS IN CIVIL RIGHTS HISTORIOGRAPHY

The study of race and civil rights history is at a crossroads. Historians have
exercised extraordinary imagination in exploring left-wing activism in the
civil rights movements of African American and other minorities.[4] Yet the
topics being pursued have become more obscure and overlook criticisms
of progressive ideas. The glorification of unionism, for example, ignores
the negative role unions often played with regard to race.[5] Likewise, works
emphasizing the American struggle for civil rights leave Communist activists
"off the hook" for aligning with an ideology inimical to human rights.

The overemphasis played upon the Communist role in civil rights activism
is striking. One oft-cited work is Robin D. G. Kelley, *Hammer and Hoe: Alabama Communists during the Great Depression* (1990).[6] Kelley, like others,
is driven by the belief that "we needed a revolutionary socialist movement
committed to antiracism and antisexism."[7] He describes himself as a "Marxist
Surrealist feminist."[8] New Left activist-scholar Mark Naison's *Communists
in Harlem during the Depression* (1983) is also widely cited in the historiography of race.[9] Naison asserts that "No socialist organization has ever had a
more profound effect on black life than the Communist Party did in Harlem
during the Depression."[10] Glenda Gilmore's *Defying Dixie: The Radical
Roots of Civil Rights* (2008) also locates the beginning of the black civil
rights movement in the pre-World War II era, with Communists inspired by
Stalin's Soviet Union playing a prominent role.[11] Erik Gellman writes about
the alliances of Communist activists with the National Negro Congress before
World War II in *Death Blow to Jim Crow: The National Negro Congress and
the Rise of Militant Civil Rights* (2014).[12]

Many historians of civil rights rage against the "New Right"—a label
academic leftists misapply to classical liberals. Books and articles on U.S.
civil rights history routinely cite "conservative backlash," "color-blind
conservatism," and the disinterest of white workers as a call to educate
the benighted masses. Influential historians in this field, such as Jacqueline
Dowd Hall, are self-conscious movement activists. For them, history is not
a critical pursuit of truth, but a means to an end—promoting "progressive"
alternatives today by highlighting the role played by leftist activists in the
past. Hall's 2005 article "The Long Civil Rights Movement and the Political
Uses of the Past" unites race and class in her anticapitalistic interpretation
of a "long" movement that she traces back to the 1930s and 1940s, when
"a powerful social movement sparked by the alchemy of laborites, civil

rights activists, progressive New Dealers, and black and white radicals, some of whom were associated with the Communist Party" forged the "first phase" of the black civil rights movement. These groups laid the basis for the "short civil rights movement" of 1954–1965 (the period starting with *Brown v. Board* and ending with the Voting Rights Act). To combat the New Right's supposed cooptation of the civil rights movement during and after the Reagan era, Hall looks to the "civil rights unionism" of this earlier period to challenge not only racism but "free market individualism" and "the rhetoric of colorblindness" that supposedly empower the New Right.[13] A decade later, a prominent scholar noted how Hall's essay "has profoundly influenced the direction of most subsequent civil rights scholarship . . . . It has decisively framed the debate."[14]

Paradoxically, despite railing against capitalist-funded foundations, the "Long Civil Rights Movement Project" at University of North Carolina received $1 million from the Andrew Mellon Foundation to subsidize the publication and dissemination of this Communist-Labor Left interpretation of civil rights.[15] The current head of the Mellon Foundation, Earl Lewis, is a historian who has published on his own and with Robin Kelley promoting this interpretation of history.[16] Scholars writing in this vein have produced well-researched accounts of the positive role played by Communist activists but, at the same time, they exaggerate the role Communists played in civil right struggles. Moreover, they ignore the criticisms of black anticommunists, such as labor organizer A. Philip Randolph.[17]

"White America" is another bogy of the academic Left. Progressive scholars working on the "long civil rights movement" have viewed whites, with few exceptions, as adversaries rather than potential allies. Since the 1990s, many other scholars have focused on "whiteness" itself as the problem, thus developing "whiteness studies." Postmodernism, with its emphasis on the social construction of reality, influenced this literature on the ways "nonwhite" groups (Irish, Jews, Italians, others) were eventually accepted by others as "white." David Roediger's *Wages of Whiteness* (1991) is particularly influential: Roediger emphasized the economic value of whiteness. His work has been cited over 4,000 times—a measure of its remarkable impact.[18] Echoing earlier labor historians, an underlying thesis of whiteness studies is that capitalist employers divide and conquer workers by exploiting racial divisions that the elite helps them "construct." As with the "Long Civil Rights Movement" literature, whiteness studies is driven by a partisan desire to overcome the New Right—the bogy of the academic Left.

A leading critic of whiteness studies, Eric Arnesen, views this literature as a flawed reading of the past inspired by outrage that white workers did not act along the class lines Marxists predicted. Arnesen is particularly critical of the whiteness scholars for overlooking the important role religion played in the life of workers. Religion often divided workers more than race or class.[19] Arnesen is correct: any history that attempts to understand bigotry against immigrants and blacks must incorporate the study of religion, not only as something that divided Americans but as an instrument of liberation.

Peter Kolchin criticizes "whiteness" scholars for failing to situate their sources in proper historical context, misusing evidence, overgeneralizing, exaggerating the role of race as something dividing "whites," and being swept away by the desire to use whiteness studies to revive socialism. Even worse, what makes Kolchin (and myself) uneasy is the notion that race is a dangerous myth that has caused irreparable harm (true) yet also something that is acceptable for nonwhites to embrace while demonizing "whites" and "whiteness."[20] Several whiteness scholars argue for the "abolition of whiteness" because it has been used to cause harm in the past.[21] The motto of *Race Traitor: Journal of the New Abolitionism* was *"Treason to whiteness is loyalty to humanity."*[22] The problem, however, is that *race* has been used to cause harm. Why not call for the abolition of racial categories themselves? The color-blind treatment of individuals, regardless of race, certainly has a long history driving the classical liberal struggle for freedom.

This belief in the liberating force of color-blind law—which inspired generations of civil rights activists—is now dismissed as "color-blind racism" by Critical Race Theorists operating in law schools. For them, as for "whiteness" historians, "white supremacy" remains even after *intentional* discrimination is gone and color-blind law is achieved. According to the UCLA School of Public Affairs:

> CRT [Critical Race Theory] recognizes that racism is engrained in the fabric and system of the American society. The individual racist need not exist to note that institutional racism is pervasive in the dominant culture. This is the analytical lens that CRT uses in examining existing power structures. CRT identifies that these power structures are based on white privilege and white supremacy, which perpetuates the marginalization of people of color.[23]

These two paradigms—the Communism-Labor-Left and "whiteness" interpretations—shed light on facets of the many-sided truth of U.S. civil rights history. However, the obsession with the civil rights Left and whiteness studies has exaggerated the role played by those two factors. Political bias, while not itself objectionable, has further blinded scholars to the possibility of other interpretive frameworks illuminating our historical past. Nonetheless, scholars seeking fresh subject material will find an abundance of research topics on civil rights and classical liberalism.

The decades-long obsession with new variants of Marxism, postmodernism, and "whiteness studies" has run its course. The next generation of scholars have much research to do to uncover figures, issues, and events imbued with classical liberal values (natural rights, individual freedom, color-blind law). Figures as diverse as Frederick Douglass, Booker T. Washington, Louis Marshall, Branch Rickey, Kelly Miller, and Clarence Thomas were inspired by classical liberal principles, including capitalism as the friend of minorities against the coercion of racist State power and lily-white unionism. A marketplace of ideas is needed now more than ever, as the lack of spirited ideological debates has led to a decline in civility on college campuses. In short, it *can* be done and History will be a richer discipline for making its civil rights tent bigger.

II. A CLASSICAL LIBERAL HISTORY OF RACE AND CIVIL RIGHTS

Classical liberal ideas on race are rooted in the American experience—espousal of classical liberal values resulted in greater freedom and equality for all Americans, including a wide range of racial and ethnic minorities. Reading arguments for liberty, individualism, colorblindness, the rule of law, and capitalism *out of* the history of race in America is like Hamlet without the prince.

There was no overarching classical liberal history of race prior to publication of *Race and Liberty in America: The Essential Reader* (2009). In that anthology, I laid out my conception of a classical liberal history of race, as supported by documents and readings. As a "first word," of sorts, I wrote *Race and Liberty in America* hoping that younger scholars might explore some of the figures, ideas, events that make up the long classical liberal struggle for civil rights.

The following section is drawn from *Race and Liberty in America: The Essential Reader* (Lexington: University Press of Kentucky, with The Independent Institute, 2009), 1–10. Revised for this book chapter.

Classical liberals fought slavery, lynching, segregation, imperialism, and racial distinctions in the law. As immigration advocates, they defended the "natural right" of migration to America. My book, *Race and Liberty* recaptures this tradition through the writings of men and women missing from other civil rights anthologies. Academic booklists reflect the politically correct view that left-wing liberals or radicals completely dominated the struggle for racial freedom.[24] Consequently, classical liberals are the invisible men and women of the Long Civil Rights Movement.

Classical liberals espoused values shared by many other Americans: "unalienable Rights" from God, individual freedom from government control, the Constitution as a guarantor of freedom, color-blind law, and capitalism. These values distinguish classical liberalism from left-wing liberalism, with its emphasis on group rights, government power, and hostility to free market capitalism. Left-wing liberalism trended toward the secular, while classical liberals typically argued for a Creator as the source of our "unalienable Rights." In short, most classical liberals believed in individual freedom, Christianity, the Constitution, colorblindness, and capitalism.

Classical Liberals on Race

These five core beliefs greatly influenced the classical liberal tradition of racial freedom. Together, they form a coherent worldview that informed the struggle for racial freedom well into the twentieth century. The core beliefs outlined below framed the classical liberal response to slavery, Jim Crow, lynching, voting rights, racial preferences, and immigration restriction. Here, a few examples illustrate the influence of each factor; the anthology develops the themes in much greater detail.

Individual Freedom

On issues of racial freedom and immigration, classical liberals advocated freedom from government control. This included the right of businesses to freely contract with labor—whether those workers were African Americans or immigrants seeking entry to the United States. This position pit classical liberals against progressives on the left, who wanted the government to make "reasonable" exceptions for labor unions and immigration restriction. On the right, nativist conservatives joined with progressives in opposing "open borders," while classical liberals staunchly defended immigration: whether Chinese or Czech, immigrants had a natural right to migrate.

Individual freedom from State control extended far beyond the right to work, however. Antebellum newspaper editor William Leggett denounced proslavery forces that used gag rules or violence to censor-free speech. During the Reconstruction era, Congress guaranteed constitutional protection of the individual right to bear arms, a right-defeated Confederates tried to limit to white citizens. Classical liberals also defended the natural right to life by introducing anti-lynching legislation. Finally, classical liberals from Louis Marshall (1910s) to Ward Connerly (2000s) sought to rid race from government classification. Removing this power to classify by groups would prevent—or at least hinder—the government from undermining individual freedom.

Christianity and Judaism

Religion inspired many classical liberals to advance the Golden Rule as a guide to civil rights. Of course, classical liberals had no monopoly on faith; others followed the Social Gospel of the Left or a southern brand of Christianity that defended slavery by citing passages from the New Testament. Nevertheless, religion played an important role in the history of classical liberalism. Christian evangelism was integral to the antislavery movement. For example, Lewis Tappan was a well-known evangelical Christian who used his church ties to create a network of antislavery men and women. Frederick Douglass, an ordained minister, repeatedly used references to the Creator in rebuking—and inspiring—his fellow Christians.

Senator Joseph Hawley (R-CT) opposed the Chinese Exclusion Act (1882) partly because of his missionary work with the Chinese, both in the United States and abroad. Louis Marshall's Judaism impelled him to fight for free immigration and against Jim Crow laws. Kelly Miller viewed religion as a "solvent of the race problem." To oppose the Ku Klux Klan's bigotry, President Calvin Coolidge delivered an address on religious and racial toleration. Justice Pierce Butler's Catholicism influenced his dissent in the infamous *Buck v. Bell* case (1927), which upheld forced sterilization by the states— a "progressive" eugenic policy of weeding out the "imbeciles" among the so-called inferior races. Branch Rickey explained his recruitment of Jackie Robinson as "a call from God."

The Constitution

Prominent classical liberals argued that the Constitution was fundamentally sound on the issue of race. Lysander Spooner, Frederick Douglass, Lewis Tappan, and others argued that, strictly speaking, there was no constitutional sanction of slavery. Moreover, the Constitution provided a means of change within the political system. This position contrasted sharply with abolitionist William Lloyd Garrison's view that the Constitution was a diabolical compact with slavery and should be scrapped, along with the Union it sustained. Later, classical liberals looked to the Constitution as a guarantor of individual civil rights. When government denied those rights, classical liberals took to the courts, using arguments based on the founding principles of the Constitution and the Declaration of Independence. That vision has united classical liberal civil rights advocates since the early nineteenth century.

The Fourteenth and Fifteenth amendments, guaranteeing legal equality and voting rights, led classical liberals to insist that all Americans were equal before the law. By embracing the Constitution and the Declaration of Independence as documents of their civic religion, they aligned patriotism with civil rights. Thus, President Calvin Coolidge publicly rebuked a white

racist who objected to a black Republican running for Congress: after noting
the patriotic contributions of blacks to the recent war effort, Coolidge stated,
"Our Constitution guarantees equal rights to all our citizens, without discrimination on account of race or color . . . . A colored man is precisely as much
entitled to submit his candidacy in a party primary, as is any other citizen."[25]

Colorblindness

Consistent with this view of the Constitution, classical liberals rejected class,
caste, or group distinctions in the law. The government should not interfere
with fundamental rights that belong to all Americans, regardless of race,
color, or creed. Likewise, they often extended this "hands-off" approach
to immigration, arguing that the government should not pick and choose
the races it admits to this country. As demonstrated by Andrew Kull in *The
Color-Blind Constitution,* this powerful ideal inspired generations of civil
rights activists, although the Supreme Court never fully accepted it, and left-
wing liberals reject it.[26] The countervailing view is that courts may uphold
"reasonable" racial distinctions—a position taken in support of segregation
and affirmative action. Classical liberals argued that this "reasonableness"
standard substitutes the rule of men and women (politicians, bureaucrats,
judges) for the rule of law. Therefore, they favored a ban on racial legislation.
     Although many writers have expressed the color-blind ideal in law, none
have done so more eloquently than Supreme Court justices John Marshall
Harlan and Antonin Scalia, separated by a century but espousing the same
sentiment: "Our Constitution is color-blind, and neither knows nor toler-
ates classes among citizens," Harlan wrote (*Plessy* dissent, 1896). Scalia
pronounced that "under our Constitution there can be no such thing as
either a creditor or debtor race. . . . In the eyes of government, we are just
one race here. It is American." The Constitution's focus, he argued, was
on the individual (*Adarand,* 1995). This "color-blind" philosophy inspired
NAACP lawyers to fight on until the Supreme Court struck down racial
segregation.

Capitalism

Marxists and black radicals have long held that capitalism is inherently racist.[27] Historian Manning Marable quotes Malcolm X: "You can't have racism
without capitalism. If you find antiracists, usually they're socialists or their
political philosophy is that of socialism."[28] Many labor historians argue that
capitalist employers used racism to "divide and conquer" the working class,
thus preventing development of an interracial labor movement. This theme
permeates historians' handling of labor-management relations and their negative view of the courts that upheld freedom of contract between capitalists

and workers.[29] To rid capitalist societies of racism, the government must force employers to "be good."

Classical liberals turn this view upside down: capitalism undermines racism by penalizing those who act on irrational prejudice.[30] Firms willing to recruit workers and market goods without regard to color or national origin have a competitive advantage. Streetcar companies fought segregated seating because it added to their cost of doing business. The "desegregating of the dollar" also occurred as large corporations reached out to the "Negro market."[31] This theme appeared in the business press, and in the writing of Booker T. Washington, Kelly Miller and the popular works of economists Milton Friedman, Thomas Sowell, and Walter Williams.

Capitalism also provided wealthy individuals with funds to advance the cause of racial freedom. Examples include merchant Lewis Tappan's funding of antislavery activists and the legal defense in the *Amistad* case; Julius Rosenwald's bankrolling of fifty-five hundred "Rosenwald" schools for southern blacks; and Booker T. Washington's fund-raising for the NAACP's crusade against lynching and segregation.

Capitalism provided African Americans and other minorities with options foreclosed by restrictive licensing laws and racist labor unions. Thus, Booker T. Washington's *Up from Slavery* (1901) became a self-help bible for generations of black entrepreneurs, including John Johnson (publisher of *Ebony* and *Jet*); Chicago businessman S. B. Fuller; and A. G. Gaston, who amassed a $150 million fortune in Birmingham, Alabama—one of the most racist environments in America. Washington's classic autobiography also inspired the philanthropy of Rosenwald and other businessmen who believed in self-help.[32]

Classical Liberalism: Neither Left nor Right

Classical liberalism deserves further study as a distinctive civil rights tradition that is neither left nor right. Why, for example, do we know so much about W. E. B. DuBois but little about lawyer Moorield Storey, cofounder and president of the NAACP? In *Buchanan v. Warley* (1917), Storey won the first Supreme Court case ruling segregation unconstitutional—thirty-seven years before *Brown v. Board.* Why is Louis Marshall forgotten? Marshall fought all racial classifications and spearheaded the defense of free immigration to the United States. In the 1920s, he fought quotas limiting the number of Jews entering college. Marshall also succeeded Storey as lead lawyer for the NAACP and won *Nixon v. Herndon* (1927), a Supreme Court case striking down racist "white primaries." Progressive contemporaries characterized both Storey and Marshall as "ultraconservative" because of their laissez-faire economics, but laissez-faire also motivated their unswerving devotion to a color- and caste-blind Constitution.

The current canon ignores these classical liberals, or distorts their record, partly because they rejected government meddling in race relations—whether the meddling was done by the Right or the Left. On the right, conservatives advocated the "state right" to discriminate in favor of native-born whites. On the left, the progressive credo might read: *government was sometimes the problem but always the solution.* Thus, the solution to segregation was not the elimination of government interference in race relations but rather its transformation from "negative" to "affirmative" discrimination. Similarly, the solution to the supposed racism of capitalism was governmental control of business.

The standard academic dismissal is to lump classical liberals with unsavory conservatives rather than address classical liberal thought as a distinctive tradition. Many writers depict today's classical liberals (Ward Connerly, Clarence Thomas, and Shelby Steele) as examples of conservative "backlash." Angela Dillard, author of *Guess Who's Coming to Dinner Now? Multicultural Conservatism in America,* expresses the received wisdom: "the conservative movement, overall, is predominantly white and Christian and has, in both the past and present, used racism, ethnocentrism, homophobia, and anti-Semitism . . . to achieve its goals."[33] Writers like Dillard label classical liberals "conservatives" and then sweep them together with racists, homophobes, and antiSemites! No wonder both Democratic and Republican administrations have kowtowed to the nativist Right's stance on immigration restriction and the Left's agenda on affirmative action; they have no historical compass to guide them elsewhere. When it comes to classical liberalism and civil rights, misinformation prevails in academic and political circles. The following section offers topics for exploration that may clarify our understanding of civil rights and classical liberalism.

III. FUTURE RESEARCH TOPICS

Race and Liberty in America introduced individuals who need further research. Several of the individuals in the anthology were consistently classical liberals: for example, Lysander Spooner or Frederick Douglass. Many others exhibited an aspect of classical liberalism—for example, Ronald Reagan's defense of immigration. Whether they are "pure" classical liberals (if such individuals exist) or not, the figures discussed below deserve further attention and are excellent topics for dissertation or book-length treatments.

Digital archiving has made many topics easier to research. The advent of commercial newspaper databases has enabled scholars to search across countless newspapers and magazines, including those read by African Americans, immigrants, and other minorities, as well as the business press. Digitized government documents, court rulings, oral histories, and entire personal archives are also available, thus enabling scholars to explore topics that were almost impossible to research.[34] Print materials remain important but even those are more accessible with online finding aids.

Kelly Miller, dean of Howard University and the most widely read African American writers of the 1920s, is an individual with classical liberal views who can now be more fully explored with digital access to his books, pamphlets, and the newspaper databases that contain his "Kelly Miller Says" column—read by a half million blacks weekly. Miller's popularity with black readers "attests to the fact that he was more influential to them than any other black intellectual featured in the pages of *The Crisis* [edited by W.E.B. DuBois] or *The Negro World* [Marcus Garvey's newspaper]."[35] Opposed to unions, Miller realized that capitalists and black workers were natural allies. He viewed religion as one "solvent of the race problem" and refused to join other black leaders in opposing immigration. Like other classical liberals, Miller was an anti-imperialist who emphasized the struggle of dark-skinned peoples abroad and at home.

While several dissertations and one short book have explored Miller's thought, none have delved deeply into his journalistic career. Previous scholars discuss Miller's books and conflict with DuBois or Booker T. Washington but have yet to research how he reached so many people through newspapers. We need to know more about his commentary and his high repute among independent-minded writers, both black and white (including H. L. Mencken, the most popular white newspaperman of the 1920s).[36]

R. C. Hoiles, who founded the Freedom Newspaper chain, is another journalist worth studying. Classical liberal in the extreme, Hoiles' "freedom philosophy" guided the editorial comment of his newspapers. His California newspaper was one of the few (along with the Chicago *Tribune*) to denounce Japanese American internment as an infringement on individual freedom. A fervent Christian, Hoiles also criticized public school segregation because it was legally and morally wrong. On immigration, Hoiles believed in the natural right of all persons to migrate regardless of national borders.

Until recently, it was difficult to research Hoiles and his Freedom Newspapers. When the newspaper chain went bankrupt in 2009, former employee Richard A. Wallace secured Hoiles' columns spanning decades, along with private correspondence with many leading classical liberals (e.g., Ludwig von Mises, F.A. Hayek, Ayn Rand). Hoiles' columns and correspondence are being digitized and will be available for research at Chapman University and on the Internet.[37] There is no book-length biography of Hoiles.[38]

The business press offers insight into the role market capitalism played in the history of civil rights. Business leaders were vocal advocates for liberal immigration policies and the "right to work" of African Americans in the face of union opposition. Part of this story is known from legislative testimony and corporate lobbying efforts, but we may learn more from researching the business press. Proquest has digitized the *Wall Street Journal* (1889 to the present), along with English-language newspapers in China, India, and other nations of interest to American business. "American Business: Mercantile Newspapers, 1783–1900" is a Readex database covering 500 newspapers in 40 states. This national and regional coverage may provide insight into how businesses addressed issues such as immigration, segregation, and the long-running conflict between employers and unions over the hiring of blacks, Chinese, and Japanese.

The career of journalist and publisher John Foster Carr deserves greater exploration. Carr was a prolific author who defended the reputation of immigrants. He created the Immigration Publication Society to provide immigrants with foreign language material to smooth their transition to American life. Carr's work was financed by the Connecticut chapters of the Daughters of American Revolution (DAR) and the American Library Association. If "whiteness" were something valuable to be withheld from the supposedly "nonwhite" Italians, Jews, and Poles, why did the WASP-dominated DAR work so hard to defend these immigrants and provide them with assistance needed to succeed? Carr and his DAR backers explicitly rejected the nativist notion of "America for the Americans" because these newcomers were also Americans (or soon would be).[39] Carr's career offers a challenge to "whiteness" studies. Since he worked with a network of people (journalists, librarians, DAR, labor leaders, immigrant societies) we can gain a better understanding of the assimilation process stripped of notions of "white privilege" as something to be gained against native-born white opposition.[40]

If anyone were born with "white privilege," it was Hamilton Fish III (1888–1991), member of one of the founding families of New York. Several members of the Fish Family were active in antislavery politics and served in Congress, Lincoln's Cabinet, and as ambassadors to various nations. During World War I, Hamilton Fish was an officer with the 369th Infantry Regiment ("Harlem Hellfighters")—a black fighting unit assigned to the French Command because the U.S. military refused to let them fight alongside white American soldiers. After the war, Fish cofounded the American Legion, introduced the Tomb of the Unknown Soldier, and spent two decades in Congress fighting for anti-lynching bills, which passed the House of Representatives but fell to Senate Democratic filibusters. A fierce critic of Franklin Roosevelt's foreign policy, Fish contrasted FDR's humanitarian rhetoric with his failure to allow Jews refuge from Nazi-occupied Europe. There is no biography of Fish but researchers can mine his papers at the New York State Library. The NAACP Papers, digitized by Proquest, also contain files on Fish's civil rights activities.[41]

The earliest NAACP lawyers need to be woven into the larger narrative of American civil rights history. For example, few texts discuss attorney Moorfield Storey, the NAACP's first president; he won the first Supreme Court desegregation case (1917) and defended free immigration. Consistent with his civil rights work, he headed the American Anti-Imperialist League.[42] Another NAACP lawyer, Louis Marshall, argued more cases before the Supreme Court than any other lawyer of his era. Marshall defended Jews, blacks, religious minorities, and immigrants. He has only recently received biographical treatment.[43] His papers are located at the American Jewish Archives in Cincinnati, Ohio.[44]

Classical liberal "cause lawyering" continues to the present, with the Institute for Justice (IJ) litigating on behalf of minorities (and others) discriminated against by occupational licensing laws and urban renewal. In *David's Hammer: The Case for an Activist Judiciary* (2007), IJ cofounder Clint Bolick recounts the strategies of classical liberal lawyers.[45] Since the 1970s, other groups have litigated against government-sponsored discrimination or advocated liberal immigration policies. These groups include the Pacific Legal Foundation, the Center for Individual Rights, and the Center for Equal Opportunity—all major players in civil rights court cases.[46]

We need to know more about the voluntary sector and its contribution to racial and religious liberty. Classical liberals believe individuals may serve their interests through cooperative associations—businesses, churches, groups committed to racial or religious fellowship, etc. John Sibley Butler has documented the nexus of black businesses, historically black colleges, and fraternal or professional societies. David Beito has explored mutual aid societies for a variety of groups. Beito underscores the common values held by these aid societies across race, class, and gender lines. Examining the voluntary associations of those studied by "whiteness" scholars leads one to question how important "whiteness" really was to Italians, Jews, Irish, and others.[47] A volume edited by Beito, Peter T. Gordon, and Alexander Tabarrok, *The Voluntary City* (2002), provides thought-provoking essays on the historic vitality of the voluntary sector in cities.[48]

The Fellowship of Christian Athletes (est. 1954) is one group that broke racial and religious barriers. FCA took off with the backing of Branch Rickey who believed individuals ought to be judged by merit and not by their skin color.[49] From the beginning, FCA camps and meetings included athletes of all races. Protestant-Catholic hostilities were healed when the founders invited Catholic athletes to participate. The intention was to promote Christianity through sport in a way that was color-blind and denomination-blind. While the nation's politicians fought bitterly over racial segregation, FCA founders knocked down racial barriers without agitation or division. This sports ministry currently reaches two million athletes and is served by over 1,000 staff in two dozen countries.[50] Although insiders have written books about the FCA, the organization has not received the scholarly treatment it deserves.[51] Interesting questions arise: How did southerners react to a multiracial Fellowship? How did the FCA model translate to the cultures of other nations?

Classical liberal perspectives on immigration history are much needed. Historically, business groups have been most conspicuous in defending free or liberal immigration policies. This has sometimes made for odd bedfellows, including the recent partnership of the National Association of Manufacturers (NAM) and the National Council of La Raza to legalize undocumented immigrants "because it provides the skilled workers manufacturers need, and it is simply the right thing to do."[52] An entire history of business and immigration could be written from the archives of the NAM, among other groups, and from coverage of immigration issues in the business press.[53]

Once immigrants arrived in the United States after the 1965 Immigration Reform Act (lifting strict quotas), the federal government classified many new arrivals as "disadvantaged" groups because of historic discrimination. The irony is that new Asian, Latino, and African immigrants never faced this discrimination; nevertheless, they were granted racial preferences along with native-born minorities. A host of issues arise challenging the "whiteness" approach to history. First, several groups—Hasidic Jews and Italian Americans in New York City—secured affirmative action status by recasting their history of *religious* discrimination as racial bias.[54] Arab Americans have lobbied to be taken out of the "white" category and listed as "Middle Eastern Americans"—thus opening the door to government protection and preference. But that strange grouping of individuals from Morocco to Iran will also include Israeli Jews. This irony of affirmative action—"whites" seeking to be labeled nonwhite deserves the attention of historians.

While many historians dwell on the civil rights contributions of Communists, labor unions, and others on the Left, classical liberal scholars have demonstrated the liberating influence of market capitalism. In *The Economics of Discrimination* (1957), Gary Becker provided a model for understanding how and when racial discrimination is most effective in the marketplace. The freer the marketplace, the less effective the racial discrimination. In a free marketplace, those who discriminate based on race (rather than merit, price, or other objective business criteria) pay a price by losing a good employee or customer to the business that does not discriminate.

Historically speaking, however, the marketplace was never free of government coercion in business decisions. For example, streetcar companies resisted the costs of segregating blacks and whites but were ultimately forced to do so by state mandates. In *Competition and Coercion: Blacks in the American Economy, 1865–1914,* Robert Higgs documented black gains through a competitive marketplace but noted the limits of Becker's model.

The insecurity of property rights, threatened by discriminatory courts and private violence, limited black advancement. State coercion, together with private lawlessness, was so severe that "discrimination *outside* the market sector had an important influence in determining the opportunities open to blacks *inside* the market sector."[55]

After the Civil War, African Americans improved their standard of living by migrating within the South to better job offers from white planters in labor-short regions. Historians have delved deeply into migration *out* of the South but we know little about the tremendous migration of blacks *within* the South. Economic incentives played an important role: labor-short white planters outbid other white planters by offering better pay to black workers. By migrating, blacks earned higher wages; those left behind also saw their wages rise as white farmers tried to retain their remaining workforce .White emigrant agents acted as middlemen to recruit blacks from one area and move them—often *en masse*—to other states. David Bernstein explores this fascinating pre-World War I southern migration. The digitization of newspapers and other sources opens important topics for future research. For example, Confederate veteran "Peg-Leg" Williams championed black worker mobility with the motto "A man in this country has the right to go where he pleases." Williams moved nearly 100,000 blacks to better jobs—against the fierce opposition of white planters losing their labor. This is one prime example of classical liberal economics opening our eyes to the ways economics could trump racial prejudice.[56]

Looking forward into the twentieth century, Bernstein, Richard Epstein, and Paul Moreno have illustrated how racist labor unions and progressive reformers used the monopoly power of the state to undercut the mutually beneficial ties between businesses and minority workers.[57] Laws mandating minimum wages or favoring union labor were color-consciously designed to exclude blacks from rising up the economic ladder. Businesses fought many of these "progressive" measures. When that failed, employers moved to states with "right to work" laws (mostly the South and West). This resulted in blacks returning to the South in search of better job opportunities. When Congress and the courts stuck down Jim Crow laws, many facially race-neutral laws remained on the books (e.g. occupational licensing requirements). Moreno, Epstein, and Bernstein have demonstrated how these laws were rooted in white racism but much more work can be done. In short, asking questions of purportedly "progressive" legislation, classical liberals challenge the myth of minority-friendly unionism or progressivism.

As the literature on classical liberal civil rights grows, scholars will need to address tensions within the tradition. For example, when is government action required to address discrimination or racial violence that threaten life, liberty, and property to such an extent that local law enforcement needs to be regulated? The debate over the federal anti-lynching laws focused on this issue. Opponents of anti-lynching laws argued that the Constitution did not specifically authorize such federal action. A competing classical liberal view was that life was a natural right threatened by rampant private violence abetted by the failure of local authorities to act.

Freedom of association is another area where conflict between classical liberals exists. Barry Goldwater opposed the Civil Rights Act of 1964, in part, because it mandated nondiscrimination in "public accommodations" (restaurants, hotels, and other businesses open to the public). Richard Epstein challenges Goldwater's view by detailing how government regulation restricted free association and competition. Free association was limited by local and state-sponsored regulation, not only of race but of economic entities (e.g., utilities, railroads) that impeded Northern entry to compete for black business on a color-blind basis. At the same time, emigrant-agent laws, vagrancy, and forced labor statutes slowed black exit to freer labor markets of the North. Epstein writes that it was "the totalitarian nature of the Old South, and much of the rest of the United States, which undercut the assumption of free entry and exit on which the economic theory rests." Opening new retail or service businesses was risky due to hostile zoning boards and utility regulators Moreover, the political power of a white majority, together with racist private violence (tolerated by state authorities) stifled entry of nondiscriminatory businesses that would have allowed blacks to eat or sleep as they traveled.[58]

Still, according to Epstein, freedom of association is wrongfully violated when "new human rights laws" forbid private discrimination in a way that undermines the mission of religious associations or businesses. A baker who believes making a gay wedding cake violates her religious beliefs should not have to give up her right of free association. There is no barrier to the gay couple going elsewhere for service. The situation is not analogous to the "totalitarian" apartheid of the pre-1964 South.

The above topics scrape the surface of issues classical liberal authors have begun to tackle. Other topics of interest: the "collision course" of affirmative action developing at the moment of 1965 immigration reform—bringing millions of immigrants entitled to race preferences. That unintended consequence of reform cut into the preferences aimed at African Americans.[59] Government designation of group categories is also murky: many of the original decisions on who counted as "Asian" (Pakistanis, yes; Afghans, no) was arbitrary and made by mid-level bureaucrats on the basis of a crude "people of color" ideology. Or, so it seems.[60] Historians can flesh out that story by researching government records and legal cases. Lastly, the corporate embrace of "diversity" as a rationale for "affirmative discrimination" needs further exploration. Most accounts credit this shift from civil rights compliance to "diversity" as a result of Human Resource staff retooling affirmative action at a time when it was threatened (the 1980s and 1990s), much like their counterparts at universities. But that story is only partly told.[61] As a rule, classical liberals view "diversity" as old wine (racial discrimination) in a new wine skin. Research into university and corporate records can test that assumption.

This chapter challenges historians to re-examine the history of civil rights by exploring classical liberal contributions to racial equality. Civil rights is a contested terrain with various voices, intellectual traditions, and social movements. The Left certainly played a role but, by ignoring competing perspectives, recent historical scholarship has blinders on to important topics that deserve attention. The general public will also benefit from a more balanced and complete history of race. At the very least, we may all become better informed citizens regarding the American dilemma of race.

NOTES

1. A portion of this chapter was previously published in Jonathan Bean, "Introduction," in *Race and Liberty in America: The Essential Reader*, ed. Jonathan Bean (University Press of Kentucky, 2009): 1–12.

2. See, e.g., Naomi Klein, *The Shock Doctrine: The Rise of Disaster Capitalism* (Macmillan, 2010).

3. Jonathan Bean, *Race and Liberty in America: The Essential Reader* (Lexington: University Press of Kentucky, with The Independent Institute, 2009).

4. For a survey of the literature on the African American civil rights struggle, see Hasan Kwame Jeffries, "Searching for a New Freedom," chapter 29 in *A Companion to African American History*, edited by Alton Hornsby, Jr. (Oxford: Blackwell, 2005), 499–511. On other groups, see Reed Ueda, ed., *A Companion to American Immigration* (Oxford: Wiley-Blackwell, 2011).

5. Paul D. Moreno challenges the labor history view of unions in *Black Americans and Organized Labor: A New History* (Baton Rouge: LSU Press, 2008).

6. Robin D.G. Kelley, *Hammer and Hoe: Alabama Communists during the Great Depression* (Chapel Hill: University of North Carolina Press, 1990).

7. Robin D.G. Kelley, *Freedom Dreams: The Black Radical Imagination* (Boston: Beacon Press, 2002), ix.

8. http://news.stanford.edu/news/1998/july29/kelley729.html (accessed 31 May 2016).

9. Mark Naison, *Communists in Harlem during the Depression* (University of Illinois Press, 1983).

10. http://www.press.uillinois.edu/books/catalog/56ddt8pm9780252072710.html (accessed 31 May 2016).

11. Glenda Gilmore, *Defying Dixie: The Radical Roots of Civil Rights, 1919–1950* (W. W. Norton, 2008).

12. Erik S. Gellman, *Death Blow to Jim Crow: The National Negro Congress and the Rise of Militant Civil Rights* (University of North Carolina Press, 2014).

13. Jacquelyn Dowd Hall, "The Long Civil Rights Movement and the Political Uses of the Past." *The Journal of American History* 91, no. 4 (1 March 2005): 1233–1263 [quotes on 1245 and 1238].

14. John A. Salmond, "'The Long and Short of It': Some Reflections on the Recent Historiography of the Civil Rights Movement," *Australasian Journal of American Studies* 32, no. 1 (July 2013): 53–61 [quote on 53]. For a sharp criticism of Hall's interpretation, see Eric Arnesen, "Reconsidering the 'Long Civil Rights Movement,'" *Historically Speaking* 10, no. 2 (2009): 31–34.

15. See https://lcrm.lib.unc.edu/blog/index.php/about-2/ (accessed 1 June 2016).

16. See Robin D. G. Kelley, and Earl Lewis, *To Make Our World Anew: A History of African Americans* 2 vols (Oxford: Oxford University Press, 2005).

17. Eric Arnesen, "No 'Graver Danger': Black Anticommunism, the Communist Party, and the Race Question," *Labor: Studies in Working Class History of the Americas* 3, no. 4 (2006): 13–52.

18. See, e.g., Noel Ignatiev, *How the Irish Became White* (New York: Routledge, 1995); Matthew Frye Jacobson, *Whiteness of a Different Color: European Immigrants and the Alchemy of Race* (Cambridge: Harvard University Press, 1998); Jennifer Guglielmo and Salvatore Salerno, eds. *Are Italians White? How Race Is Made in America* (New York: Routledge, 2003); Eric L. Goldstein, *The Price of Whiteness: Jews, Race, and American Identity* (Princeton University Press, 2006); Jason E. Pierce, *Making the White Man's West: Whiteness and the Creation of the American West* (Boulder: University Press of Colorado, 2016).

19. Eric Arnesen, "Whiteness and the Historians' Imagination," *International Labor and Working Class History* 60 (Fall 2001): 3–32.

20. Peter Kolchin, "Whiteness Studies: The New History of Race in America." *Journal of American History* 89, no. 1 (June 2002): 154–173.

21. See David R. Roediger, *Towards the Abolition of Whiteness: Essays on Race, Politics, and Working Class History* (London: Verso, 1994).

22. See http://racetraitor.org/ (accessed 2 June 2016).

23. UCLA School of Public Affairs, "What is Critical Race Theory?" https://spacrs.wordpress.com/what-is-critical-race-theory/ (accessed 6 June 2016). See also Richard Delgado and Jean Stefancic, *Critical Race Theory: An Introduction*, 2d ed. (NYU Press, 2012); Derrick A. Bell, *Race, Racism, and American Law*, 6th ed. (Aspen Publishers, 2008); Eduardo Bonilla-Silva, *Racism without Racists: Color-Blind Racism and the Persistence of Racial Inequality in the United States* (Rowman & Littlefield, 2006).

24. Clayborne Carson, *Eyes on the Prize: America's Civil Rights Years: A Reader and Guide* (New York: Penguin, 1987); Clayborne Carson, *The Eyes on the Prize Civil Rights Reader: Documents, Speeches, and Firsthand Accounts from the Black Freedom Struggle, 1954–1990* (New York: Penguin, 1991); Peter B. Levy, *Let Freedom Ring: A Documentary History of the Modern Civil Rights Movement* (New York: Praeger, 1992); Jonathan Birnbaum and Clarence Taylor, *Civil Rights since 1787: A Reader on the Black Struggle* (New York: New York University Press, 2000); Manning Marable, *How Capitalism Underdeveloped Black America: Problems in Race, Political Economy, and Society*, rev. ed. (Cambridge: South End, 2000); Raymond

N. D'Angelo, *The American Civil Rights Movement: Readings and Interpretations* (Guilford, CT: Dushkin, 2001); Manning Marable, Nishani Frazier, and John Campbell McMillian, *Freedom on My Mind: The Columbia Documentary History of the African American Experience* (New York: Columbia University Press, 2003); Ronald H. Bayor, *The Columbia Documentary History of Race and Ethnicity in America* (New York: Columbia University Press, 2004).

25. "Cal Coolidge Tells Kluxer When to Stop," Chicago *Defender*, 16 August 1924, 1.

26. Andrew Kull, *The Color-Blind Constitution* (Cambridge: Harvard University Press, 1992).

27. Marable, *How Capitalism Underdeveloped Black America*.

28. Manning Marable, "By Any Means Necessary: The Life and Legacy of Malcolm X," *Black Collegian Online*, 21 February 1992, http://www.black-collegian.com/african/lifelegacy200.shtml (accessed 20 July 2008).

29. Moreno, *Black Americans and Organized Labor*, "Appendix: 'Divide and Conquer': The Folklore of Socialism."

30. Gary Stanley Becker, *The Economics of Discrimination* (University of Chicago Press, 1957). See also Harold Demsetz, "Minorities in the Market Place," *North Carolina Law Review* 43, no. 2 (February 1965), 271–297.

31. Jennifer Roback, "The Political Economy of Segregation: The Case of Segregated Streetcars," *Journal of Economic History* 46, no. 4 (1986): 893–917; Robert E. Weems, *Desegregating the Dollar African American Consumerism in the Twentieth Century* (New York University Press, 1998).

32. Booker T. Washington, *Up from Slavery: An Autobiography* (Garden City, NY: Doubleday, 1901); John H. Johnson and Lerone Bennett, *Succeeding against the Odds* (New York: Warner, 1989); Mary Fuller Casey, *S. B. Fuller: Pioneer in Black Economic Development* (Jamestown, NC: Bridgemaster, 2003); A. G. Gaston, *Green Power: The Successful Way of A. G Gaston* (Birmingham: Southern University Press, 1968); Peter Max Ascoli, *Julius Rosenwald: The Man Who Built Sears, Roebuck and Advanced the Cause of Black Education in the American South* (Bloomington: Indiana University Press, 2006).

33. Angela D. Dillard, *Guess Who's Coming to Dinner Now? Multicultural Conservatism in America* (New York University Press, 2001), 12–13.

34. Leading vendors of digitized material include Proquest, Readex, LexisNexis, and foundation, government or university-funded sites. The Library of Congress is particularly rich in digital material. https://www.loc.gov/

35. Sylvie Coulibaly, "Kelly Miller, 1895–1939: Portrait of an African American Intellectual," (PhD diss. Emory University, 2006), 7–8.

36. See Larry McGruder, *Kelly Miller: The Life and Thoughts of a Black Intellectual, 1863–1939* (PhD. diss., Miami University [Ohio], 1984); Ida Jones, *The Heart of the Race Problem: The Life of Kelly Miller* (Littleton, Mass.: Tapestry Press, 2011); H.L. Mencken, "Negro Spokesman Arises to Voice His Race's Wrongs," [1917] in *The Impossible H.L. Mencken: A Selection of His Best Newspaper Stories*, ed. Marion Elizabeth Rodgers (New York: Anchor, 1991), 186–191. Selected works by Miller: *Race Adjustment: Essays on the Negro in America* (Neale Publishing, 1908); *Out of*

the House of Bondage (Neale Publishing, 1914); *The Disgrace of Democracy: Open Letter to President Woodrow Wilson* (n.p., 1917); *Kelly Miller's History of the World War for Human Rights* (Washington: Austin Jenkins Company, 1919); *The Everlasting Stain* (Associated Publishers, 1924).

37. Richard A. Wallace and Jonathan Bean, telephone conversation 21 June 2016.

38. See Carl Watner, "To Thine Own Self Be True: The Story of Raymond Cyrus Hoiles and His Freedom Newspapers," http://voluntaryist.com/articles/018.html (May 1986) [accessed 20 June 2016]; Brian Doherty, "R.C. Hoiles, American Original," http://reason.com/archives/2007/04/10/rc-hoiles-american-original/singlepage (accessed 20 June 2016).

39. John Foster Carr, *Some of the People We Work For* (New York: Immigrant Public Society, 1916), 12–13.

40. Carr's papers are available at the New York Public Library. http://archives.nypl.org/mss/477.

41. For a bibliography and list of archives with Fish papers: See http://bioguide.congress.gov/scripts/guidedisplay.pl?index=F000142 (accessed 26 June 2016).

42. William B. Hixson, *Moorfield Storey and the Abolitionist Tradition* (New York,: Oxford University Press, 1972). Storey's papers are at the Library of Congress.

43. M.M. Silver, *Louis Marshall and the Rise of Jewish Ethnicity in America: A Biography* (Syracuse: Syracuse University Press, 2013). See also *Louis Marshall: Champion of Liberty; Selected Papers and Addresses,* ed. Charles Reznikopp (Philadelphia: Jewish Publication Society of America, 1957).

44. "A Finding Aid to the Louis Marshall Papers. 1870–1943 (bulk 1890–1929)," Manuscript Collection No. 359 http://findingaids.cjh.org//LouisMarshall.html#series1 (accessed 22 June 2016).

45. Clint Bolick, *David's Hammer: The Case for an Activist Judiciary* (Washington: Cato Institute, 2007).

46. See Lee Edwards, ed., *Bringing Justice to the People: The Story of the Freedom-Based Public Interest Law Movement,* 1st ed (Washington.: Heritage Books, 2004); Steven M. Teles, *The Rise of the Conservative Legal Movement: The Battle for Control of the Law* (Princeton University Press, 2010); Ann Southworth, *Lawyers of the Right: Professionalizing the Conservative Coalition* (University of Chicago Press, 2008); Damon Root, "Conservatives v. Libertarians: The debate over judicial activism divides former allies," *Reason* (July 2010), http://reason.com/archives/2010/06/08/conservatives-v-libertarians (accessed 28 June 2016).

47. John Sibley Butler, *Entrepreneurship and Self-Help among Black Americans: A Reconsideration of Race and Economics,* 2nd ed. (Albany: State University of New York Press, 2005); David T. Beito, *From Mutual Aid to the Welfare State: Fraternal Societies and Social Services, 1890–1967* (Chapel Hill: The University of North Carolina Press, 2000).

48. David T. Beito, Peter Gordon, and Alexander Tabarrok, eds., *The Voluntary City: Choice, Community, and Civil Society* (Ann Arbor; Oakland, Calif.: Independent Institute, 2009). See also Edward Peter Stringham, *Private Governance: Creating Order in Economic and Social Life* (Oxford; New York: Oxford University Press, 2015).

49. As keynote speaker at FCA's first national camp, Rickey advocated using Christian faith and sportsmanship to overcome racial differences. "Branch Rickey's

Speech to FCA," August 1956, audio clip. http://timeline.fca.org/branch-rickeys-speech/ (accessed 29 June 2016).

50. http://downloads.fcaresources.com/organization/2013annualreportweb.pdf (accessed 29 June 2016).

51. Wayne Atcheson, *Impact for Christ: How FCA Has Influenced the Sports World* (Grand Island, NE: Cross Training Publishing, 2000).

52. "Manufacturers Launch Radio Ads in Support of Immigration Reform," *Reform Is the Pathway to the American Dream* http://www.nam.org/Communications/Articles/2013/08/Manufacturers-Launch-Radio-Ads-in-Support-of-Immigration-Reform.aspx# (accessed 21 June 2016).

53. "National Association of Manufacturers records," Manuscripts and Archives Department, Hagley Museum and Library, http://findingaids.hagley.org/xtf/view?docId=ead/1411.xml (accessed 21 June 2016).

54. Liana Kirillova, "Exceptional Cases of White Ethnic Inclusion in Affirmative Action Policy Since 1970," (M.A. Thesis, Southern Illinois University Carbondale, 2016).

55. Robert Higgs, *Competition and Coercion: Blacks in the American Economy 1865–1914* (New York: Cambridge University Press, 1977).

56. David E. Bernstein, *Only One Place of Redress: African Americans, Labor Regulations, and the Courts from Reconstruction to the New Deal* (Duke University Press, 2000); Bernstein, "Peg-Leg Williams," in *100 Making Constitutional History: A Biographical History*, ed. Melvin I. Urofsky (Washington: CQ Press, 2004).

57. Bernstein, *Only*; Bernstein, *Rehabilitating Lochner: Defending Individual Rights against Progressive Reform* (University Of Chicago Press, 2011); Richard A. Epstein, *Forbidden Grounds: The Case Against Employment Discrimination Laws* (Cambridge: Harvard University Press, 1992); Richard A. Epstein, *The Classical Liberal Constitution: The Uncertain Quest for Limited Government* (Cambridge: Harvard University Press, 2014); Moreno, *Black Americans and Organized Labor*.

58. Richard A. Epstein, "Public Accommodations Under the Civil Rights Act of 1964: Why Freedom of Association Counts as a Human Right," *Stanford Law Review* 66, no. 6 (1 June 2014): 1241–1292 [quote on 1254].

59. Hugh Davis Graham, *Collision Course: The Strange Convergence of Affirmative Action and Immigration Policy in America* (New York: Oxford University Press, 2002).

60. George R. La Noue and John C. Sullivan, "Deconstructing Affirmative Action Categories," chap. 3 in *Color Lines: Affirmative Action, Immigration, and Civil Rights Options for America*, ed. John D. Skrentny (University of Chicago Press, 2001).

61. Erin Kelly and Frank Dobbin, "How Affirmative Action Became Diversity Management: Employer Response to Antidiscrimination Law, 1961–1996," chap. 4 in *Color Lines: Affirmative Action, Immigration, and Civil Rights Options for America*, ed. John D. Skrentny (University of Chicago Press, 2001); Frederick R. Lynch, *The Diversity Machine: The Drive to Change the "White Male Workplace"* (New York: Free Press, 1997); Jennifer Delton, *Racial Integration in Corporate America, 1940–1990* (New York: Cambridge University Press, 2009).

Chapter 7

The End or Ends of Social History?

The Reclamation of Old-Fashioned Historicism in the Writing of Historical Narratives

Hans L. Eicholz

I. THE GHOSTS OF MATERIALISM IN THE
GEIST OF SOCIAL *MENTALITÉ*

From the standpoint of liberalism in its classical form, history is that domain of understanding in which we attempt to explain the scenes of past human activity where particularity and spontaneity intersected with the forces of necessity and circumstance. Of course, not every historian who has viewed the past in this way has been politically liberal, but every historian who takes this perspective does so because he or she finds the varieties and possibilities of individual experience simply too compelling to be submerged entirely under the weight of external forces.[1] Critics of this perspective often decry against "great man theory," but innumerable examples of histories can be shown where the balance is maintained between individual innovation and social context which one would hope are sufficient to dispel such simplistic either/or reasoning. Yet the temptations to assert the "decisive explanation," something akin to a naturalistic exogenous account of why things are as they are, has proven all too alluring for even otherwise sophisticated historians. The once impressive edifice of social history has seen its position gradually erode precisely because of its implicit grounding in such determinism.

The initial promise of social history was to liberate the field from the pretensions of elites and, at the same time, make the discipline of history more objective in its orientation to facts. This hope was at the root of social history's origins in early Marxist aspirations to "scientific history."[2] With time, however, Marx's materialism, and the commitment to dialectical determinism in particular, ran athwart the all too apparent fact that revolutions had failed to materialize where they had been predicted to occur or came "too early" to places where the industrial proletariat had not yet fully formed.[3]

137

Rather than discarding materialism, though, social historians first sought to bury their theoretical tensions under large quantities of data amassed through new and innovative tools of statistical and analytical research, and for a time the field appeared to be sweeping the discipline of all other approaches.[4]

But then something curious began to happen. The varieties of social experience revealed by this new quantitative data just kept on multiplying. It was not simply that labor was divided among many organizations, that certain of its leaders opposed radical measures, that some workers' groups fought other workers' groups (though all this was difficult enough to fit within traditional Marxist categories), or that capitalists themselves were not all of one piece. Indeed, the oppressed were not always workers, but, as the mounds of new evidence seemed to affirm, also included races, genders, and various other groupings, each with its own aims and organizations, and very often prone to being exploited in very different ways by very different opponents. By the end of the twentieth century few historians could dare to venture the notion that any material necessity compelled a particular social or ideational outcome. But it got even more interesting. What Gary Nash initially called a "glorious disarray" turned out, in the end, to be nothing less than a complete about-face.[5]

What was meant by social historians to be a "science" has quietly and steadily merged into subjectivist channels where ideas, meanings, and discourses predominated. Its main tools have become in fact the old-fashioned ones of textual interpretation and linguistic analysis and ideas, with generous portions of biographical narrative added in for good effect. What few seem willing to admit is that social history, when done well, has simply become history, little different theoretically from where intellectual historians stood well over a century ago. Unnoticed and unappreciated, old-fashioned historicism has resumed its place as the preeminent form of historical presentation.[6] Yet, the spirit of the original claims of social history lingers on in the form of political commitments and inclinations, even as the methods of social history have changed. Social historians are still inclined to raise claims of class and class consciousness, but now they do so within narratives whose theoretical foundations no longer quite serve the materialist interpretation they were originally meant to invoke. What in the world has happened?

Social history now invariably seeks text and intention, and of necessity draws on biographical elements in the re-creation of narrative. What these newer histories imply is everywhere a belief in meaningful historical contexts and individual agency. The reasons for this tectonic shift, however, are rarely explicitly acknowledged. The turn to language and subjective interpretation of meanings was a tactical move that resulted from an early collision with economic history under the leadership of Max Hartwell in the debates over the quality of life in the early Industrial Revolution. And it was that altercation that has produced the current tensions within the histories social historians produce and the claims they wish to make. It is high time then to expose the remaining inconsistencies of those asserting the old mantle of the "social" and bring practice back into line with theory, reaffirming historicism in its original aims and aspirations, while rejecting the last vestiges of determinism and its scientistic pretensions.

II. RED TIDE CRESTING

When looking back over the period in which theory and practice have diverged in modern social history, it is important to understand the early roots of modern historical thought to fully appreciate just how dramatic a transformation social history has undergone. When using the term *historicism*, it is necessary to bear in mind that it refers here to the predominant use of the word as translated from the German, *Historismus*.

The concept of historicism was first used in the late 1790s to designate the attempt to imaginatively recreate the mind-set of persons living in a particular time and place.[7] It was this understanding that Friedrich Meinecke utilized when he spoke of the development of *Historismus* as belonging "to the essence of individuality (that of the single man no less than the collective structures of the ideal and the practical world) that it is revealed by a process of development," and by process he meant nothing like a specific goal or determined end, but simply the to and fro of history, "with its greater degree of spontaneity, plastic flexibility and incalculability."[8] It is also what Herbert Schnaedelbach referred to as historicism types one and two which were roughly to be equated with the practices and approaches of the historian, rather than the philosophical systems of philosophers.[9] Consequently, history was produced out of the intersection of ideas coming from social context and the unique configurations given to those beliefs by both particular persons and groups. Texts and their interpretation with biographical narrative were thus always an essential mode of historical explanation and analysis.[10]

Contrasting this earlier understanding of history with the course of social history at its height in the early seventies and eighties and its current theoretical topography, indicates not a consistent adaptation of social history over time, but a complete revolution of the field's conceptual landmarks. We need only recall just how indomitable social history, with its one-sided assertions of such externalizing variables as "material modes of production," "social structure," and "class" once seemed to gain a full perspective on just how dramatic the transformation has been.

In the late seventies and eighties, a student was hard pressed even to find a course offering in intellectual history, let alone American intellectual history.

Having entered U.C. Santa Cruz in the early eighties, I well remember that
American intellectual history was no longer offered, despite some very prominent founding faculty members like Page Smith who had worked in the older
styles of narrative history. Only one intellectual historian, a leading figure
in the area of American educational history, Laurence Veysey, remained in
the department, and he had been persuaded by his colleagues to desist from
teaching his own topic. The subject was viewed as elitist, narrow, and not the
wave of the future. In fact, Veysey had even written a review of the discipline
in 1979 that was counted by some to be the very flag of surrender.[11]

Fortunately, I was able to persuade Veysey to conduct an independent
study and through this avenue, could pursue such classics as Page Smith's
John Adams, Avery Craven's *The Coming of the Civil War*, and R. R.
Palmer's *The Age of the Democratic Revolution*. It was not that Veysey
agreed with all he assigned, far from it, but he appreciated good writing, the
use of textual sources, and the focus on *intentions*, with goodly amounts of
biographical detail. I particularly remember his criticism of all sorts of determinisms, and especially technology-driven interpretations that made agency
subservient to rational necessity. This is not to say that he was unappreciative
of the newer research tools which had made the "new" social history seem
so indomitable. In fact, it was quite the opposite. He worried that the new
methods were making the task of doing history so arduous that historians
might give up on these new resources out of sheer exhaustion. But his more
fundamental concern was left understated.

Veysey assumed that traditional political and intellectual history would
limp along as a kind of academic curiosity, the province of a small minority
that still relished the complexity of thought. Ideas and intentions, spontaneity and freedom, would thus be exiled to a small isolated peninsula of the
historical profession.[12] What he could not anticipate was that these elements
of classical liberal history were due for a resurgence. What indeed is history
without them but a collection of facts without an understanding of human
agency? Veysey wrote at the crest of the tide. What he could not yet see was
the degree to which social history would eventually be compelled to transform itself through its own internal tensions and contradictions.

In the same year that Veysey's piece appeared, Tony Judt, perhaps the
foremost social historian of the time and an outspoken public intellectual, saw
a very different picture from his vantage point within social history, one that
was exactly the opposite of Veysey's prediction and for which he was far less
gentle in his attribution of motive and responsibility.

Judt attacked point blank the new methods of statistical analysis as an
"obsession" that bespoke a collective "loss of faith in history," and then took
aim at a trend just beginning to come to light: the move to interpret language
and texts, rather than class. As Judt saw it, this newer shift in approach

threatened the whole theoretical underpinning of social history as it had been originally conceived. One group was becoming obsessed with the new technical gadgets at their disposal, *without* extending their theoretical commitments to a material base, while the other group, was not only *not extending* social theory rightly understood, but was actively jettisoning it altogether for an implicitly elitist and reactionary method. It was this last group that dominated the remainder of his treatment. This bunch represented the move to interpret "symbols and meanings" or what would come to be called the "linguistic turn" in the analysis of "social discourse."

For Judt, this trend represented, not exhaustion with the newer and more difficult technical methods of data collection as Veysey had feared might happen, but an "obvious" lack of theoretical understanding about *class and its relation to power*. And he left little doubt about his meaning. The reasons for ignoring the concept of class were, he argued, either ignorance or betrayal of the older Marxian idea of politics as the expression of economic power. When Judt used the term politics, he very specifically meant the political manifestation of forces rooted in the modes of production.

Surveying the work of his younger colleagues, Judt observed that "an odd thing happens" when historians attempt to account for "*differences* in attitude or beliefs." They begin to resort to psychological explanations for the attitudes of the oppressed, as though they were unmediated by the powers that oppressed them: "It is," he wrote, "the *refusal to consider class-based relations of power* which encourages such limited pseudo-psychological accounts of the history of individuals." Rather, he insisted, motives should be viewed collectively in terms of class conflict, located in particular historical situations and understood primarily as struggle. From this vantage point, "their behavior looks very different." Agency was for him only perceivable when its "essential components" are anchored in "parties, ideologies, power, class," and even then, only in the context of revolution or conflict. Only then, he argued, can we have a meaningful discussion about social relations. Only then does agency appear relevant, or even apparent in the historical record.[13]

On the other hand, a "particular emphasis on the 'voluntarist' element," Judt went on, "results in a wider failure to grasp the nature of social relations under capitalism." Thus, he concluded, the problem within social history was "directly related to the refusal to write the word 'capitalism.'" And yet, oddly, Judt complained but a few pages later, that modern social history was robbing past groups of their *active participation* and *choice*, making the ideas of working men and women mere epiphenomena: "At no point, do peasants and workers themselves," he wrote, "men or women, acquire *any* political identity of their own. They never *chose*, or were politically conscious. They rebelled blindly, or followed a lead."[14] But here we see the very tensions to which the entire theoretical apparatus of social history was succumbing. It was not that Judt was really opposed to choice, but rather that he was insisting that it be located in "class." Was this not a voluntarist element itself? Yes, and then, no.

Judt's review was a general indictment, naming prominent figures like Charles Tilley, Lawrence Stone, and Joan Scott. But while many were bludgeoned, Judt seemed too willing to let the limitations of his own theoretical orientation slide, most especially as it related to motive and agency. Only two pages after lamenting the loss of a sense of choice among the working classes, he went on to assert that it was "the fear of Marxism" that was engendering most of the confusion in the field. "When the term 'social class' is employed," he insisted, "it is divorced from any relationship to a mode of production, and becomes a mere ascriptive category, interchangeable with any other." There was no concern for the reductionism inherent in the Marxian legacy itself, no cognizance of the original claim to scientific status, nor the determinism that is blatant in the very concept of social relations rooted in "the means of production." As a consequence he seemed blind to the reasons why so many of his colleagues were increasingly uncomfortable with Marxist assertions of motive.[15] Can this circle be squared?

Certainly Judt must have realized that it was Marx himself who classified thought as epiphenomenal. The theorists most complained of in his essay were Michel Foucault and Max Weber. From them was supposed to have come the loss of faith in objective social relations, especially among the new Left of the 1960s which now "openly denied objective social and economic categories, and claimed the right to identify itself just as it chose and with whomsoever it wished. The individual rather than class became the revolutionary 'unit,' and occupational or subjective 'strata,' such as students or intellectuals, became the collective nouns for such units."[16]

Of course he was right about the shift in theory, but he seemed oblivious to the fact that the linguistic turn, meaning the interpretation of texts and intentions, was taken in large measure because his own answer was no answer at all. And that fact had become all too apparent to most of his colleagues, even if they didn't like to speak of it openly. Indeed, the real reasons for the turn to texts and language are almost never discussed. It was not the political inclinations of social historians that were changing. It was not some newly found interest in personal agency or 1960s style free expressionism. It was simply that in the area of material facts, Marxian categories were not holding up, but you will very rarely ever hear a recounting of the debates that brought this into the open or about the scholar who first took on the materialist challenge. Whether or not Judt was himself fully aware of this history is not clear, but he certainly recognized the contradictions that it posed to his field. Despairingly, he concluded "It is not hard to envisage a reaction, a few years hence, in favor of 'old-fashioned' history, with the social kind dismissed as a soft option for the 'unserious.'"[17]

To that particular bill of lading, the time has come to mark *delivered*.

III. HARTWELL VERSUS HOBSBAWM AND THOMPSON

What few social historians care to remember, and in fact almost never mention, is the debate between Max Hartwell and the two great champions of labor history in England, Eric Hobsbawm and E. P. Thompson.[18] The term "social history" meant something a bit more general and diffuse in the United Kingdom than in the United States, but no one should doubt the influence of Hobsbawm and Thompson on social history in the United States, of which labor history has always been a preeminent expression.[19] And few have had such a profound impact on theory and method as these two scholars. Judt cited both without any of the critical fire he had reserved for others in his field. In fact, closer attention to Thompson, he argued, would have saved one poor rube from missing the clear "relationship between the social history of the English working class and their developing consciousness."[20] But nary a word is to be found of Hartwell's devastating critiques of both.[21]

The truth of the matter is Hobsbawm had had his more thoroughly Marxist presuppositions seriously shaken by Hartwell on grounds of both economic data and conceptualization. From this, it became painfully apparent to anyone paying the slightest bit of attention that a turn to the subjective was the only route remaining to escape with any chance of survival. It also meant that the political would come to more openly drive the social historian's self-understanding and in this endeavor, Thompson was one of the first to point the way out, though not without serious internal tensions, as Hartwell also made devastatingly plain.

Clues to this development can be found in interviews conducted with both Hartwell and Hobsbawm later in their lives. It is no accident that Hobsbawm commented on the cultural and linguistic turn right after his elaboration of the debates with Hartwell. It is also equally significant that he recognized the beginnings of the cultural approach with the appearance of Thompson's work just two years after that fateful exchange. For Thompson, this development had become obvious when Hartwell had compelled Hobsbawm to recognize a modest but undeniable rise in the material standards of living among the working classes in the first few decades of the nineteenth century. And it was precisely from this seemingly small material point that Thompson then took his alternative theoretical and narrative turn. What is also rarely remembered is that Hartwell had also engaged Thompson for the way in which he chose to do this.[22]

IV. HAVING OUR DETERMINISMS
AND CHOOSING THEM TOO

In 1965, Hartwell published in the December issue of *Economic History Review* a very meticulous analysis of Thompson's *The Making of the English Working Class*. Here already were all the signs of the linguistic and cultural turn with respect to the nature of class, as Hobsbawm himself acknowledged in his 2008 interview. "There is no question," Hobesbawm said, "that our generation in the 1950s and 1960s, while they didn't completely neglect culture, did not actually give it sufficient weight in our analyses."[23] The most gripping aspect of Thompson's interpretation, he went on, was his innovative use of eye-witness testimony. In his review written shortly after publication, Hartwell fully acknowledged the powerful draw such evidence has. Here were real persons speaking for themselves, real agents, and not mere instruments.[24] The working class "was not the spontaneous generation of the factory system," Thompson insisted, "Nor should we think of an external force—the 'Industrial Revolution'—working upon some nondescript undifferentiated raw material of Humanity." But rather, "The working class made itself as much as it was made."[25]

The difficulty here, as Hartwell carefully noted, was that the interpretation was inconsistent. The author wanted to have his freedom and determinism too. For all his protestations about real agents, he was *still* driven by the Marxist concept of class. "I do not see class as a 'structure,' nor even as a 'category,'" Thompson asserted in his preface, "but something which in fact happens ... in human relationships." Class consciousness forms from experiences and should be handled in cultural terms "embodied in traditions, value systems, ideas, and institutional forms." Class is "defined by men as they live their own history, and in the end, this is its only definition."[26]

In the very midst of all this, however, we find that the culture of the working class has for some reason still to be produced through the modes of production. Thompson actually applied a stronger word, *determined*: "The class experience is largely determined by the productive relations into which men are born—or enter involuntarily." Why? Because somehow individuals have come "to be in this 'social role.'" Otherwise there would be no class "but simply a multitude of individuals with a multitude of experiences." So, in the end, class becomes a category after all, one that is applied by the historian to illuminate a relation that would otherwise be composed of very particular experiences.[27]

And here is where Hartwell got the better of Thompson. Are there not multiple working classes? Multiple experiences? Multiple interests? Admitting a moderate improvement in material conditions over the first four decades of the nineteenth century (the essential point that Hartwell had scored against

Hobsbawm two years before), Thompson had for some curious reason come to the conclusion that this improvement could only give rise to only *one* experience: "they [the members of the English working class] had suffered and continued to suffer this slight improvement as a catastrophic experience."[28] His was a reading still haunted by the ghosts of Marxism past.[29] Acceptance of material improvement, however slight, was a remarkable admission, and a revelation as to why the subjective turn was taken. "Admitting this," Hartwell wrote, "he poses a paradox of his own making."[30]

Thompson explicitly attacked quantitative evidence when used to determine averages and tendencies, but he would certainly avail himself of such data when it supported his case for a unitary class experience. What is truly amazing, however, is the extent to which, whatever the material condition, class *position* was asserted to assure the conclusion of immiseration. "This is having it both ways too much," Hartwell noted wryly. What it was not, and what Hartwell made plain, is consistent theory: "On the one hand there is the interpretation of Marx: the degradation and immiseration of the proletariat to the point of revolution. On the other hand, there is the long list of working-class achievements. . . . But degradation and self-improvement are unlikely bed-fellows." It was not even a very satisfactory *description* of evidence, but a very selective one, drawn from records that virtually guaranteed the author's negative conclusions.[31]

Despite such flaws in Thompson's project, Hartwell proved correct in another way: he predicted that the book would be "widely read and influential." Thompson's influence through prominent social historians like Herbert Gutman, Gary Nash, Thomas Dublin, and Lynn Hunt, has abounded on both sides of the Atlantic.[32] Following his lead, these writers have steadily moved social history from the quantitative and technical modes that had seemed so daunting to Veysey at the end of the 1970s to the textual and biographical analyses of ideas and language that Judt had feared. By the mid-1990s Patrick Joyce could even ask in the pages of *The Journal of Social History*, if this new turn amounted to "The end of social history?"[33]

But of course the question was meant rhetorically. The field was thriving, Joyce believed, precisely "because whatever the collective subjects involved, the 'linguistic turn,' in looking at how such subjects are put in place, is pointing to the manner and mode in which hegemony is achieved: for instance, collective identity and political mobilization can be very valuably reinterpreted in terms of the narrative patterns that enunciated them."[34] The field was booming precisely because the range of groups about which narratives could now be told had multiplied. Where Thompson used texts to find but one class, however, the new social history was finding many, and not just classes, but all sorts of what Joyce called "collective subjects." Thompson's need to tie class, however remotely, to the relations of production had been jettisoned.

Most dramatically, the cultural turn had become the "linguistic turn," and the new mantra was to celebrate a kind of free-floating assertion of all sorts of power relations.

V. FOUCAULT AND THE QUIET DEATH OF THEORY

At the heart of Joyce's adulations, as with the fears of Judt, was the influence of Michel Foucault: His was not so much a theory we are told, as practice in action. Deeply influenced in the postwar years by the writings of Friedrich Nietzsche, Foucault had come to believe in the possibility of overcoming the standard tropes of historical understanding through a kind of "will to see" certain specific relational meanings in texts through recognizing disjunctures of newer from older textual expressions.[35] Rather than Marxian class analysis which was anchored to economic power, or liberal bourgeois perceptions of the state, Foucault embraced a free-form notion of power in what he considered the genetic tracing of textual linguistic relations back in time as the most historically promising approach. Supposedly such "tracing" would permit the historian to bypass preconceptions about power's meaning, its aims, or even its forms, and simply *see it* in action.

Of course how Foucault "saw it" has always been a main criticism of his work. From what standpoint, if not the state? From what, if not class? He saw patterns in speech and text, but how did he know to say this or that aspect signified "power"? O'Brien observed that to "step into Foucault's circle" is to "recognize nothing as given." But without any schema for interpretation, the question is begged and begged again: "How do you know power when you see it?" Neither Foucault nor O'Brien has answered that question. While some scholars have thought his understanding a bit unhinged, others felt liberated, in just the fashion Judt had warned about.[36] The historian could reveal changes from, or retrogression to, older forms of power in whatever way he or she happened to perceive them. No need to worry about cause, but merely the presentation of "ruptures and breaks," without apparently any need for an explicit theory to explain how you know what it is you are seeing.

For Joyce, this all pointed to new possibilities. "Attention to the creation of subjectivity, to new 'social' subjects and to the manner in which subjectivity is produced all suggest a new agenda for reconfigured 'social history.'" And Foucault was his man: "It is Foucault's work that most emphatically liberates us from the limits of traditional approaches to society and the social ... ."[37] But to do what? Supposedly by such subjectivity, historians would be empowered to discover how "different groups, individuals and institutions identify and organize themselves, and handle power." Yet Joyce never explained how this was to happen. He concluded with vague references to human agency and the evolution of meanings, citing others on "the duality of structure," or asserting that "social structures are both constituted by human agency, and yet at the same time are the medium of this constitution."[38] But these are assertions bordering on platitudes, not explanations.

Where Judt proclaimed the problem to be an unwillingness to spell out the word "capitalism," it is apparent the real problem was the social historians' refusal to spell out the word for the agents themselves, *the person*. All is not exogenous. All is not the collective imposition of structures. And Joyce could do nothing but recognize the problem, *this fact* of agency, directly: "If the social world is at bottom a human construct, it is only by looking at the principles of its construction that headway will be made, and this applies to the history of the social, as well as to the theory of the social." Let us just articulate what the implications of all this actually are. Joyce gives a clue: It is to be found in the "recreative, representational activities of actors as they make the social world (one example would, again, be narrative itself …)."[39]

I suppose calling individuals "actors" sounds less bourgeois, less liberal, perhaps more "structural" and "collective" or perhaps even "scientific." But the fact that Joyce explicitly signaled the rebirth of the narrative form is powerfully laden with implications that most social historians simply have not wanted to admit outright.

VI. WRITING HISTORY WITH ONLY HALF A THEORY

Narrative above all is a story, and a story is about something that happens. If that story is to be something other than outright grand teleology in either the Whig or Marxist sense, then it must be, as Joyce intimated, about the actors themselves. What gives Thompson's history its power? Hartwell had said it. It was the degree to which he had let the "actors," at least some of them anyway, speak for themselves. And the degree to which social historians succeed today, is in fact the degree to which they have been compelled to incorporate the elements of lives lived and the thoughts that animated them. It has not, however, been something they like to draw much attention to in any kind of overt theoretical way.

In 2002, Lynn Hunt observed a general decline in the explicit application of theories in the writing of social history and of theorizing in general by historians. She attributed this to a sense within the discipline that one should now get on with the writing of good histories. Citing concerns over plagiarism among historical popularizers, Hunt thought perhaps historians were spending more time focusing on standards of evidence or source criticism. As support for this, she noted, we are witnessing a new season for encyclopedias, which are cropping up everywhere like mushrooms, as people try to nail down the contours of the various conceptual and factual aspects of the field.[40] But I think there is a deeper reason.

Because social history has been compelled to move in a subjectivist direction, it finds itself coming full circle to the original grounds of the old historicist project itself. Yes, the themes have changed, but I mean here the theory.[41] No one is going to recreate Ranke's history of Prussia in modern garb, but the subjects were only ever incidental to the original theory anyway.

Every historian, as John Burrows recently noted in his magisterial *History of History*, chooses his/her own subjects.[42] That much will always be the case, but how we approach the materials requires some sense of what *the person* is, if you want to tell a story that is in fact the product of historical actors. And the linguistic or hermeneutical turn is especially tied to this sort of narrative, one that seeks to understand events as contemporaries understood them. How one achieves such *understanding* becomes the critical factor in the process of interpretation. But, unfortunately, as social historians have increasingly become cultural historians, they have not wanted to face the implications of what Patricia O'Brien has recently brought out into the open: "Social history has brought us to the brink of a new history of culture, where society may not be primary after all and culture may not be derivative. The result is a period of confusion and perhaps crisis in the rise and fall of paradigms."[43] That would also explain the interest in encyclopedic summaries.

Encyclopedias are intellectual cartography. They help us locate ourselves in the disciplinary mix of things. A good way to gauge the climate of a field is to see what the surveys focus on. In a 2003 historiographic review of social history, Peter Stearns could do no more than cite the great masters with an up-beat promise that "There's more to come."[44] If we then turn to the latest entry for "social history" in the *Sage Handbook of Historical Theory*, we find that it has only been more of the same. Here the author of the entry, in addressing the supposed disillusionment of social history with the return of narrative, could find no more recent counter examples of such dissatisfaction than those from the early eighties, such as Tilly, Braudel, and Stone, all of whom attempted in some form or other to return back to a discussion of the material conditions of life.[45] But these are now old attempts and oceans of water have gone under the bridge since. Surely the writer could have updated his entry by now.

The truth is, social historians have run aground on the shoals of historical theory. At best, they will conjure up terms like "social relations," "social structures," "imbedded meanings" because these terms have an exogenous collective feel to them. In this way, "individuals" might still be rendered as the largely passive receptors of imposed norms, where discourses of power can then be described as shaping and structuring relations within society as a whole. But such language inevitably leads to interesting internal tensions within the older social historical frameworks. In reality, writing about norms, ideas, and culture without a clear sense of the schema necessary to identify agents and what they are actually doing with all those subjective meanings and signifiers, is to work with only half a theory, without any clear means of locating alterations and changes in contexts to which those agents may have contributed.

And here is where old-fashioned historicism comes back into the picture, and where the classical liberal historian in particular must play a part. The very idea of context grew out of the belief that historians must somehow get into the mind-set of persons to know how each thought about the world of his or her day to explain the actions taken. The hermeneutical turn grew out of this notion of *understanding*. It is no accident that Thompson refers to Weber, or that Foucault drew upon Nietzsche. Each came out of a tradition from which historicism, or *Historismus*, was itself the unique contribution to the very notion of historical context and by which it was to be undertaken through the processes of *verstehen*.[46]

From the very moment the idea of contextual *understanding* was formulated by Gustav Droysen in the late nineteenth century, it meant *all* of the social relations that social historians embrace as their primary concepts *plus* a conception of mind that would account for change. All the later historicists up to and including Max Weber carried forward some version, some variation of this idea through close attention to the personal and biographical elements in historical narrative.[47] As some have subsequently pointed out in the realms of sociology and psychology, this constitutes a kind of positive feedback loop.[48] But whatever we may call it, the point is, the idea of narrative history demands an articulation of a concept of the person, without which any analysis of change is half formed and incomplete. Of course, most "social historians" now do this in practice, but they remain silent about it in theory and even seem content to remain blissfully unaware of their methodology's own historical roots. And this is the reason I suspect so little is now being said on the matter of theory.

VII. BACK TO INDIVIDUALS AND CONTEXT

Whereas Judt insisted that the problem with social historians was a growing failure to write the word "capitalism," in reality it is the failure to accept the ultimate foundations of historical change where context and choice actually intersect: in the minds of persons. In responding to the determinisms of his own day, one of the leading institutional and intellectual historians of the early twentieth century, Otto Hintze, helpfully expressed the essence of the original historicist position with admirable clarity:

The common motivating forces [in society] are expressions of the common element in individual attitudes and are forged into an accepted intellectual system
(*objektive geistige Macht*). Even where they are reinforced by being embodied
in institutions, they are not permanent and immutable factors, but change constantly as a result of alterations in the individual impulses which prompt them.
The more primitive the social development, the more it imposes uniformity on
the individuals of a community, and the individual cannot liberate himself from
the beliefs of the community; nonetheless, all progress is based on differentiation, and on the contrast between the mind of the individual and the mind of
the community. The individual factor cannot be disregarded in its effects on
the development of the collective mind; it must be seen not only as the source
of the specific character of a group, it is also the most vital factor in its further
evolution.[49]

This is hardly the shibboleth of "great-man history" so often attributed to
an earlier methodological individualism. Hintze was in fact a practitioner of
comparative social institutions of a very sophisticated sort. The unique patterns of meaning that each person reflects back onto the social stage are the
necessary ingredients to explain change. It is in practice an interplay of factors that good historians have always tried to accomplish in their narratives.
It is in fact what good social history has done in actual practice, at least in
its most compelling aspects. In his *Urban Crucible*, for example, published
the same year that both Judt and Veysey came out with their very different
assessments, Gary Nash applied the Thompsonian framework to American
colonial cities, producing an elegant narrative very much in the same style. It
too succeeded because of the liberal use of textual and biographical data. But
like Thompson, the theoretical apparatus was left undeveloped and in critical
places in tension with itself.

For Nash, change is seen to be a kind of mysterious by-product of social
conflict. When differences are explicated, the narrative pays close attention to persons and thoughts, and not structures or modes of production.
From the "mini-revolution of 1689," when New Englanders overthrew
Governor Andros in Leisler's Rebellion, to the culmination of 1776, we
are presented with the various ideas of millenarian Protestantism and
republican ideology as the solvents of the culture of traditional English
deference to authority. Thoughts and norms thus take a prominent, if not
the central part of the explanation for the actions of actual persons.[50] Citing Thompson, Nash too argued that class is thus "a social and cultural
formation, arising from processes which can only be studied as they
work themselves out over a considerable historical period." But also
like Thompson, he insisted that the modes of production still have their
place in this history because each drew on republican theory selectively
"depending on their position in society."[51] And yet, his evidence is replete

with examples of persons who did not do this, but broke the mold of their expected social standing.

Thus from the outset we meet Mr. Samuel Sewall, prominent Boston dairy merchant, "whose hands had never been roughened by artisanal labor," proclaiming that "all men have equal right to Liberty," to the great consternation of another of his class. Or the operators of the "United Company of Philadelphia" who "stood far above the ruck in Philadelphia," but were each of unique and mixed backgrounds. Clearly, as Nash tries to emphasize, they were closer in their relations to the artisans and poor, but they were also up and coming, and it is only by examining them in their personal histories that we can *understand* their actions.[52] Their *actual* class position, however, does relatively little for the explanation as a whole.

Of course other American historians, self-consciously political and intellectual in their orientation, have noticed just how poorly the notion of social class as a concept and theory of agency works in the American case. Bernard Bailyn made his reputation with his path-breaking article, "Politics and Social Structure in Virginia," published in 1959. Here he revealed how American elite opinion was never a carbon copy of English aristocratic class consciousness.[53] Not social structure, but personal experiences in the context of very different environments were far more important factors. What then does the current state of social history portend for the future?

VIII. THE END OR THE ENDS OF SOCIAL HISTORY?

A recent edition of *The Journal of Social History* was dedicated to just this question through an assessment of the legacy of Thompson and the cultural turn. The picture surveyed, with but one exception, was a continuation of the flaws noted by Hartwell in the work of the original master. Most of the contributions simply substituted Thompson's focus on the English working class for a different group, without addressing any of the deeper conceptual flaws.

The introductory piece by the *Journal*'s editorial panel actually noted those very same flaws, but only to ask if they could be overcome. More particularly they noted that the problem of agency in Thompson's idea of class still had within it that deterministic germ of modernism characteristic of an earlier Marxism or stage theory of development. Thus, they noted, "Traces clearly remained here of a view of progressive historical stages, despite Thompson's attempt to rid himself of such a cast of mind."

Yet most of the contributions to the volume do not attempt to rise above this defect. Whether it is gender in England or labor in America or Greece, the pieces remain descriptive in a very predictable fashion. Attitudes are explored, but the coherence of the collective categories chosen, like Thompson's notion of class, was simply assumed. And so, as with Thompson, the particular collective theoretical assumptions assured that each paper would result in "a fairly predictable view of who might speak for the working class" in U.S. courts of law, in Greek politics, or for women at Greenham Common, Greenham Common.[54]

The one contribution that stands out as the exception is notable because the author makes a very direct attack on class and Marxism in particular. Here the author looks to the very complicated case of the Indian peasantry, and what has been found is neither uniform, nor amenable to the analysis of merely exogenous factors to explain the multiplicity of identities that exist. Indeed, the author of this piece, Parthasarathy, applies the idea of culture with a rigor and consistency that raises an interesting problem for explanation in general, revealing characteristics of deep description more reminiscent of anthropology or sociology, than history. It develops the intersection of trades and castes with all the attendant problems for conceptualizing meanings for different groups across different regions. In doing this, the author has in fact addressed Hartwell's original question to Thompson, whether consciously or not: Why just one experience, why not multiple?[55]

It also becomes clear that capitalism itself is not just a single exogenous system. Parthasarathy is quite direct in criticizing the deterministic models of more traditional Marxists who simply assert that India is the victim of exogenous globalized forces. Rightly, the essay directs attention inward and finds multiple layers of experience, including quite dramatic evidence for the sort of corrupted or crony capitalism that was once a hallmark of some earlier left interpretations, such as that identified with Gabriel Kolko. The only real difficulty is that such deep description by itself makes for a very unwieldy narrative of change. What all this seems to indicate is the necessity for historians to once more take up the history of their own particular fields and ask, what are they in fact doing? This sort of reflection is not an idle pastime, but a necessary means of orienting ourselves as a discipline. When done in a more rigorous fashion, I venture to predict that history in all its narrative fullness, including the now temporarily subdued specialties of political, intellectual, comparative, and diplomatic history, will see a resurgence. In this vein the recent flourishing of the cultural approach to economic development is to be counted as a singular instance of the very beginnings of this process to understand the dynamics at work globally in the unfolding history of the open society, where the notion of context openly embraces the variations emanating from individual experiences as a necessary part of the explanation of change.[56]

The aims of historical research in the original historicist understanding of the nineteenth century should not be judged solely by the subject matter those historians chose to investigate, but also by the theoretical and conceptual means they developed to ground their narratives. Those means entailed close attention to meanings and practices carried on in society, and the distinct experiences and expressions of actual persons. These were the elements of narrative stories that permitted the successful analysis of change in context. The application of source criticism assured the continual testing of facts to preserve the claim to historicity, and that application remains the hallmark of history rightly understood. And in the end, these ideas will be honored in practice, if not in the explicit theoretical expositions of historians, regardless of their subject matter, whether it be social, economic, political, or intellectual. And there are numerous examples of social history that seek just such a balance of factors personal and social without suffering any of the conceptual confusions.[57]

As for social history in general, however, if the last Thompson festschrift is any indication, social historians seem determined to pursue a one-sided, singular emphasis on the exploration of a *political agenda*, or as the editors freely admit: "the real and potential relationship between historiography and social movements on the left."[58] Thus the one unifying theme that seems to define their current efforts is not the approach to evidence, not the illumination of fundamental relationships within which real persons actually lived and chose to act, but just the political proclivities of the historian. And that is unfortunately, as Judt worried, merely a soft option for the unserious.

NOTES

1. One can trace these ideas through various debates across national traditions. See for example the attack by Lord Acton (perhaps the quintessential classical liberal historian of the nineteenth century) on Henry Thomas Buckle in the 1880s or Otto Hintze's contribution to the Lamprecht Streit in Germany over a decade later: Lord Acton, "Buckle's Philosophy of History," in *Essays in Religion, Politics and Morality: Selected Writings of Lord Acton* vol. III, ed. J. Rufus Fears (Indianapolis 1988), 443–459; Otto Hintze, "The Individualist and the Collectivist Approach to History," in Felix Gilbert, ed., *The Historical Essays of Otto Hintze* (New York, 1975), 357–367.

2. Fritz Stern, *Varieties of History* (New York, 1972), pp. 145–169; Page Smith, *The Historian and History* (New York, 1966), 141–142.

3. John Burrow, *A History of History* (New York, 2008), 455–46; Georg Iggers, *Historiography in the Twentieth Century: From Scientific Objectivity to the Post Modern Challenge* (Middletown, CN, 1997), 78–94.

4. Laurence Veysey, "The 'New' Social History in the Context of American Historical Writing," *Reviews in American History* 7 (March 1979), 1–12.

5. Gary Nash, "Social Development," in, Jack P. Greene and J. R. Pole, eds., *Colonial British America: Essays in the New History of the Early Modern Era* (Baltimore, 1984), 233–261.

6. This point was actually made by Lawrence Stone in 1979, a prominent year for making predictions, but seems to have gone resolutely without notice by some of the more prominent historiographers of American social history. This was not so in England, where Eric Hobsbawm took notice, but disputed Stone's main contention. See Lawrence Stone, "The Revival of Narrative: Reflections on a New Old History," *Past and Present* 85 (November, 1979), 3–24; E. J. Hobsbawm, "The Revival of Narrative: Some Comments," *Past and Present* 86 (February, 1980), 3–8.

7. The first to deploy the word was Friedrich Schlegel to indicate the quest to understand a period in its own terms and is thus inextricably bound to the idea of historical context, with emphasis on understanding the thoughts and ideas of contemporaries. The term has retained this connotation in Germany. It decidedly does not refer to the usage employed by Karl Popper who meant any directionally determined orientation to the past, or that of certain Austrian School economists who have a very particular set of theoretical ideas in mind associated with the peculiarities of the German Historical School of Economic thought. See Georg G. Iggers, "Historicism: The History and Meaning of the Term," *Journal of the History of Ideas* 56 (January, 1995), 129–152; See also Fredrick Beiser, *The German Historicist Tradition* (New York 2011), 1–6; and on the criticism of Karl Popper's use of the term see Helen P. Liebel, "The Enlightenment and the Rise of Historicism in German Thought," *Eighteenth-Century Studies* 4 (Summer, 1971), 359–385, see esp. 384.

8. Friedrich Meinecke, *Historism: The Rise of a New Historical Outlook*, trans. J.E. Anderson (New York, 1972), lvii.

9. Herbert Schnaedelbach, *Geschichtsphilosophie nach Hegel: Die Probleme des Historismus* (Muenchen, 1974), 20–21.

10. A very nice overview of this perspective was given by one of the leading historians of American financial institutions, Fritz Redlich, in an appendix to his *Essays in American Economic History* (New York, 1944), 191–199. The overview is usefully read alongside Otto Hintze's work cited above at n. 1.

11. Laurence Veysey, *The Emergence of the American University* (Chicago, 1965). On the significance of his work see the festschrift, Christopher P. Loss, "Introduction: Laurence R. Veysey's *The Emergence of the American University*," *History of Education Quarterly* 45 (Fall, 2005), 405–406.

12. Veysey, "'New' Social History," 4.

13. Tony Judt, "A Clown in Regal Purple: Social History and the Historians," *History Workshop* 7 (Spring, 1979), 66–94.

14. Ibid., 82–83.

15. Ibid., 85.

16. Ibid., 73, 84.

17. Ibid., 68.

18. In Judt's otherwise extensive review, for example, nary a mention of Hartwell is to be found. Nor in Alice Kessler Harris' "Social History," in Eric Foner, ed., *The New American History* (Philadelphia 1990), 163–184, and yet references to Hobsbawm and Thompsen are replete.

19. See Hobsbawm Interview Transcript, London, 17 June 2008 at Making History: www.history.ac.uk.>resources>inerviews

20. Judt, "A Clown in Regal Purple," 90 n 21.

21. There is, however, a very slight, though unmistakable recognition of that ear-lier historiographical contest. It is where Judt warned that it is "not just Marx who is jettisoned, but whole schools of conservative economic historians with him." Hartwell was certainly the leader of this bunch in Post War England. See Ibid., 85.

22. The point from which Thompson begins his distinctive foray into subjec-tive interpretation of language and texts is precisely the point which Hartwell had scored against Hobsbawm: "Over the period 1790–1840," Thompson concede, "there was a slight improvement in average material standards." See E. P. Thomp-son, *The Making of the English Working Class* (New York, 1966), 212. See also Hartwell's discussion that parallels Hobsbawm's account in the video interview, "A Conversation with Max Hartwell," *The Intellectual Portrait Series*, Liberty Fund., Inc. Indianapolis, 2000.

23. Hobsbawm Interview, 2008; R. M. Hartwell and R. Currie, "*The Making of the English Working Class,*" in R. M. Hartwell, *The Industrial Revolution and Economic Growth* (London, 1971), 361–376.

24. Ibid., 164.

25. Thompson, *Making off the English Working Class,* 194.

26. Ibid., 10–11.

27. Ibid., 9.

28. Ibid., 212; Hartwell, "*Making,*" 364, 368–369; See also, Stanley L. Engerman, "Reflections on 'The Standard of Living Debate': New Arguments and New Evi-dence," in John A. James and Mark Thomas, eds., *Capitalism in Context: Essays on Economic Development and Cultural Change in Honor of R. M. Hartwell* (Chicago, 1994), 71, 78.

29. One could say that Thompson and social historians in general have assumed the negative position as their peculiar contribution to history, much like the young Marx who remarked to Louis Napoleon, "The tradition of all dead generations weighs like a nightmare on the brains of the living." See Karl Marx, *The Eighteenth Brumaire of Louis Bonaparte.* 1852 at https://www.marxists.org/archive/marx/works/1852/18th-brumaire/ch01.htm

30. Hartwell, "*Making,*" 373.

31. Hartwell, "*Making,*" 364, 373; See also the video interview, "A Conversation with Max Hartwell," *The Intellectual Portrait Series*, Liberty Fund., Inc. Indianapolis, 2000.

32. Hartwell, "*Making,*" 374–375; Herber G. Gutman, *Work, Culture and Society in Industrializing America* (New York, 1976), 33–34, 85–86; Gary Nash, *The Urban Crucible: Norther Seaports and the Origins of the American Revolution* (Cambridge, MA, 2009), 7, 10–11; Thomas Dublin; Lynn Hunt, ed., *The New Cultural History* (Los Angeles, 1989), 4–5, and see also the review in the same work by Suzane Desan, "Crowds, Community, and Ritual in the Work of E. P. Thompson and Natalie Davis," 47–71.

33. Patrick Joyce, "The End of Social History?" *Social History* 20 (January, 1995), 73–91.

34. Ibid., 85.

35. Lynn Hunt, "Introduction: History, Culture, and Text," in Lynn Hunt, ed., *The New Cultural History* (Los Angeles, 1989), 1–22, and on the question of Foucault's focus, or lack there of, see especially 8–9; Patricia O'Brien, "Foucault's History of Culture," Ibid., 25–46.

36. Ibid., 35, 37; 39, and on the abjuring of theory and "drifting free" through sheer "practice," see especially, 43–44.

37. Joyce, 77; 82–83, 85, quotation on 86.

38. Ibid., 90.

39. Ibid., 91.

40. Lynn Hunt, "Where have All the Theories Gone," *American Historical Association Perspectives* (March, 2002).

41. Even as he praised Foucault as the pole star of future research, Joyce couldn't help but notice renewed interest in Georg Simmel who is a principle figure in old historicist theory. Historians of course, as Joyce noted, need a concept of agency or a theory thereof, and as O'Brien made clear in her earlier article, that is precisely what Foucault could not provide. Joyce, "End of Social History?" 90. On Simmel see Beiser, *The German Historicist Tradition*, 468–510.

42. John Burrows, *A History of Histories: Epics, Chronicles, Romances and Inquiries from Herodotus and Thucydides to the Twentieth Century* (New York, 2008), xv, 470.

43. Patricia Obrien, "Foucault's History," in *Hunt*, ed., *The New Cultural History*, 26.

44. Peter N. Stearns, "Social History Present and Future," *Journal of Social History* 37 (Autumn, 2003), 9–19.

45. Brian Lewis, "Chapter 14: Social History, A New Kind of History," in Nancy Partner and Sarah Foot, ed.s, *The Sage Handbook of Historical Theory* (Los Angeles, 2013), 93–104.

46. Beiser, *The German Historicist Tradition*, 4, 55, 66, 75, 77–79, 85, 106–109, 168–170, 381–384, 546–547.

47. Ibid., 298, 547.

48. Ralph H. Turner, "Personality in Society: Social Psychology's Contribution to Sociology," *Social Psychology Quarterly* 51 (March, 1988), 1–10; Dawn T. Robinson, "Control Theories in Sociology," *Annual Review of Sociology* 33 (April, 2007), 157–174.

49. Otto Hintze, "The Individualist and the Collectivist Approach to History," in Felix Gilbert, ed., *The Historical Essays of Otto Hintze* (New York, 1975), 363.

50. Nash, *Urban Crucible*, 42, 350.

51. Ibid., 6.

52. Ibid., 43, 336.

53. Bernard Bailyn, "Politics and Social Structure in Virginia," in James Morton Smith, ed., *Seventeenth-Century America: Essays in Colonial History* (Chapel Hill, NC, 1959), 90–115; On the special role of individuality in social structure in Bailyn's work see, Hans L. Eicholz, "A Revolutionary Historian: Appreciating Bernard Bailyn," *Claremont Review of Books* 5 (Spring, 2005), 55–58.

54. Rudi Batzell, Sven Beckert, Andrew Gordon, Gabriel Winant, "E.P. Thompson, Politics and History: Writing Social History Fifty Years after The Making of the

English Working Class," *Journal of Social History* 48 (Summer, 2015), 753–758; see esp. 756; Gabrielle Clark, "'Humbug' or 'Human Good?': E. P. Thompsen, the Rule of Law and Coercive Labor Relations Under Neoliberal American Capitalism," *Journal of Social History* 48 (Summer, 2015), 759–758; Lisa Furchtgott, "Tents Amid the Fragments: The Law at Greenham Common," *Journal of Social History* 48 (Summer, 2015), 789–802; Nikos Potamianos, "Moral Economy?: Popular Demands and State Intervention in the Struggle over Anti-Profiteering Laws in Greece 1914–1925," *Journal of Social History* 48 (Summer, 2015), 803–815.

55. D. Parathasarathy, "The Poverty of Marxist Theory: Peasant Classes, Provincial Capital, and the Critique of Globalization in India," *Journal of Social History* 48 (Summer, 2015), 816–841.

56. The cultural approach to economic development has taken a variety of perspectives. Mokyr has, like Weber and other members of the early twentieth century historical school, has included ideas, information and institutions, and even invoked Foucault, but to give a textual and evidentiary context to define what he means by ideas of power. Appleby has presented a very Weberian reading with emphasis on the ethics and values of scientific endeavor. Deirdre McCloskey, while highly critical of earlier answers such as that propounded by Weber, speaks to ethical concepts as liberating forces. All look to context but also to the innovative role of persons as motive forces in the narrative of economic change: See Joel Mokyr, *The Enlightened Economy: An Economic History of Britain* 1700–1850 (New Haven, 2009), 34–36; Joyce Appleby, *The Relentless Revolution: A History of Capitalism* (New York, 2010), 20–31; Deirdre N. McCloskey, *Bourgeois Dignity: Why Economics Can't Explain the Modern World* (Chicago, 2010), 1–19; Joyce Appleby, Hans Eicholz, Hendrick Hartog, "The Early Modern Origins of Capitalism: A Roundtable," *Historically Speaking* XII (November, 2011), 9–15; Deirdre N. McCloskey, *Bourgeois Equality: How Ideas, not Capital or Institutions, Enriched the Modern World* (Chicago, 2016), xi–xxxvi.

57. One thinks here of the classic of colonial Pennsylvania by James T. Lemon, *The Best Poor Man's Country* (New York, 1972); or more recently the works of Stephen Innes such as his "Puritanism and Capitalism in Early Massachusetts," in John A. Adams and Mark Thomas, ed.s, *Capitalism in Context: Essays on Economic Development and Cultural Change in Honor of R. M. Hartwell* (Chicago, 1994), 83–113.

58. Rudi Batzell, Sven Beckert, Andrew Gordon, Gabriel Winant, "E.P. Thompson, Politics and History," Ibid., 755.

Chapter 8

"History through a Classical Liberal Feminist Lens"

Sarah Skwire

As Jane Austen noted in *Northanger Abbey*, reading traditional history can leave one feeling as if history is made up only of, "The quarrels of popes and kings, with wars or pestilences, in every page; the men all so good for nothing, and hardly any women at all."[1] Reading many feminist histories creates a similarly disorienting effect wherein history becomes a story of women's successes and failures at persuading the state to back their desires and preferences with force. Just as traditional history is accused, often justly, of not attending to the voices of those who do not operate within the ranks of power and privilege, so feminist history may, equally justly, be accused of not attending to the voices of those who do not operate within the ranks of government, the state, and the current political system.

The Australian politician Joan Kirner has argued that "There is no such thing as being non-political. Just by making a decision to stay out of politics you are making the decision to allow others to shape politics and exert power over you. And if you are alienated from the current political system, then just by staying out of it you do nothing to change it, you simply entrench it."[2] Even Bella Abzug—the member of the U.S. House of Representatives who famously said that, "The inside operation of Congress—the deals, the compromises, the selling out, the co-opting, the unprincipled manipulating, the self-serving career-building—is a story of such monumental decadence that I believe if people find out about it they will demand an end to it"[3] was happy to insist that what women wanted was "an equal share in government." The solution to inequities entrenched in the state, in other words, seems to be not so much to solve them as to have an equal share in directing their distribution.

June Hannam's article, "Women's History, Feminist History" notes that feminist history has long been, "the history of less powerful groups—'history from below'"—and challenged conventional wisdoms about what should be

159

seen as historically significant.[4] While that is both true and admirable, the combination of that focus with the influence—also noted by Hannam—that Marxism has had on feminist history means that political power becomes increasingly the focal point for thinking about women's influence. Added to the popular tendency to "keep score" of women's progress by tracking changes in their political status—full citizenship, voting rights, election to political office, and so on, this may make women who are, at best, skeptical of the state seem somewhat out of the loop of modern feminism and somewhat divorced from the concerns of more traditional feminist historians.

As has been noted often, however, there is no such animal as feminism. There are, instead, a multiplicity of feminisms, and one of the much-neglected feminisms is classical liberal feminism, most particularly in its instantiation as a feminism of women against the state.[5] This has operated in areas of concern to most other feminisms—areas such as religious expression; marriage and legal standing; war and peace; and health and reproductive freedom. Such a deep and broad history deserves extensive treatment. And yet that treatment is virtually nowhere to be found.

There are three methods by which considering history through the lens of a classical liberal feminism can serve as a way to radically undermine the assumption that a feminist approach requires a close alliance with government power. The first of these is the historian's choice of subject matter. Second is the historian's choice of questions asked about the subject. Third is the often very small and very subtle question of word choice and phrasing used when discussing and writing history.

SOME THOUGHTS ON SUBJECT MATTER

In the same way that some of the greatest gains of feminist history have been attained by a dogged insistence on recovering the voices of neglected female historical figures,[6] a classical liberal feminist history can turn the same dogged insistence to recovering the voices of women who spoke against the state.[7] Looking for forgotten voices can, but need not, take us far outside the scope of study that is considered traditional history. Areas such as religion, law, and peace activism, are widely accepted as legitimate locations for feminist historical work, and they also provide rich material for a classical liberal version of that work. The catalog that follows is not meant, in any way, to be exhaustive. Instead it is meant to begin to indicate the wealth of materials that await the classical liberal feminist historian who takes on the task of applying her particular lens to the subject matter of history.

With some rare exceptions, organized religion has not been particularly kind to women, nor has it been kind to those who resist the state.[8] However, in much the same way that traditional feminist history has been able to re-envision such prophets as well as cloistered convents, dissenting sectarians, and other religious communities of choice as locations of power and influence for women, a classical liberal feminist history should be able to emphasize the important ways in which they were not just about female power, but about female power explicitly exercised in intentional opposition to the state.

Figures who might attract attention of classical liberal scholars are women like Saint Salaberga and Saint Fara who founded religious communities in Europe and Ireland in the first millennium. The nuns at the abbey of Las Huelgas chose their own confessors until the 12th century. The many female mystics in medieval Europe such as St. Hildegard von Bingen, St. Julian of Norwich, and St. Theresa of Avila offered, through their ecstatic visions of personal union with the divine, an alternate path for the soul longing for something more immediate and impassioned than the traditional road to salvation. In 1666 Margaret Fell, Quaker activist and wife of the movement's founder George Fox, wrote "Women's Speaking Justified" in which she used sophisticated scriptural exegesis in order to defend the rights of women to preach.[9] Anne Hutchinson fought with equal vigor in the American colonies for her right to preach and to teach. Several early modern women became known for their prophetic visions at around the same time. Anna Trapnel and Eleanor Davies envisioned the overturning of current systems and institutions in favor of a new world of religious radicalism where the measure of merit was one's relationship to the divine. Poets like Aemelia Lanyer who created her own retelling of the Passion and offered a ringing defense of Eve in *Salve Deus Rex Judaeorum,*[10] as well as female translators of the Psalms and other religious texts, co-opted the male voices and stories of scripture and made them uniquely their own. Across centuries, women like Mother Ann Lee of the Shakers, and Mary Baker Eddy of the Church of Christ Scientist have founded successful and devout religious sects.

The 19th and 20th centuries have been notable as women around the world have fought, achieved, and continue to fight for the right of ordination in many denominations, as well as for the right to practice their faiths in ways that are most compatible with their individual understandings of divine law. Recently, Ayaan Hirsi Ali has been a notable voice in the struggle of Muslim women against oppressive theocracies, and Rabbi Miri Gold spearheaded the movement to see Reform Judaism recognized as a legitimate theology alongside Orthodox Judaism in Israel.

Equality under the law, from the right to appear in court, to the right to own property, to vote and run for office, has long been a struggle for women. It is another area that should attract the attention of the classical liberal feminist historian. While individual women—sole heirs to large families or dynasties, or royal widows, for example—might historically have been given property rights to preserve social order, this was the exception rather than the rule. Arts patron Lady Anne Clifford, for example, became Baroness de Clifford in title when her father died in 1605. But it was only after nearly 45 years of legal wrangling that she was able to obtain the family estates, instead of only the £15,000 left to her when her father willed the estates to his brother. Women less wealthy, persistent, and capable than Clifford, however, found themselves hemmed in on all sides by legal strictures like coverture, primogeniture, and entail, all of which limited their access to property. The 20th and 21st-century legal contests over women's health care and abortion, custody and harassment cases, Sharia law, and other areas where gender complicates legal status mean the question of equality under the law continues to be of pressing interest, and should be a focus on classical liberal feminist historians.[11]

Marriage, which was a key limiting factor in women's rights to own property in many times and places, provided other legal challenges for women as well. Roman and English common law considered children the property of their fathers. Thus, it was not until Barbara Addick sued for custody of her children in 1813 that child custody in the United States ceased automatically reverting to the father in cases of divorce. Roman and English common law also held that it was impossible for a husband to rape his wife. Despite the best efforts of early advocates for equality in marriage rights, it was not until the early to mid-20th century that countries in the Soviet Bloc and Scandinavia began to overturn these laws. Most countries waited for the final decades of the 20th century. In 1993, North Carolina became the last of the United States to remove the spousal exemption for rape.

The question of suffrage becomes surprisingly complicated when viewed through a classical liberal feminist lens. Early 20th-century anarchist essayist and poet Voltairine de Cleyre, for example, makes an anarchist argument against political participation by arguing that all governments, regardless of their form, will always be manipulated by a small minority.[12] Emma Goldman's famous essay against suffrage argues that voting will merely increase the power held by those who have enslaved women for centuries.[13] Agitating for the vote then becomes morally questionable, as it is either a power grab or a reification of power that is already in place and already oppressive. A classical liberal feminist approach may be uniquely suited to drawing out the unpleasant complications in the relationship between the women's suffrage movement and the Negro suffrage movement in the United States. Despite the long alliance between leaders of both movements, the 15th Amendment's promise to extend suffrage to black American men led several leaders of the women's suffrage movement to campaign against it on the ground that the franchise should have been extended to women as well. This led to an unpleasant and temporary "Baptists and Bootleggers" alliance between some feminist leaders and some racist southern groups. Continued fights for suffrage around the globe might provide some interesting case studies for classical liberal feminist history as well.

Given such early peace workers as Julia Ward Howe, peace advocacy has long been an area of interest to feminist historians, but the classical liberal feminist historian may well be particularly interested in the ways in which such advocacy explicitly positions the advocate against the state. Figures deserving of their notice are women like Sophie Scholl, of the White Rose Society, executed for treason in 1943, and Irena Sendler, a Polish Catholic social worker who saved the lives of 2500 Jewish children by smuggling them out of the Warsaw Ghetto, providing them with false documents, and finding shelter for them.

Complicating matters for those who turn a classical liberal eye to the feminist history of peace activism, is the fact that women who resist the state have not always chosen to do so through peaceful means. Some have chosen to turn the state's war-making powers against it. The Trưng sisters, Trưng Trắc and Trưng Nhị, assembled an army in 39 C.E. in Vietnam, composed largely of women, after the Chinese had executed Trưng Trắc's husband for rebellion. They recaptured more than 60 citadels from the Chinese and fought them successfully for over two years. Boudicca, the Queen of the Celtic Iceni, led a revolt against the Romans, destroyed Camulodunum and the site of a temple to the former emperor Claudius, and routed an entire Roman legion. Yaa Asantewaa was leader of the 1900 Ashanti uprising against the British that became known as the War of the Golden Stool. She rallied her people with a famous speech that included the words "If you, the men of Asante, will not go forward, then we will."[14] The challenges for feminist history and for classical liberal history that can be raised by attention paid to this more militaristic resistance against the state would be fascinating, and would surely provide useful and interesting context for such 21st-century concerns as the opening of selective service to women as well as men.

The history of women's work outside the home should be of great interest as well. Historians of women's work have often tended to approach their subject from the left, with a great deal of attention given to the history of women in the labor movement, for example. Here, historians like Ruth Milkman, Martha May, and Alice Kessler-Harris have rightly noted the problematic way in which, from its earliest days, much of the business of the labor movement was to protect organized white male labor by protecting itself from competition against immigrant labor, non-union labor, and female labor. But there is work to be done by specifically classical liberal feminist historians as well. Of particular interest, I suspect, will be women like Rheta Childe Dorr and Doris Stevens, who campaigned against the 1923 push for an Equal Rights Amendment on the grounds that it interfered with women's right to contract for their labor on the same terms as men. This is also an area in which a good deal of work has been done on the history of immigrant women. Suzanne Sinke's work on Dutch immigrant women, Hasia Diner's on Irish and Jewish immigrant women, and Donna Gabaccia's work on Italian immigrant women have all added to the history of women's work outside the home as well as turning attention beyond the anglosphere.

Of equal interest are the actions of individual women as entrepreneurs, inventors, and innovators in the world of work. As inventors women have been responsible for windshield wipers, disposable diapers, vacuum-packed canning, the technology underlying the cell phone, Liquid Paper, the programming language COBOL, and Kevlar. The scientific achievements of Marie Curie are commonly acknowledged, but the contributions of women like Ada Lovelace are only beginning to be recognized, though recent works like Janet Abbate's *Recoding Gender: Women's Changing Participation in Computing,* and Margot Lee Shetterley's *Hidden Figures: The American Dream and the Untold Story of the Black Women Mathematicians Who Helped Win the Space Race* are beginning to remedy that neglect.

Women entrepreneurs are similarly neglected as themes for serious study. In 17th-century New Amsterdam (later, New York), the wealthiest woman was the shipping magnate Margaret Hardenbrook Philipse. Eliza Lucas Pinckney managed a successful indigo enterprise in the 18th century. In early 20th-century Indianapolis, Madame C. J. Walker took her formula for a homemade shampoo and hair restorative and turned it into a thriving business that employed 1000 female sales representatives. She used her profits to expand her business and to fight for the equal treatment of black soldiers and against lynching. In the 1950s Brownie Wise invented the classic Tupperware party, and with it the whole idea of the "party plan" system of marketing that continues to be a major facet of women's work to this day. With contemporary debates over the minimum wage, "equal pay for equal work," and other issues of women in the workplace taking center stage in many current political campaigns, the time is right for extensive studies on women's participation in entrepreneurship and in capitalism.[15]

SOME THOUGHTS ON QUESTIONS

But arguing that a classical liberal feminist history is needed will require more than simply turning to a new set of subjects for study. A classical liberal feminist history will also need to ask new questions, or ask old questions in new ways.

In an article on the history of women in the labor movement, I urged classical liberal feminists to reconsider the question posed by Alice Kessler-Harris

"How do we ... come to terms with the failures of organized labor with regard to women? How do we explain the persistent failure of women to make their way to positions of power inside trade unions? [Ruth Milkman] laid the absence of common goals at the door of an exclusionary and male-oriented trade union movement and pleaded with feminists not to turn their backs on it. But her description of organized labor's years of neglect of women and their concerns yields no source for optimism and her argument offers few hints of any possibility of change. Whether the trade union movement can ever become a vehicle for non-sexist activity on behalf of all its members is still a major question for women." Kessler-Harris and Milkman attribute the lack of female representation in powerful positions in the labor movement to "years of neglect" and to the sexism of the individuals involved in the movement. A classical liberal feminist history would have to—as I do—use the analytical tools of Public Choice theory to ask whether that lack of representation is about personal, individual misogyny and neglect, or whether it is a structural issue, purposefully built into the institutions of the labor movement by those who created the unions and by the government institutions with which they have become so closely allied. Attending to the insights of Public Choice theory encourages a healthy skepticism about institutions and policies that may well be based on good intentions but still have deleterious results that all historians should bring to their work. Classical liberal feminist historians should particularly relish Public Choice theory for its ability to cut through political rhetoric and ask important questions about results. With such a framework in place, a classical liberal feminist looks at the history of the labor movement—and its simultaneous appeals to and exclusion of female workers is promising territory for future classical liberal feminist historical research.

A similar example of rethinking a feminist question from a classical liberal feminist perspective appears later in that same piece. At the 2014 Association for Private Enterprise Education annual conference, Utah State Economists Lindsey McBride and Grant Patty considered the way in which occupational licensing specifically relates to women. As reported by Jared Meyer from the Manhattan Institute, McBride and Patty looked specifically at lower-income professions and determined that "women are most adversely affected by occupational licensing laws in Utah. Approximately 70 percent of the people who needed licenses to work in these professions were women." As a feminist, this struck me as outrageous. But as a classical liberal feminist, it also raised further questions. It would not be surprising if Utah, because of its strong Mormon culture, were an outlier in any number of economic and social measurements. Do McBride and Patty's findings seem likely to hold if the rest of the United States is bundled in? While the Institute for Justice has produced landmark studies in the problems of occupational licensing, the data they have collected do not specifically consider gendered issues. There must be rich fruit for study in a classical liberal feminist history of occupational licensing that attends to the questions of whether occupational licensing disproportionally affects women.

Lastly, the history of the tax code would benefit from a classical liberal feminist approach. Vivien Kellems's battle against the U.S. income tax, recorded in her book *Toil, Taxes, and Trouble* would be an appealing place to begin such inquiries. And while *Taxing Women* by Edward McCaffery provides a surprisingly gripping history of women and taxation, I suspect much could be done by a classical liberal feminist scholar who is as much a tax lawyer as a historian. This seems particularly true since the traditional feminist movement has limited its current discussion of economic issues to non-data-driven debates over the gender wage gap. Meanwhile, the outrages of the tax code are ignored. McCaffery writes, for example, that, "Major elements in the tax code were put in place in the 1930s, 1940s, and 1950s. This was a time when the traditional family—in which the man as father and husband worked outside the home, and the woman as mother and wife worked inside it—was dominant. Tax law changes were put in place to foster and reward this single earner household. These changes were left in place, all but unexamined, as the system kept growing. The tax system's strong bias in favor of single-earner families now sits uneasily under modern conditions." Who better than a classical liberal feminist to question the tax code's enshrining of the ahistorical notion of the "traditional family" and the damage it has done to the working women, to the lower-income families, and indeed, to the stability of the very same "traditional family" it sought to protect?

SOME THOUGHTS ON PHRASING

Subject matter and the questions we pose about it are large-scale issues for classical liberal feminist historians. I suspect, however, that there are important small ways in which a classical liberal feminist approach can influence the discussion and study of history. In this, I look to the importance which more traditional feminists have placed on the use of language—insisting on using humankind rather than mankind, for example, and pointing out that "he" is a gendered pronoun, not a neutral one. While often the cause of a certain amount of mockery, the fact remains that it matters how we say things, and that often the way we speak of a historical event directly influences the way that we think about it.

Take, for example, the question of rights—particularly those rights enumerated in the Constitution's Bill of Rights. I have pointed out elsewhere that the way we speak about the origin of rights reflects and influences the way that people from different perspectives think about what a "right" is. We speak, often, of rights being granted by the government rather than of rights as originating with the individual and then being recognized by the government. This means that when the 21st century speaks about equality in common parlance we tend to speak of it, without much thought, as having been brought about by particular policies. The Civil Rights Act of 1963 established racial equality. The 19th amendment established women's right to vote. The ERA, had it passed, would have established gender equality. Even more common is the use of the word "gave" in this context. On exams, for example, students are routinely asked to identify which amendments gave which rights to blacks, or women, or people over the age of 18.

The frequent use of constructions that imply and enshrine a top-down approach to rights that makes them appear to be inextricably a part of the "made order" of government regulation, legislation, and policy can be problematic, particularly for those who are concerned with equality. The suggestion of such a construction is that "the people" are not equal until the government makes them equal. What we lose when we adopt these constructions—or when we unthinkingly read right over them—is the radical voice of individuals asserting that their equality always already exists.

That radical voice of individuals asserting their equality is the voice that classical liberal feminist historians are well placed to hear and to explore seriously. And that is a voice that is well worth recapturing, not only for its historical radicalism, but also as a model for a modern-day political rhetoric that puts the focus on actions and rights of individuals rather than governments. This same phrasing question—about rights that are "granted by the government" or that exist already and cannot be infringed by the government—has long been central to debates over same-sex marriage, over privacy, and over gun ownership. Close and careful attention to this kind of linguistic matter both in the material we explore and in our discussions of that material may be the smallest, but most significant, value that classical liberal feminist history can add.

The U.S. legal scholar Gary Chartier observed recently in conversation that "As long as there is an entity that has the aggressive power of the state, there will be those who have a closer relationship with it and that will affect their material welfare."[16] The challenge for those who do classical liberal feminist history is to focus on those women who have resisted the temptation to form that tempting alliance with the state in an attempt to leash its aggressive power to their desired ends and have instead worked toward those ends from a position outside of and in opposition to the power of the state, to ask new questions about them and about long-established topics, and to attend closely to the language in what we study and in what we produce. These individuals and the events they have shaped are not hard to find. Those with an interest in telling the classical liberal stories of women's history just need to remember to look for them and to remind others of their existence.

NOTES

1. Jane Austen, *Northanger Abbey* (Boston: Little Brown and Co., 1903), 129.

2. Joan Kirner at *Women Into Power Conference*, Adelaide, October 1994 (Accessed online at http://www.australianinspiration.com.au/Quotes/Authors/K/ KirnerJoan.aspx).

3. Bella Abzug. (Accessed online at http://womenshistory.about.com/cs/quotes/a/ qu_bella_abzug.htm).

4. June Hannam, "Women's History, Feminist History." *Making History: The Changing Face of the Profession in Britain* (Accessed online at http://www.history. ac.uk/makinghistory/resources/articles/womens_history.html).

5. Classical liberal feminism is not, of course, limited to an anti-state feminism. This is, however, the aspect of classical liberal feminism which is most neglected. Other parts of classical liberal feminism such as the history of voluntary associations, opposition to a wide range of injustices, and the fight for suffrage are studied more often as a part of a general women's history. On voluntary associations, see: Anne Firor Scott, *Natural Allies: Women's Associations in American History.* University of Illinois Press, 1992 and Sara M. Evans, *Born for Liberty: A History of Women in America.* Free Press, 1989, particularly chapter 4, "The Age of Association." Academic discussions of suffrage and of feminist opposition to injustice are too numerous to catalogue here, though Bonnie S. Anderson and Judith P. Zinsser provide an extensive discussion of both in *A History of Their Own: Women in Europe from Prehistory to the Present.* Harper and Row, 1988.

6. See, for example, the works of scholars like Elaine Hobby, Margaret Ezell, and Linda Woodbridge, as well as the Women Writers Project begun by Brown University and carried on by Northeastern University.

7. Scholars like Wendy McElroy and Sharon Presley have revived interest in early classical liberal/libertarian/anarchist women like Voltairine de Cleyre, the Grimke sisters, Suzanne la Follette, and others. John Blundell's collection of short biographies in *Ladies for Liberty* provides useful starting points for young researchers. Roderick Long and Charles Johnson's essay "Libertarian Feminism: Can This Marriage be Saved?" gives a useful outline of the history of libertarian feminism, particularly in 19th-century England and America. Joan Kennedy Taylor's *Reclaiming the Mainstream* outlines the participation of individualist feminists throughout the history of the women's movement, and Aileen S. Kraditor's *The Ideas of the Women's Suffrage Movement 1890–1920* is at the same time a useful look at the multiplicity of feminisms active in the early 20th-century women's movement and a document from the women's movement of the 1960s.

8. Charlotte Otten's editorial and introductory material in *English Women's Voices, 1540–1700,* Ed. Charlotte Otten (Miami, Florida International University

Press, 1992) provides a useful introduction to some of these issues about the treatment of women by organized religion in an early modern context.

9. Margaret Fell, "Women's Speaking Justified." 1665/6 (Accessed online at http://www.qhpress.org/texts/fell.html).

10. Aemilia Lanyer, "Salve Deus Rex Judaeorum," in *The Poems of Aemilia Lanyer*. Ed. Suzanne Woods. Women Writers in English 1350–1850. Oxford: Oxford University Press, 1993.

11. General discussions of the history of questions of legal equality for women can be found in works like *Feminist Legal History, Essays on Women and the Law,* Tracy A Thomas and Tracey Jean Boisseau (NYU press, 2011), *Feminist Legal Theory: A Primer,* Nancy Levit, et al. (NYU Press, 2016) and *Women and the Law: Stories,* Elizabeth Schneider, et al (Foundation Press, 2010).

12. Voltairine De Cleyre, "Why I am an Anarchist." 1897. (Accessed online at http://praxeology.net/VC-WIA.htm).

13. Emma Goldman, "Woman Suffrage," in *Anarchism and Other Essays*. Second Revised Edition (New York & London: Mother Earth Publishing Association, 1911), 201–217.

14. D.L. Chandler. "British Rulers Spark 'Golden Stool' War With Ashanti Tribe On This Day In 1900." (Accessed online at http://newsone.com/2312442/queen-asantewaa-ghana).

15. Margaret Dawes and Nesta Selwyn's, *Women who Made Money: Women Partners in British Private Banks, 1752–1906* and Anne Laurence, Josephine Maltby, and Janette Rutterford, eds., *Women and Their Money, 1700–1950: Essays on Women and Finance* (New York: Routledge, 2009) provide some useful starting points but little or no extended analysis of the businesswomen they consider. Nicola Phillips *Women in Business 1700–1850* takes a more thorough look at similar subject matter.

16. Personal conversation with the author.

Chapter 9

Classical Liberalism in Eastern Europe

Very Vibrant but So Mild

Leonid Krasnozhon and Mykola Bunyk

1. INTRODUCTION

In Eastern Europe, classical liberalism entered academic and aristocratic circles in the eighteenth century. Even members of the royal families displayed their trendiness by espousing a familiarity with Voltaire or Diderot. While classical liberal movement was very vibrant in Eastern Europe between the eighteenth and the nineteenth centuries, it had no profound effect on political development until the early twentieth century. In the 1920s a Russian classical liberal, Alexander Chayanov (1888–1937), applied Mykhaylo Tugan-Baranovksy's theory of cooperation in the debate on collectivization policy with Vladimir Lenin. The debate received attention from international scholars and influenced Lenin's decision to replace the War Communism Policy (1918–1921) with more liberal policy, the New Economic Policy.[1] After the death of Lenin in 1924, the Stalinist regime reversed the New Economic Policy, imprisoned Chayanov for a political crime in 1930, and executed him in 1937.

Except for a Ukrainian-born historian and political economist, Mykhaylo Tugan-Baranovsky (1865–1919),[2] many Eastern European liberal scholars are ignored in the European history of classical liberal movement. Sima and Nikodym (2015)[3] described a very vibrant tradition of classical liberalism in the Czech Republic. They wrote that Emil Sax, professor of economics in Prague, published *Grundlegung der theoretischen Staatswirtschaft* (1888), which Friedrich Hayek (1934) called "the first and the most exhaustive attempt to apply the marginal utility principle to the problems of public finance." Some of the Czech thinkers rubbed shoulders with the giants of the classical liberal movement. Sima and Nikodym (2015) wrote that Ludwig von Mises praised a Czech classical liberal, Sigfried von Strakosch, who

coauthored an essay with him in 1919 "for being the only advisor to the
Austria's minister of agriculture who realized that regulation and protection
of agriculture are steps toward socialism." However, the European history
of classical liberalism mostly ignores Czech, Ukrainian, Russian, and other
Eastern European liberal thinkers.

This chapter outlines the key thinkers in the Eastern European classical
liberal tradition. Mykhaylo Drahomanov, Ivan Franko, Mykhaylo Tugan-
Baranovsky, and Bogdan Kistyakivsky presented a vibrant classical liberal
tradition among Russian and Ukrainian historians. Their movement had unifying features of support of gradual social change, rejection of Marxist socialism, skepticism of big government, and opposition to imperialism. Also, the
liberal thinkers who were Ukrainian-born raised a very important question
of how to create a classical liberal society in Ukraine while managing the
political economy issues of self-determination, state-building, and economic
development short of war with the Russian Empire. Though the Ukrainian
liberals held various convictions about the right answers, they believed that
their main task was to adapt European liberalism to the Ukrainian circumstances. Their main concern was that Marxist socialism would sway general
public and revolutionary youth if the liberal movement failed to make concessions on social issues.

2. BETWEEN RATIONALISM AND PLURALISM

In Eastern Europe, classical liberal thinkers developed political theories by
building on their experience of having watched the liberalism unfold in the
Habsburg Empire. Russian-born classical liberal thinkers also had to look to
the west for historical examples of liberalism because the Russian Empire
lagged behind the European liberal movement. If the Habsburg Empire abolished serfdom in the 1780s, the Russian monarchy emancipated serfs only in
the 1860s. A Ukrainian-born historian, Mykhaylo Drahomanov (1841–1895),
who was comparing a state of political freedom in Austria and Russia noted
that "in 1878 a political dissident would be sentenced to three months in Gali-
cian jail in Austria but from six to twelve year in Siberian prison in Russia."[4]
A fear of political prosecution was another unifying feature of the Russian
classical liberal thinkers. Drahomanov who was the leading figure in the classical liberal movement in the Russian Empire lost his faculty position at the
Kyiv University because of his political activity and he had to immigrate to
Switzerland.

The economic crisis of 1873, however, discredited liberal ideas in the eyes
of intellectuals and general public by pushing them closer to socialism. The
growing labor movement raised social issues and questioned an ability of

liberalism to solve various socioeconomic issues ranging from social justice to equality. At the same time, the Western European thinkers struggled to resolve an internal conflict of the liberalism between equality and liberty by separating an egalitarian and a liberal (Lal, 2010).[5] Since J. S. Mill's *Principles* the historical development of economic liberal thought had always left place for public financing of the "deserving poor." The growing labor movement, however, believed that public financing of the "deserving poor" would not resolve the socioeconomic issues and exploitation of workers by capitalists. In the aftermath of the 1873 economic crisis, the rise of revolutionary attitudes in the labor movement made liberal thinkers realize that the internal conflict of the movement would have to emphasize a social safety net.

2.1 Mykhaylo Drahomanov as a Leader of the Eastern European Liberalism

In *Rationalism, Pluralism, and Freedom* (2015) Jacob Levy argues that European liberal thought evolved along a rationalist/pluralist distinction:

> On one side of this divide lies a liberalism I will call "pluralist": skeptical of the central state and friendly toward local, customary, voluntary, or intermediate bodies, communities, and associations. On the other side we see a liberalism I will call "rationalist": committed to intellectual progress, universalism, and equality before a unified law, opposed to arbitrary and irrational distinctions and inequalities, and determined to disrupt local tyrannies in religious and ethnic groups, closed associations, families, plantations, the feudal countryside, and so on.

Mykhaylo Drahomanov (1841–1895) was the key figure in the rationalist liberal movement in the Russian Empire. He was a graduate of the Department of History and Linguistics at the Kyiv University, where he worked as a Docent of Ancient History until he was dismissed for political activity and immigrated to Switzerland. Several years before his immigration, Drahomanov spent three years conducting archival research in Heidelberg, Berlin, Rome, and Vienna. During his years in Geneva (1876–1889), he continued scholarly and journalist activity, including founding the first Ukrainian-language sociopolitical journal *Hromada*, with a readership audience in both Austrian and Russian empires. Drahomanov spent his last years as a professor of history at Sofia University.

Drahomanov's political thought developed along two main principles: personal liberty and personal happiness. Similar to Aristotle, he envisaged a liberal social order as a socially cooperative union of language-based voluntary associations that would establish a sociopolitical equality among European countries. Drahomanov ([1878] 1937a) argued that the main social value was not the highest public good rather it was individual happiness. "People join a community only in order," Drahomanov ([1878] 1937a) wrote, "to achieve an individual happiness." He argued that voluntary association should not constrain a personal liberty and it should be free of aristocratic privilege:

> Union of people, big or small, will consist of free people who come together for joint work and mutual help. There is no state that has this social order in the world. ... Our goal is anarchy where each individual, each community, each union is free.

Drahomanov, however, drew a distinction between community-based anarchy and social utopia. He stated that his theory was not practical; rather it was a philosophical ideal that every society should strive for. To achieve the ideal, people should follow the principles for social reform (cultural rationalism, political federalism, and social democracy) and pursue the goals of social development (public education, intellectual progress, and secularization).

Drahomanov (ibid.) explained why public education, intellectual progress, and secularization were the essential goals of social change:

> The ideal society has no place for clergy and religion where the latter produces clergy, which is a hierarchy and aristocracy by itself, and causes conflict among people. Free science should replace religion so that scientific progress will give people opportunities to do any kind of work such as manual, intellectual, and administrative. None will do only one kind of work. The intellectual work is only aristocratic privilege now. As a result, the learned people are separated from the unlearned ones. And these things (intellectual work) are not easy or short.

Next, Drahomanov argued that social change should be gradual instead of revolutionary. A community-based bottom-up gradual change, as he believed, should drive a social reform. He even coined a new term for social change—*évolution sociale* instead of *révolution sociale*. Drahomanov (ibid.) pointed out that:

> in Europe those who are better off lead the social reform while those are worse off follow them. The most successful reforms are found in those places where the old regime went through the largest number of small changes, not the smallest number of small changes.

Drahomanov ([1878] 1937a) adamantly opposed the violent methods of social change which were popularized by *narodnyky* and Russian liberal socialists in that period of time:

As a matter of fact, I gradually became increasingly opposed to Russian revolutionaries. In addition to their pan-Russian centralization, anti-cultural tendency, *narodnyky* illusions, and Machiavellian methods, I differed from them in their high regard for political assassination as a principle of revolutionary change, which they referred to as "terror." I considered terror as a natural, though pathological, response to a government terror.[6]

Beginning in the 1860s, the radical youth movement, *narodnyky*, emerged in the Russian Empire. As the term implies, the radical young intelligentsia identified with the people (*narod*), mainly peasants. That movement idealized peasant and rural commune, which seemed to demonstrate the peasant's natural opposition to self-interest and inborn tendency toward socialism (Subtelny, 2009).[7]

The *narodnyky* proposed to transition from rural communal society to socialism by skipping a stage of capitalism. A heated debate developed among the radical youth about the most effective means of transition toward socialism. One group led by Russian anarchist Mikhail Bakunin called for violent actions that would ignite a massive uprising. Another group headed by Russian *narodnyk* Petr Lavrov favored a gradual approach to revolution by preparing masses through education and propaganda. Drahomanov ([1880] 1937b) demonstrated skepticism of Marxist socialist political philosophy adapted by *narodnyky* and Russian liberal socialists:

we tend to believe that federation and anarchy have been sacred words for Russian socialists since the times of Herzen and Bakunin, but their activity is similar to Jacobinism, rather than a federalization that we discussed earlier.[8]

Since Drahomanov rejected the idea of political terror as a means of social change, he advocated for a cultural and gradual approach to social change ([1878] 1937a):

Unless there would be a change in mentality, customs, and economic order, neither rebellion nor revolution would achieve its goal … . An uprising can begin to awaken the public mind, can end the old orders which have been undermined by all other methods, but it cannot create a new order, neither social nor economic. Even overthrown order, especially social and economic, eventually comes back 'the next day after the uprising' when a new order cannot satisfy economic needs of people. As a rule, people do not wait too long to satisfy their economic needs.

To Drahomanov, liberalization was a spontaneously emergent order that evolved and moved in a bottom-up direction through a system of voluntary associations of individuals by gradually eradicating the state as an institution of coercion. He wrote that the main objective of liberalization was "to reduce the power of the government and make it subservient to individual and community and to lay down the living rule of law of anarchy, free of aristocracy and state." Drahomanov's theory of social change focused on two main ideas: one, a dichotomy between a voluntary association of individuals, the civil society, and an institution of coercion, the state; two, liberalization as a bottom-up gradual social reform.

Since Locke, civil society has been "the self-contained and unified political society that can apply a general law and that excludes external claims to political power" (Levy, 2015). Marx and Hegel changed our understanding of civil society by conjoining commercial civil society and legal civil society. They coined a term of *bourgeois society* to describe the legal regime that recognized only bourgeois citizens as free and equal. As a Ukrainian-born liberal thinker, Drahomanov (ibid.) theorized that even though there was no sovereign Ukrainian state, Ukrainian civil society continued to persist. The Russian Empire, as he conceived, was the institution of coercion and national hegemony. The empire needed to be replaced with a federation of sovereign nations. It could be achieved through a gradual bottom-up liberalization of people, communities, and nations and through cooperation with other nations. That would be the solution to the Ukrainian question of how to manage self-determination and nation-building short of war with Russia.

Drahomanov (ibid.) wrote that:

> Ukraine will not be alone in its gradual liberalization which is an effective and smart approach. Other federalists from different nations and from the Russian empire will step on the path towards federalization.

Finally, Drahomanov (1883) disagreed with the dialectics method of historical study of social change. He argued that you should not look at human behavior through production-exploitation relationship framework because human behavior was driven by multiple factors, including cultural and geographic.[9] Drahomanov (1937c) wrote that:

> Human life is so complex that we cannot explain it by focusing on a single determinant. But I do not oppose to a unilateral theory as long as it encourages a new study. Unfortunately, Marxists rarely research their theories; they simply prescribe *a priori* historical and political models, often quite unrealistic.[10]

2.2 Tugan-Baranovsky's Eclectic Liberalism

Mykhaylo Tugan-Baranovsky (1865–1919), a Ukrainian-born historian and political economist, was a representative of pluralist liberal thought in the Russian Empire. His political thought evolved in a very eclectic theory under influence of Neo-Kantianism, Darwinism, Classical School of Economics, and Marxism. The eclecticism of his work influenced many Eastern European liberals. As a young scholar, Tugan-Baranovsky came under the influence of Marxism and later he read Menger's *Principles* (1871) (Kachor, 1969).[11] Menger had a major influence on him as a thinker. First, Tugan-Baranovsky used Menger's marginal theory of value to attack Marx's labor theory of value. Second, he accepted the Mengerian theory of spontaneous order in his work on cooperation.

Tugan-Baranovsky argued that liberalism was historically predetermined to fail in Russia because most intellectuals held anti-bourgeois beliefs. In *Russian Intelligentsia and Socialism* ([1910] 1996: 57) Tugan-Baranovsky wrote that:

> In Western Europe, individual did not have to make a choice between socialism and liberalism. Liberalism emerged naturally through social reforms and economic development. By contrast, Russian intellectual was disconnected from realities of his motherland and thus he chose an ideology from a rational point of view. Socialism attracted them by its cosmopolitanism and superhistorical ideology.[12]

In Russia, education was available only to aristocracy and clergy. Unlike in Western Europe, Russian intellectuals did not come from families of farmers or manufacturers and they did not develop any appreciation for a role of market economy in the social development. He wrote:

> In Russia, aristocrats envisaged socialism as a topic for intellectual discussion, not as a threat to their rule. Russian aristocracy was awakened only when several aristocrats organized uprising of revolutionary socialism (in 1905). (ibid.)

In the 1903 *Notes on the Newest History of Political Economy*, Tugan-Baranovsky demonstrated another feature of his eclectic theory by defending capitalism against Marxist socialism and agreeing that Marxist socialism would replace capitalism. Contra to Marx, Tugan-Baranovsky (ibid., 418) argued that one could not prove logically the imminent end of capitalism: "despite its popularity, Marxist theory has not been formulated and proved yet."[13] In his attempt to broaden social issues of the liberalism, he drew a distinction between socialism and Marxism. While the former was feasible and consistent with ethics, the latter was economically impossible and inconsistent with ethics:

> the crisis of Marxism, in my opinion, proves that socialism is not in demise, rather on its rise ... . The Kantian idea of the self-centeredness of individual is sufficient to ethically justify socialism. All ethical pathos around socialism stems from this idea which is consciously or subconsciously presumed by every

socialist. The logic of the Kantian idea inevitably leads to socialism ... . That Marxist social philosophy fundamentally denies ethics is self-inflicted error.[14]

Moreover, Tugan-Baranovsky offered an eclectic socioeconomic system that would combine a capitalist organization of economic life with a socialist organization of social life. The hybrid system would achieve a harmony between equality and liberty:

> private property, profit motive, and self-interest drive economic development though these forces create economic inequality. Abandonment of these economic principles will be equal to destroying humankind. Capitalism economy must be upheld and adopted to provision of public goods.[15]

The proposition that market economy was a social spontaneous emergent institution which he adopted from Menger implied that it would take a social change to disrupt the evolution of market economy and to replace it with the new social order. Tugan-Baranovsky (1903: 420) wrote that:

> spontaneous emergent institution cannot stop its evolution—new economic order may emerge as a result of voluntary social change which adapts society to new and superior ethics. New economic order will emerge when a current economic order will be abandoned by new social order.

However, he pointed out that (Zlupko, 1993: 158):

> Russian anarchists (*narodnyky*) who call for social revolution force their will upon others and thus they lead us to state socialism that is a coercive order of the society. Social coercion of individual liberty is immoral. Kant, the greatest philosopher of our time, said that ideal society must have free individuals.[16]

Tugan-Baranovsky considered free will the highest public good. The question of how to secure individual liberty without violating liberty of others preoccupied his thinking. Tugan-Baranovsky conjectured that neither capitalism nor state socialism could solve that question. He wrote (ibid.):

> Free will is the highest public good. If I had to choose between prosperity and free will, I would always choose the latter. Poverty does not strip you of the dignity; deprivation of free will takes your dignity away. Without the free will, civilization and culture cannot exist because humankind that is deprived of free will loses all morality. Hardship does not belittle a person; the loss of free will enslaves a person by turning a person into a tool of someone's; it destroys humanity.

When Tugan-Baranovsky (ibid., 159–161) considered capitalism as an ideal society, he pointed out that capitalism could not solve the tradeoff between liberty and equality:

> There is no doubt that a formal personal liberty, which exists in capitalist society, does not represent realistically freedom of all people. On the contrary, economic inequality, which emerges in capitalist society, curbs liberty of majority of the population and gives more liberty to economically powerful minority. As a result, the capitalist society cannot achieve a harmony between personal liberty and collective liberty.

In his opinion, socialism was more a harmonious social system than capitalism, though socialism had a tendency toward totalitarian regime:

> In terms of the ideal of a free society, state socialism trumps capitalism. State socialism subjects individual interest to collective interest and thus social will is greater under socialism than under capitalism because the latter subjects the will of a majority to the will of a minority. Contra to free will, both socialism and capitalism use coercion … . State socialism will leave no room for individual decision-making, socialist society will plan every part of our lives … . Thus, *correct socialism* must have two parts: coercive state and free state.

Tugan-Baranovsky searched for a social order that he referred to as *correct socialism* which would secure equality, personal liberty, and free-market economy. In search of a model for the *correct socialism*, he developed a theory of cooperation that, as he thought, combined both economic principles of capitalism and social principles of socialism (ibid., 173–174):

> As a social order, cooperation has the broadest scope of liberty. Unlike anarchy, it is realistic. Anarchy is simply a social order with absolute personal liberty. Cooperation is non-coercive social order and built on freedom of association. Individual interest will give in to group interest naturally through cooperation … . As an alternative to capitalism, cooperation is the next evolutionary stage of social development which leads to anarchy. In future, society will consist of many cooperatives without any state, any centralization, and any coercion.

Tugan-Baranovsky had formulated his eclectic theory of social order in the 1916 *Social Foundations of Cooperation* that became the study guide for every member and scholar of cooperative.[17] The primary objective of cooperation was to combine socialist welfare with capitalist economy. As a profit-maximizing enterprise in free-market economy, the cooperative would provide social safety net to its members. Since everyone would join cooperatives, everyone would work in a capitalist economy with a universal welfare system. Cooperation would free people from mutual exploitation. Cooperatives would have two types: producer and ownership. The former would perform the following functions: distribution, consumption, banking, and construction. The latter would guarantee employment and production. The crux of his theory was to show that cooperation would solve the political economy issues of self-determination and nation-building. He argued that a union of cooperatives would establish a democratic decentralized system of governance that would be similar to federalism. The cooperative social order would not lead to interventionism or totalitarianism and it would make Ukraine an equal partner of Russia.

Tugan-Baranovsky developed his theory of cooperation by building on his experience of watching the development of cooperative movement in Kharkov province, his birthplace. The fact that the wave of the Russian cooperative movement started in Kharkov in 1811, preceding the Rochdale cooperative in England, had a major influence on his thinking. It was a very important historical fact for Tugan-Baranovsky because his early work had studied the history of the British industrial revolution.[18] Furthermore, he attended the Kharkov University (now V. N. Karazin Kharkov National University) that was established by a prominent cooperator, Vasily Karazin (1773–1842). In 1854, Kharkov led the cooperative movement of Eastern Europe as a home for the biggest agricultural cooperative, *Kharkovskoe Tovarishestvo*. The cooperative started its operations with fourteen regional offices across Ukraine and Russia. In 1912 it grew into the biggest cooperative in Eastern Europe with thirty-four regional offices, including a whole-sale store in Minneapolis, USA (Ancyferov, 1929).[19] The Bolshevist Revolution of 1917 led by Vladimir Lenin brought communists and Marxist socialist to the power in the Russian Empire. To them, a cooperative was a product of bourgeois society and incompatible with socialism.

2.3 Toward Contractarianism and Constitutionalism

Ivan Franko (1856–1916), a Ukrainian historian and political economist, dedicated most of his work to understanding a nature and role of the state. He received a PhD in History from the University of Vienna. Along with other historians, Ostap Terletsky (1850–1902) and Ivan Lutschizky (1845–1918), Franko belonged to the Ruthenian (now Ukrainian) group of classical liberal historians.[20] The Ruthenian group shared liberal views of the younger German Historical School and followed the *Social-Politik* movement for social reform of historians and economists, led by Gustav Schmoller (1838–1917), across German-speaking Europe. Nonetheless, Ruthenian historians differed from the younger German historicists in their vision of social reform. To them, it served as a means of nation-building for a stateless nation, not imperialism.

Franko who studied the effect of the social reforms implemented by the Austrian rulers, Maria Theresa (1740–1780) and Joseph II (1780–1790), supported active social policy but he remained skeptical of government. In Europe, at that time, general public perceived liberalism as a state-initiated social reform led by a liberal government.[21]

To Franko (1904), the state was a natural outcome of human progress and its power needed to be constrained by the rule of law:

> In every economy, there is an inborn tendency for someone to govern others. The bigger is economy, the greater is power of those who govern. With the greater power comes the greater responsibility of protecting each individual.

But he warned that Marxist socialism had a natural inclination toward totalitarianism (ibid.):

> In general, the omnipotence of communist state, as formulated in all ten points in *Communist Manifesto* (1848: 33), would lead to the triumph of new bureaucracy over society and all aspects of social, material, and spiritual life.[22]

It is interesting that Franko has formulated his political theory in the 1903 *"What is Progress?"* in response to Lenin's address to the 1903 Congress of the Russian Social Democratic Party.[23] Contra to Lenin, he argued that inequality was inevitable and pivotal driving force of human progress. A permanent and natural competition between people, as Franko thought, was the foundation of human nature and it always caused inequality. Franko (1903) wrote that:

> survival of the fittest is the source of human progress. People are in eternal competition with each other … . By contrast, equality is the greatest misfortune for people because it leads people towards indifference and inertness. But we should not be afraid of it because the nature makes sure that there is always inequality among people.

Another driving force of human progress, as Franko conceived, was the division of labor. On the one hand, he believed that the division of labor generated a social hierarchy that divided a *civil society* into rulers and ruled (ibid.):

> State divides people in lords and servants, imposes taxes on many and distributes wealth from many to a few, and sends people to war. The state enters our minds through education and religion by promoting its interests and eradicating opposing views … . The state curbs individual freedom by making individuals subservient to groups, groups to communities, communities to provinces, provinces to states, and states to the tyranny of elected officials.

On the other hand, Franko argued that the division of labor led to a personal and social progress. Like other representatives of Eastern European political thought, Franko struggled to reconcile a perceived skepticism of government with a natural need for a government and the internal conflict of liberalism between equality and liberty.

Finally, as a response to the growing Marxist socialist movement, Franko questioned political philosophy of the Marxist theory of state and its acceptance by Russian and Ukrainian social democrats (ibid.):

> Trust in omnipotent state in future society is the main feature of social democracy. According to this belief, every person will be a public employee and then he will receive retirement benefits: the state will give him all necessary things; assign him an occupation; incentivize and reward him; and when he will get older or sick, the state will feed him ... . Who will guard the guardian? Who will rule the state? Social democrats do not tell us anything; though these people will hold such a great power over lives and destinies of millions of their comrades that even tyrants cannot dream of. Then the old problem, inequality, that was kicked out through the doors would come back through the window: there would be no exploitation of workers by capitalist but there would be omnipotence of bureaucrats—it does not matter whether they are aristocrats or elected—who would be in control of millions of citizens. If they hold such a great power for a short period of time, it will be so easy for them to seize it forever!

Another representative of the Eastern European rationalist movement was Bogdan Kistyakivsky (1868–1920), Ukrainian-born Russian legal scholar and sociologist. He received a PhD in History from the University of Strasbourg in 1898 where he was influenced by the younger German Historical School, Wilhelm Windelband (1848–1915) and Georg Friedrich Knapp (1842–1926). Kistyakivsky described his political thought in the 1898 dissertation *Society and Individual*. Contra to German historicists, he opposed a pursuance of active state-initiated social reform. Kistyakivsky ([1898] 1996: 238) limited a role of government to protecting life, liberty, and property under the rule of law:[24]

> The state evolves from unjust wars that lead to the subjugation and enslavement of weak and small nations by great and powerful ones. The state always relies on coercion and puts it above all; by being the embodiment of power, the state makes all people bow to it ... . Historically, the states that used coercion and violence against their people ceased to exist and new states emerged in order to play a natural role of state, meeting the needs of the people.

The state, as he thought, was a part of civil society where the state and a *cultured individual* are interdependent. By using the term *cultured individual*,

Kistyakivsky implied that civil society needed educated and well-mannered individuals. He put emphasis on legal education or teachings of justice. The role of government should be limited to pursuing common interests and achieving the Aristotelian highest public good (ibid., 239). Nonetheless, Kistyakivsky demonstrated skepticism of government by making a distinction between the *rule of law* and the *police state*. The rule of law was an outcome of social development and the highest form of government that served individual interest and protected personal liberty.

To Kistyakivsky, the rule of law limited the power of government while the police state was an institution of unconstrained coercion. He metaphorically spoke of the Russian Empire as the police state and the Austrian Empire as the rule of law (ibid., 243):

> The rule of law puts state in certain boundaries which it cannot overstep. Individualism and personal liberty constrain the state. The rule of law or the constitutional state recognized that personal self-determination and self-expression should be beyond the state control.

The police state, as he conceived, was juxtaposition to the rule of law (ibid., 253):

> There is no other form of governance in the world, beside the police state, that hurts human dignity so much. By scorning a person, the police state also loses any personal and public initiative. It is replaced by detailed and formulated regulation casuistically. Any public or private initiative is seen as a threat to the state and thus public associations are outlawed and people are disengaged.

The more Kistyakivsky thought about the rule of law, the deeper grew his appreciation of constitutional democracy. His theory of constitutional democracy was strikingly similar to the American and French constitutional thinkers:

> A state did not create inalienable rights of individuals; on the contrary, the inalienability feature implied that a person received it directly. The following inalienable rights are the foundation for the constitutional state: freedom of conscience ... it implies the freedom of religion ... it implies freedom of speech and freedom of press ... it implies the freedom of union and association ... it implies universal suffrage. Voting should not have any aristocratic or group privileges. Every vote must be equal. To ensure universal suffrage, voting must be direct and secret .... Today the requirement of universal, equal, and direct suffrage by secret vote is the main requirement of democracy.[25]

Next, Kistyakivsky (ibid.) believed that the police state would lead to anarchy because it was incompatible with the social justice:

In society where the rule of law is enforced by command and control the public is prevented from self-governance and thus it has no incentive to enforce a socially cooperative behavior. A wave of anarchy will hit this society when an old rule of law will fall apart and a new rule of law is not designed yet. In a police state the rule of law is never sustainable in the long-run if it is not grounded in social justice. Police state is antagonistic to active social justice. The latter is always seen as public intervention in the state domain … . By contrast, the rule of law precludes anarchy because people govern themselves by performing legal and executive activities. By being founded on and adapting to social justice, the state changes when the social justice changes. In addition to the rule of law, the state involves broad public and social associations which promote its governance.

However, Kistyakivsky's political thought started gravitating toward liberal socialism when he was describing an ideal society. The ideal society, as he thought, would reach harmony, on the one hand, by using a means of public learning of ethics and individual rejection of both egoism and materialism, and, on the other hand, by using a means of increasing cultural opportunities, expanding *solidarity*, and strengthening human dignity. His concept of *solidarity* assumed an abolishment of private ownership of means of production as a safeguard of decent human existence and safeguard against anarchy. At the same time, as a legal scholar, Kistyakivsky rejected Marxist socialism because it lacked any description of socialist law. Marxists considered the rule of law a part of *bourgeois society* and thus dynamic laws of historical development would replace the rule of law with the socialist law. Kistyakivsky (ibid., 272) agreed that socialism would come out of inexorable necessity but he stressed that the socialist law would be a system of social justice as the next stage in historical development of the rule of law. Thus, he believed that an ideal socialism should enforce and secure both social justice and personal liberty.

It is interesting that the Eastern European liberal thinkers have had a historical precedent on their side. In the late nineteenth century, socialists and *narodnyky* acknowledged that the Ukrainian village was the main obstacle to the spread of their ideas throughout Eastern Europe. Individualism and private land ownership historically evolved as the unifying social values for Ukrainians (Subtelny, 2009; Hrushevs'kyi, 1941). Ukrainian peasants, as they conceived, developed historically an attraction to self-interest and tendency toward individualism and liberalism. Ukrainian socialist revolutionary, Mykola Starodvorsky, admitted that in Ukraine "matters are different. Our people are bourgeois because they are permeated by the instincts of private ownership" (Subtelny, 2009: 361). Starodvorsky pointed out that the national inclination toward private ownership meant that Ukraine "might serve as a barrier to the spread of the socialist idea in Russia" (ibid.).

In the mid-19th century, over 85 percent of the peasants in Eastern Ukraine (under the Russian rule) and almost 70 percent in Western Ukraine (under the Austrian rule) worked individual homesteads (ibid., 256). By contrast, 95 percent of Russian peasants worked and lived in communes (ibid). Since the earliest civilizations, individual farming was more wide-spread in Ukraine than in Russia because both fertile soil and favorable climate conditions significantly increased individual agricultural productivity in Ukraine (Subtelny, 2009; Conquest, 1986; Hrushevs'kyi, 1941).[26] In Russia that was mainly to the north of Ukraine poor sandy soil and harsh climate made it hard to farm individually. A growing season was shorter in Russia by at least a month than in Ukraine. Thus, Russian peasants historically tended to farm collectively while Ukrainian peasants could often farm individually (Subtelny, 2009).

At the same time, agricultural revolution that was unfolding throughout Europe supported liberal values by shifting farming from feudal (manor-serf) toward individual. Farmers witnessed greater yields of vegetables, including two important American crops, potato and maize (Spielvogel, 2014). For rural countries such as Ukraine, the agricultural revolution was a pivotal economic change. Peasants comprised 93 percent of Ukrainians by the end of the 19th century (Krawchenko, 1985).[27] Ukraine exported one-fourth of the world's supply of grain (Subtelny, 2009). Industrialization came to Ukraine in the mid-20th century, much later than in Austria, Poland, and Russia. The first blast furnace was built in Ukraine in 1921 (Moroz, 2012: 12).[28] Thus, the Eastern European liberal thinkers witnessed a very important historical development that was favorable toward their movement. Somehow, liberalism received very little support among farmers. Socialism won over their minds.

3. CONCLUSION

In Eastern Europe classical liberalism lost to Marxist socialism in the battle of ideas of social change though the classical liberal tradition was a substantial current. It followed the Western European liberal tradition and developed along two main strands, rationalism and pluralism. The chapter outlined the key thinkers in the Eastern European classical liberal tradition: Mykhaylo Drahomanov, Ivan Franko, Mykhaylo Tugan-Baranovsky, and Bogdan Kistyakivsky. Their movement had unifying features of gradual social change, rejection of Marxist socialism, emancipation of captive nations from imperialism, and skepticism of big government and active social policy. Most of their work was a response to the growing labor movement in the Russian Empire, led by Marxist socialist and *narodnyky*. Pressed by the advancement of Marxist socialism, the Eastern European liberal thinkers searched for theories to mitigate the internal conflict of the Western European liberalism between equality and liberty. Though they held various convictions about the right answers, the liberal intellectuals agreed that their main task was to adapt the Western European liberal tradition to the Eastern European circumstances. Their main concern was that Marxist socialism would sway away general public and revolutionary intellectual youth if the liberal movement failed to make concessions on social issues. The liberal intellectuals warned that Marxism would lead to totalitarianism and thus it would preclude Eastern European nations such as Ukraine and Poland from self-determination and state-building. Though the classical liberals looked for a theory that could reduce economic inequality short of curbing individual freedom and fringing upon private property rights, they failed to win over minds of revolutionary intellectual youth and general public.

NOTES

1. The New Economic Policy gave peasants usufruct private property rights (i.e., sale and bequest are prohibited) in agricultural land and allowed peasants to utilize farmland, to lease it, and to sell their farm produce at market prices. Joseph Stalin, Lenin's successor, feared that the thriving agricultural economy would lead to the rise of the bourgeois nationalism in the Soviet Ukraine. In the December 27, 1929, issue of *Pravda*, Stalin proclaimed in his address to the Communist Party of the Soviet Union that the state should teach the Ukrainian peasants "a lesson they would not forget," eradicate "bourgeois nationalism," and "liquidate them as a class." In 1929, Stalin reversed the New Economic Policy and returned farm collectivization.

2. Mykhaylo Tugan-Baranovsky was born in a family of aristocrats near Kharkov in Eastern Ukraine. He is less known for his work on political philosophy. But his theory of business cycles and his study of the British industrial revolution influenced Schumpeter's theory of economic development and works of British and American Keynesian economists.

3. Sima, Josef and Thomas Nikodym. 2015. "Classical Liberalism in the Czech Republic," *Econ Journal Watch* 12(2): 274–292.

4. Drahomanov, M. ([1878] 1937a). "Address to Hromada," *The Selected Works of Mykhaylo Drahomanov*, Vol. 1 in ed., Pavlo Bogatsky: Prague. Online source: http://www.ditext.com/drahomanov/selected/hromada-u.html

5. Lal, D. 2010. *Reviving the Invisible Hand: The Case for Classical Liberalism in the Twenty-first Century*. Princeton: Princeton University Press.

6. Drahomanov, Mykhaylo ([1878] 1937a). "Address to *Hromada*," *The Selected Works of Mykhaylo Drahomanov*, Vol. 1 in ed., Pavlo Bogatsky, Prague, the Czech Republic: Legiographia. Online source: http://www.ditext.com/drahomanov/selected/auto.html

7. Subtelny, Orest. 2009. *Ukraine: a history*. Toronto: University of Toronto Press.

8. Drahomanov, Mykhaylo ([1880] 1937b). "Little Russian Internationalism," *The Selected Works of Mykhaylo Drahomanov*, Vol. 1 in ed., Pavlo Bogatsky,

Prague, the Czech Republic: Legiographia. Online source: http://www.ditext.com/drahomanov/selected/internationalism.html

9. Mykhaylo Drahomanov. 1883. *Historical Poland and Pan-Russian Democracy.* Geneva, Switzerland: Rabotnik and Hromada Press.

10. Drahomanov, Mykhaylo ([1894–1895] 1937c). "Correspondence between Drahomanov and Yuriy Buchinsky," *The Selected Works of Mykhaylo Drahomanov*, Vol. 1 in ed., Pavlo Bogatsky, Prague, the Czech Republic: Legiographia. Online source: http://www.ditext.com/drahomanov/selected/shapoval.html

11. Kachor, Andriĭ. 1969. *Mykhaĭlo I. Tuhan-Baranovs'kyĭ.* Vinnipeg: Nakl. Ukraïns'koï vil'noï akademiï nauk.

12. Tugan-Baranovsky, M. ([1910] 1996). "Russian Intelligentsia and Socialism," *Russian Encyclopedia of Politics*, Rosspen: Moscow.

13. Tugan-Baranovsky, M. 1903. *Notes on the Newest History of Political Economy*, Saint Petersburg.

14. Tugan-Baranovsky, M. ([1912] 1996). "Kant and Marx," *The Selected Works of Tugan-Baranovsky*, *Russian Encyclopedia of Politics*, Rosspen: Moscow, 77. Tugan-Baranovsky, M. ([1912] 1996). "To Better Future," *The Selected Works of Tugan-Baranovsky*, *Russian Encyclopedia of Politics*, Rosspen: Moscow, 57.

15. Tugan-Baranovsky, M. 1907. *Notes on History of Political Economy and Socialism.* Saint Petersburg, 171.

16. Zlupko, Stepan. 1993. Mykhaylo Tugan-Baranovsky: a World-Known Ukrainian Economist (*Mykhaiylo Tuhan-Baranovsky: ukrainsy ekonomist svitovoi slavy*). Lviv: Kameniâř Press.

17. Tugan-Baranovsky, M. 1916. *Social'nya osnovy kooperacii.* Moskva: Moskovskij gorodskoj narodnyj universitet imeni A. L. Sanavskago.

18. Tugan-Baranovsky, M. I. 1894. *Promyshlennye krizisy v sovremennoĭ Anglii, ikh prichiny i vlianie na narodnuiu zhizn'. S prilozheniem 12 diagramm.* S-Peterburg: I.N. Skorokhodova.

19. Ancyferov, Aleksej Nikolaevič. 1929. *The cooperative movement in Russia during the war: credit and agricultural cooperation.* New Haven: Yale university press.

20. Ostap Terletsky was born in Galicia region of the Habsburg Empire. He was Ukrainian historian who received PhD in History from the University of Vienna in 1883. Ivan Lutschizky was a Russian and Ukrainian historian. He wrote *Peasants and Peasant Reform in Eastern Austria*, 1901 (Крестьяне и крестьянская реформа вь восточной Австріи) and *On the History of Land Tenure in Little Russia*, 1896 (Zur Geschichte der Grundeigenthumsformen in Kleinrussland).

21. Mantl, Wolfgang. Liberalismus und Antiliberalismus in Österreich. Eine Spurensuche, in: Liberalismus: Interpretationen und Perspektiven /hg. Von Emil Brix und Wolfgang Mantl.—Wien; Köln; Graz: Böhlau, 1996, 15–48.

22. Franko, Ivan, 1904. *History of Socialist Movement*, online source: http://www.i-franko.name/uk/Publicistics/1904/HistSocialist.html

23. Franko, Ivan. ([1903] 1986). "What is Progress?" The Selected Works of Ivan Franko, Vol. 44–47, in ed. J.P. Kyryljuk, Kyiv: Naukova Dumka press. Online source: http://www.ukrcenter.com/Література/Іван/Франко/25125/Що-таке-поступ.Lenin, Vladimir. 1903. "The Position of the Bund in the Party," *Iskra* 51 (October 22). Online source: https://www.marxists.org/archive/lenin/works/1903/oct/22a.htm

24. Kistyakivsky, Bogdan. ([1898]1996). "State and Individual," *The Selected Works of Bogdan Kistyakivsky*, Kyiv: Abris Press.

25. Ibid., 244, 250.

26. Conquest, R. 1986. *Harvest of Sorrow.* Oxford: Oxford University Press. Hrushevs'kyi, Mykhailo. 1941. *A History of Ukraine.* New Haven: Yale University Press.

27. Krawchenko, Bogdan. 1985. *Social Change and National Consciousness in Twentieth-Century Ukraine.* New York: St. Martin's Press.

28. Moroz, V. 2012. *Ukraïna u dvadtsiatomu stolitti* (Ukraine in the 20th Century), Lviv, Ukraine: Liha-Press.

Chapter 10

"Start the Economy"

Causation, Emergent Order, and Social Change in the Origins of Modern Economic Growth

Matthew Brown

A *New Yorker* cartoon features an image of the stereotypical king of popular historical imagination—crown, thrown, groveling servants—instructing his underlings to "start the economy." The cartoon helps introduce concepts such as emergent order, the elusive nature of the economic process, and misconceptions about how economic growth occurs. For our current purposes it illustrates a problem with how many historians have conceptualized the origins of modern economic growth.[1] Liberal history's focus on the interplay between human well-being and freedom warrants a, perhaps relentless, focus on how that relationship broke out of its millennia-long story of poverty and servitude. When exploring and discussing the origins of modern economic growth we confront a number of challenges which were present in the late eighteenth century when Scottish moral philosopher Adam Smith published the first great modern investigation of the topic. A topic that has been addressed in different ways, often less successfully, ever since.

Noticing a distinct trend toward greater economic activity in his own century, Smith explored "the nature and causes of the wealth of nations" in his famous 1776 book of the same name.[2] Smith's contribution goes well beyond his status as the "father of economics" as a discipline. He helped illuminate and clarify an emerging worldview and understanding of human progress that combined economic, social, ethical, and political spheres into a more coherent process and its crucial relationship to human freedom, which is a central focus of liberal history. As economist Ludwig von Mises observed in his introduction to a 1953 reprinting of the *Wealth of Nations*, Smith provided "the keystone, of a marvelous system of ideas … . They presented the essence of the ideology of freedom, individualism, and prosperity, with admirable clarity and in an impeccable literary form."[3] The unbundling of Smith's accomplishment into narrower approaches—history without Smith's insights on economics, or resource-focused economics without the bigger picture—is a source of much error in historical writing on the topic Smith tackled. Smith provides not only an early acknowledgment of, but also systematic explanation for, the emergence of perhaps the most important trend of the last quarter millennium: the divergence of incomes and economic performance among modern economies. Smith's choice of words is instructive in a number of ways.

1. Smith acknowledges a *sustained change in economic performance* and represents a solidification of the idea that economic performance was qualitatively and quantitatively different than the past. How historians have internalized this reality has had a significant influence on their resulting work for better and often worse.
2. That we *can and should identify a cause* and act on it. Smith was prescient to use the plural *causes* rather than the more pretentious and misguided contemporary academic standard *cause*, singular. But the question of causation has been central in the economic history writing about the modern world, and how the *cause(s)* are conceptualized and *what* they are explaining are crucial variables.
3. That *the nation is the unit of account*. Smith's inquiry specifically concerned the *wealth of nations*. This puts Smith squarely in the mold of modern scholarship across different topics, from economics, politics, culture, etc. that adopted the modern conception of the nation-state as the relevant unit of discussion. This approach has guided most work in the area ever since.

I will briefly, and by necessity, thinly, explore the literature related to the emergence of modern economic growth in light of Smith's three categorical identities with the goal of better understanding how a liberal approach to this most important of changes in the human condition can and should differ from (and also build upon) more dominant history writing on the topic.

1. Smith acknowledges a change in economic performance and represents a solidification of the idea that economic performance was different than the past. This is an idea so rooted in our current historical imagination as to go unrecognized as a guiding mental model in our own analysis, but it is a very modern conceptualization that would have been illogical at best, most likely incomprehensible, much before Smith's life in the eighteenth century. Studying this history of economic growth (as we typically refer to the pursuit) or economic performance[4] we tend to take the more deterministic or linear approach to history writing and assume that, growth, is just the natural way of things.

But, of course, *growth* is not the natural way of things. As economists, and classical liberal historians such as contributors to this book, point out—to the increasing frustration of historians and other humanists—*scarcity* and its off-spring *poverty* are the norm.[5] This distinction is more important than it may seem; it is not just an issue of semantics—but perhaps it is more correctly an issue of semantics *and* how they shape our understanding of not only the past, but the present, and how we conceptualize our questions and historical inquiries.[6] If *growth* and *wealth* are taken as the natural way of things it is only logical that one puts one's focus on *poverty*, particularly its *"causes,"* which is one of the failings of a great deal of modern history and humanities research—as well as twentieth-century economic policy, such as development economics, which never seemed to take the historic experiences of "developed" countries into the scope of its analysis.

Smith and most of his contemporaries were laboring under no such misleading mental model. His title gets the question right: *wealth* is the thing in need of explanation. Economic historians, with their grounding in at least some version of the economic way of thinking and its insistence on the necessity of choice based on scarcity, have generally done a good job of appreciating this, regardless of their ideological divides.[7] Historians and other humanists have not been as consistent in this regard. This is particularly obvious in various Marxian approaches, and sympathetic off-shoots, that take a more deterministic approach to history, as well as work in less-overtly Marixan critical theory in its various approaches in sociology, history, and literature. Any approach of this variety, in weak or strong forms, runs a serious risk of misdirecting the analysis away from the real issues and toward false identities created by the model.

An excessive focus on the poverty "caused" by the Industrial Revolution and related take-off of modern levels of economic growth is a prominent example of this type of error. E. P. Thompson was a leading proponent of this reimaging of the story among the "new left" with his work on the English working class in the Industrial Revolution.[8] Thompson's work, which is admirable in its focus on the records left by the workers and artisans who to that point were often left out of the historical narratives, is flawed in its over-attention paid to the damage or ravages caused by capitalism. The solidification of this mental model in the minds of many following historians has led to much mistaken analysis. Here both the assessment of the relative harm done to the poor and the distinct identifications of capitalism and not-capitalism are problematic over-simplifications. Fernand Braudel's famous trilogy on the emergence of capitalism is subject to a similar critique.[9] But Braudel does make the important distinction that fits within a liberal political economy analysis that "capitalists" are not necessarily toiling for social benefit, but rather interacting with governments to engage in rent seeking and protection or establishment of monopolies.[10] The over reliance on a model of either "capitalists are good and seek growth and human progress" or "capitalists are bad and seek exploitation and misery" are both overly simplified unhelpful mental models that shift the focus to abstract group-level analysis away from the incentives and social environment of individual agents.

This approach connects modern social/political debates about poverty and issues of income inequality directly into the historical narrative. The stories are crafted in such a way as to illuminate the human suffering and undeniable misery of this period experienced by a great many of its participants as the primary event or trend of the era. This suffering sets the stage for the ongoing tale of woe wrought by the emergence of "capitalism" on the "working class" of the modern era, continuing into the present, where said workers presumably read about their capitalist oppression on their i-phones. The failure here is twofold. First, the great story is not the Great Divergence[11] or the Great Enrichment,[12] but the suffering "imposed" on the masses of society by "capitalism." Second, and less well-recognized, is the debatable nature of this misery relative to prior periods. The strong version of these approaches paints a stark contrast between the blissful, agrarian lifestyle prior to the Industrial Revolution with the mechanical hellscape created by capitalism. This naïve view has proven unfortunately stubborn and resilient in many historical tellings, presumably not least because of the ability more recently to jettison strict Marxian approaches, which lost some luster the last quarter century, and still attach contemporary environmentalist context backward in time on to the historical narrative of capitalist exploitation—again creating emotional ties to contemporary progressive metanarratives onto the story of the past. But these metanarratives tend to always take some either pre-existence of greater human well-being or inevitable future achievement of human welfare improvement as a given. This is a big step down a very misleading path. The greater welfare of people and society is the story to be told not assumed, a distinction several important liberal scholars have thankfully got right.

F. A Hayek has argued convincingly that one important question to consider regarding the analysis of the human condition in the origins of modern economic growth is the likelihood that any one worker would have even existed without the changes to outputs and economic productivity made possible by the changing nature of the economy. Here again, other more focused approaches take that outcome as given and move on. But Hayek's challenge here is one that cannot be easily dismissed. We now also have a better understanding of the less-than-ideal nature of the agrarian life replaced by industrial capitalism. In particular, it is important to explore two issues: first, what was life like for the majority of people in the agrarian production model and second, were they forced out of that model or did they abandon it willingly. The standard progressive narrative is one that suggests a more idyllic preindustrial past. We now have a better understanding from both empirical work on living standards and nutrition and from contemporary social history accounts that it probably wasn't so idyllic.

Social historian Emma Griffin has overserved regarding the working class during the Industrial Revolution "not that there was anything new about poverty and exploitation. Toiling away for scant reward had been the lot of mankind since the dawn of time."[13] The loss of free-time argument commonly employed as a defense of the idyllic model overlooks the possibility of limits on human ability to engage in productive labor on more limited caloric rations[14] and the cyclical nature of agrarian "employment" (to use an anachronistic characterization of work then) which imposed a great deal of wide swings in the availability of basic necessities, availability which would be greatly smoothed and standardized by the more stable ongoing year-round employment of commercial and industrial society. Better understanding of the movements of labor out of the country and into cities during the commercialization of the early modern period and the modern period illustrates that rather than having their peaceful rural lifestyles ripped away from them by industrial capitalism, most couldn't get away from the country fast enough. This debate probably also critically rests on a misunderstanding of, or ignorance of, marginal analysis in economic thinking. As mentioned earlier scarcity requires trade-offs, even by history's least fortunate. Sure, everyone wants unlimited amounts of free-time frolicking in the ideal countryside, but they also want food, shelter, and better opportunities for their kids. Failing to understand how marginal decisions can lead people away from what, if trade-offs were not required, would be strictly-preferred options often leads scholars untrained in the economic way of thinking to assume the trade-offs must have been involuntary. This error would still hold even if the idyllic countryside description contained more truth as a preindustrial revolution life-setting.

Social historical analysis is still of crucial importance in this type of debate—we do not want to turn liberal history into a version of blackboard economics: all theory and no data. But it is most valuable when supplemented with good empirical economic history and theory. Growing commercial sectors mainly in the new and growing cities provided previously non-existent opportunities to escape the optionless features of rural life.[15] And the greater wealth created by commercialization, even in the early modern period, allowed for greater numbers to support themselves without working directly on the land. And we now know that urbanization created the incentives for innovations in agricultural practice that helped feed and support this process, rather than the progressive-preferred story of agricultural changes forcing unneeded labor into cities in search of hope for survival.

Recent work on the issue has helped shed some much needed factual light on to the question. Emma Griffin has utilized the recorded accounts of

workers to show that the Industrial Revolution brought more than just the
standard narrative of misery, suffering, and poverty.[16] The economic opportunity and change brought by the revolution increased choices for many in
regard not only to work but to social, personal, and cultural life as well. Fresh
examination of the record reveals the period to be one of an "unexpected tale
of working people carving out for themselves new levels of wealth, freedom
and autonomy."[17] While children, in particular, seem to have undeniably
suffered a great deal of physical calamity leading to long-term problems as
a result of the shift to large-scale factory production in England in the early
years of the Industrial Revolution, this does not suggest that the traditional
historical alternative was viewed as a better option to those living through the
time (unlike our modern wealthy perspectives might suggest): "Many parents, who remembered the gnawing hunger of their own childhood only too
well, grasped eagerly at those opportunities" for their children.[18] The question
of overall social impact and long-term impact are not so bleak as they are
commonly portrayed. Workers formed their own associations, educational
opportunities, religious offerings, and political organizations; just as with culture and fashion (discussed below) they were not helpless, they were active
self-authoring agents eager to take up the cause of their own destinies—an
outgrowth of increased economic and thus personal freedom. For the first
time in history they were becoming their own masters.[19] This is an example
of the very helpful contribution social history, when carried out at the unit of
individual analysis, can shed on our understanding of not only great questions
in economic history, but history more generally.[20] While much social history,
like most other contemporary approaches, such as the increasingly influential
so-called "history of capitalism" project, has been deployed clearly in the service of anti-liberal, anti-market narratives, with a great many contemporary
uses, that does not mean the approach itself cannot shed important light on a
liberal history. In fact social history can be much more helpful in many ways
to creating a useful and more accurate history of modern economic growth.
Relative to say other approaches, such as the emphasis on great men or intellectual history, social history gets down to the actors of the economy, in the
way it was experienced by most of society. What we, as liberal historians and
anyone else, need to appreciate is that these approaches are not as mutually
exclusive as they are generally constructed to be.[21]

One's sympathies as a classical liberal historian do not rest with business-
men, entrepreneurs, or businesses (contra the Randian heroic narrative, which
can be seen as substituting business leaders for generals and prime ministers
in the "great man" narrative), but with individual economic freedom and the
resulting relative availability of human choice. Overlooking the horrors of
early industrial manufacturing is just as ahistorical and biased as proceeding
under a lost-agrarian utopias model. Developing a more accurate picture of

the social history, and cultural history, of the early modern and modern periods is of paramount importance in understanding the emergence of modern growth. A great shortcoming of most liberty-friendly historical narratives has been this absence and tendency to focus exclusively on the great contributions of intellectuals and innovators of the era—undeniably important, but lacking in two respects. First, the great minds and great doers of the era can be only correctly understood as the products of their times.[22] Second, the emergence of modern economic growth brought with it an overwhelming restructuring of the human social order at all levels of society, which cannot be understood as, or investigated by, a top-down process of intellectual and commercial elites any more so than as one that was imposed by kings, ministers, and generals, in the manner of an exogenous shock.

The roots of the social change brought about by the origins of modern economic growth go back well before the Industrial Revolution and now can be clearly seen in the social history of the seventeenth and eighteenth centuries. The story does not fit in the traditional narrative of poverty and misery for the lower class. Diets expanded, material possession increased, tea, sugar, pendulum clocks, pottery, better nicer clothing were becoming commonplace. Working people were materially better off than those on the continent where wooden shoes were still the norm and featured in caricatures of the French. Clothing was the most obvious and commonly engaged with aspect of material transformation of the English working class. By 1700 consumer culture was materially integrating with most of the working class. Silk ribbon, silk handkerchiefs and bonnets, silver plated shoe buckles, cotton stockings, and leather shoes, and silver watches were expensive but obtainable to the working poor—desired as a sense of self-identity, status, and luxury. Some of the few things they could truly own all to themselves, very personal constructions of identity made possibly by increased economic freedom and wealth. For the first time in history the poor were able to create their own identity, construct their own traditions and social customs. This led directly to a rise of self-worth and self-respect and a long-term decline in deference to "betters."[23]

Foreign visitors raved about the high quality of the poor's dress and appearance and diet. Working-class taste could lead tastes of the elites, inverting the expected social patterns. Lower sorts abandoned wigs two or more decades before the elites. Masculinity and practicality of working-class dress was viewed as a good thing and exerted pressure on upper-class trends and fashions. Planeness, simplicity, and function were emphasized. As one shocked foreign visitor to England observed, "masters dress like their valets, and duchesses copy after their chamber-maids."[24] The increased availability and adoption of nice clothing by the lower sorts raised alarms among conservative critics who saw in the development immorality, the decline of hierarchy, threats to military power and economic performance, deception, cultural collapse, insubordination and disrespect. They thought laws should be passed to impose the old order on dress and behavior. Interactions in the city, where increased economic freedom and commercialization threw all sorts together, led to a rise in "politeness." Ranks were still respected, but people interacted with more respect. The world-historic nature of this long-term shift in social ordering can hardly be over-emphasized and cannot be properly understood without both social historical and economic historical evidence and reasoning.

While Smith's focus, in the late eighteenth century was on the wealth of nations, later scholars shifted to the Industrial Revolution as the great break in economic history that needed exploring. Given the stark shift in output and incomes that the Industrial Revolution yielded and the resulting social disruptions it is associated with, it is not surprising that it has been looked to as a cause of modern economic growth. In many ways this is the ultimate conflation of cause with effect. The industrial revolution is a part of the process of modern economic growth it is not the cause; it is part of the story that needs explaining. And as discussed above the Industrial Revolution does not represent a break from a more liberated, idyllic human past, but is part of the first sustained effort to achieve such a future.

2. _That we can and should identify a cause and act on it._ Smith's identification of the nature and causes of the wealth of nations as a key question also made explicit the goal of identifying _causes_ for great economic episodes. This is an ongoing question, increasingly so regarding the origins of modern economic growth in the economic history literature of the last twenty years, if less so in non-economic history. Smith's own work illustrates that the question of causes also includes the question of action or lessons for contemporary readers. The second being a natural outgrowth of the first when concerning issues of human well-being. Of course, the question of causation is rendered mute by linear deterministic models of historical inquiry. If the natural progression is laid out _a prior_ then it follows that searching for causes is a waste of time—a waste that might also lead to troubling questions for the predetermined model.

But even in less explicitly deterministic approaches the question of causation is problematic at best, if important, and raises a number of questions. Perhaps the most obvious being the tendency of inquiries of this sort to look for _a cause_. This is a result of both limited intellectual capacity and the need to present a "new idea" in order to get published and get discussed. "Everything affects everything affects everything," is not generally a good sales pitch for a scholar. This tendency to one grand explanation is heightened by the tendency to think of history, economic or otherwise, in discrete units. "Now it's Istanbul not Constantinople," makes sense; "Now it's capitalism, not feudalism," does not. More importantly it is an unhelpfully over-specified model that detracts from the complexity of the historical process and the search for *explanations* (perhaps a slightly better word than *cause* or *causes*). Economists are probably more guilty of this approach than many other scholars of the human experience; it follows that economic historians are thus more keen to it than historians (of course, they are also more likely to be looking at the right outcome: growth rather than oppression/poverty, etc., so we need some of each).

The construction of grand labels for historical experiences is certainly not new or a result of our inquiries into the nature and causes of modern wealth and economic activity. But they do play an outsized role in how we have gone about identifying and studying the great question. We create labels to summarize historical episodes to make it easy to make sense of experiences vastly too complex to comprehend. Just as Hayek pointed out in regard to economic planning, historical analysis is plagued by an insurmountable *knowledge problem*. Even in the much simplified surviving data historians explore we can capture only an unimaginably oversimplified sample of the historical experience. This process is further compounded when we label and linearly narativize the historical experience into discrete chronological stories. We create a simple, discrete, linear, and *authoritative* narrative that shapes our mental models about the past and how we explore it going forward. This is an unavoidable metaphysical reality of the human mind, but it also creates what Hayek described, in alternative usage, as the *pretense of knowledge*.[25] We artificially create objects to study, characterize, and explain. It's neat; it's simple; it can be helpful; it's also potentially very misleading.

Earlier analysis focused on the Industrial Revolution as the cause of modern economic growth. Coal, steam engines, mechanical production, and factories—start the economy! This is still a dominant educational model. Of course, historiographies of the Industrial Revolution, just like historiographies of the Renaissance, the "Dark Ages," and the Enlightenment, among many other great labels have demonstrated that this is a vast over simplification. And, thankfully, more recent studies have moved the "start" of the economy back in time from the Industrial Revolution. But this moving of the starting line is just a reimagining of the same problem. Many of the alternative *causes* of the previously identified *cause* (IR) exhibit the same shortcoming. They are easy to identify, categorize, and study—most importantly they are easy to comprehend: "God said, 'Let Newton be,' and all was light."[26] The years 1688–89 saw the implementation of government institutions conducive to economic investment and long-run growth.[27] Coal was conveniently present in the right place in an accessible way (and, lo! it also spurred the creation of steam engines to keep the pesky water out of the mines) and thus: growth.[28]

Here we see three oversimplified (not by much) highly regarded contenders for the great cause of the great change. One intellectual/scientific; one institutional; and one resource focused. Each has been popular, and remains so in different permutations, with various schools of thought in history and economic history. Each has a lot of interesting intellectual merit. And each is also very misleading in the sense that they are too over-specified and focused on events and things as *the* explanation. In other words they fit our mental models well and satisfy our need for the pretense of knowledge: A led to B; B led to C; C led to D; and D led to TV dinners and latchkey kids. But this approach leads to a critical shortcoming of the search for causation. We spend too much time looking at older labels to explain newer labels rather than studying and trying to grapple with the much more difficult problem of how and why those labeled great events came about. It is the difference between *input/output*-focused thinking and *process*-focused thinking. Talking about A, B, C, and D is compelling; it is easy; it makes a nice story; and it is cheap. But the real story, the hard story, in *the process*; how did we get from A to B to C to D to Mac versus PC?

In other words the story of the history of our search for *causes* has led us down the road of exploring ever more *outcomes*. The Industrial Revolution is an *outcome*. The Scientific Revolution is an *outcome*. 1688–89 is an *outcome*. The application of coal and steam to mechanization is an *outcome*. They are all great mental models constructed to help us make sense of the past in a neat storyline and they help us pass AP world history. But do they help us understand the nature and causes of the modern explosion of wealth and human flourishing in the last 250 years? Or do they just provide fancier responses to the *start the economy* puzzle?

In addition to the very useful set of tools economists apply with the economic way of thinking, such as the role of scarcity in necessitating choice and competition etc., they also unfortunately have progressed increasingly since the mid-twentieth century toward a much more mechanical Newtonian conceptualization of economic analysis away from a more holistic process-oriented (or Darwinian if you want to continue the great man analogy) approach of earlier economists. Paul Samuelson's doctoral dissertation at Harvard, ambitiously titled *Foundations of Economic Analysis*,[29] is often pointed to as the solidification of the more mechanical approach. Mechanics, and the formal mathematical modeling of economic theory celebrated by Samuelsonian economics, implies cause and effect, and clear ones at that. Economic historians, although generally thought of as somewhat less "rigorous" than their other economics colleagues, have been influenced by this trend as well. Thus the "production function" approach to economic history is naturally given to identifying causes that can be put into said production functions—land, labor, and capital being classic examples.

In terms of labor, one of the great focuses of historians studying modern economic growth has been the exploitation of labor—either the nominally free labor of the factory workers in industrial revolution England or explicitly unfree slave labor in the colonial period up to the 1800s. The arguments tend to proceed along variations of: Capitalists exploited workers and slaves to create wealth and economic growth only doing away with slavery when it became too detrimental to the maintenance of wage labor and social stability. An early leading exponent of this view was historian and political leader Eric Williams.[30] The work of Fernand Braudel, discussed above, also relied on the idea of exploitative labor inputs in the origins of modern economic performance.[31] In this story, common to variations of Marxist, New Left, and contemporary progressive accounts exploited labor allows for the accumulation of "excess" capital (money) which can be invested in new economic projects leading ultimately to industrialization. The input-based approach runs through both the late-twentieth century "Eurocentric" accounts and the twenty-first-century globalist approaches (discussed more below). For example, O'Brien and Engerman conclude that "it is difficult to envisage an alternative path of development" that would have led to the Industrial Revolution in early nineteenth-century Britain without its slave-based international economy.[32] Following the publication of Kenneth Pomeranz *The Great Divergence* in 2000 the literature took a much more "globalist" perspective, but as will be discussed below, the input and exploitation-based explanations remain central to many of the accounts.[33]

The reemergence of the exploitation hypothesis as part of the twenty-first-century great divergence literature returns to a favorite progressive explanation for modern economic growth. But this argument has always rested on a logically false extension from the idea that theft can benefit the thief to the idea that theft can create long-run growth and increased wealth. Theft redistributes wealth, and possibly as the more recent rent-seeking literature in economics shows, reduces aggregate wealth; it does not stimulate gains from trade or innovation (it may be, logically, a hindrance to innovation). This is an example of the fallacy of composition in action in economic history—what's good for the individual exploiter is not good for society. Historian Robert Wright has provided the most recent scholarly refutation of the slavery-led-to-growth argument. In his analysis of slavery in the nineteenth century, as well as other periods, Wright shows that the overall costs to society of protecting and preserving a slave system outweighs the benefits of that system to everyone other than the immediate slave-holders.[34] Nevertheless, the argument that slavery was a foundation of modern economic growth is persistent in the literature given that it fits very neatly within the broader capitalism-as-exploitation model of modern economic growth shared by various critical theory approaches to history as well as variations of Marxist and progressive scholarship while simultaneously satisfying the naïve input/output production function conceptualization of growth.

Economic historian Douglass North provides a possible alternative path around this strict production function approach with his emphasis on the importance of institutions in the emergence of long-run economic growth.[35] Recent work on institutional economics, growing out of North's work and the more recent empirical institutional work of MIT economist Daron Acemoglu and his coauthors, has led to an important shift among some scholars toward a broadening of the strict classical land/labor/capital approach to understanding economic change (although they do not abandon that approach).[36] And their works introduce an important acknowledgment that human ingenuity and decision making, that is, agency, are critical components to the story. This is a key step back in the direction of a liberal approach to the history of modern economic growth. If the rules of society do not allow for and reward investment and creativity through institutional innovations like clear, transferable property rights, financial intermediation, etc., then those types of important behaviors are less likely to occur and therefore growth is unlikely to be sustained beyond brief bursts or discrete jumps due to technological innovations, and so on.

The problem as indicated above with the 1688–89 story offered by North is that an institutional story can be reduced into an oversimplified *outcomes-based explanation*. It seems more likely that 1688–89 or other institutional markers were the codification of an *institutional evolution* with deep roots and origins. The institutions in this case got codified because they were useful to the people in a position to put the things into law and those people happened to also be people who benefited from the existing economic process and status quo. How and why is the story. That is the *cause*, so to speak, although *process* would be a better label than cause. The process of individual competition and experimentation led to an outcome that was, to borrow again from Hayek, the result of human efforts but not preconceived human designs.

We need to shift our mental models enough to move away from discrete A, B, C, and D *great label causes*, which were really *great outcomes*, and develop a more *process-oriented approach* to the study of the great enrichment/divergence, etc. As historian of capitalism Joyce Appleby has observed, "capitalism is as much a cultural as an economic system."[37] We then confront the final of the three challenges laid out in Smith's title—the one regarding the level of analysis and unit of historical account.

3. That the nation is the unit of account. Smith's inquiry specifically concerned the wealth *of nations*. This puts Smith squarely in the mold of modern scholarship across different topics, from economics, politics, culture, etc., that adopted the modern conception of the nation-state as the relevant unit of discussion. This aggregation of economic experiences into a national metanarrative is also found in most contemporary studies of economic performance as well. Indeed macroeconomics' birth in the Keynesian Revolution of the mid-twentieth century was built on, in part, the conceptualization and then measurement of the components of national income accounting like Gross Domestic Product, unemployment rates, inflation rates, rates of GDP growth, etc.—*national income accounting* became a thing; macroeconomics courses were sometimes referred to as *income theory* (as opposed to the *price theory* of microeconomics). Here again we see the terminology guiding the analysis—*national income* points the story at the nation-state as the primary player and source of differentiation.[38] This approach is somewhat less predominant in traditional Marxist approaches which are more concerned with class orderings than national categories. But again it is impossible to deny, in either approach, how the dominant categorization, guides the inquiry and narrative. Historical narratives since Smith's time have tended to double-down on the emphasis on the nation-state in the story of modern economic performance.[39] Several reasons for this can be hypothesized.

First, economic historians' focus on the nation-state fits within the broader history discipline's projects with the focus on the nation-state being the defining characteristic of the modern system.[40] Therefore it is a natural extrapolation from that to explore the modern economy on the basis of the nation-state as well. Second, a nation-state-centric focus keeps governments central to the narrative. This is bad economics if one is talking the great enrichment and explosion of human creativity and innovation. It is a natural approach if one is operating under a mental model of government-guided macroeconomic development ala the World Bank, Keynes-Samuelson macro, the Tyranny of the Two Cambridges, and contemporary progressive emphases on collective-action solutions to market failure and social problems. A government-guided approach to economic growth is apparently a great logical relief to many scholars looking to make sense of the vast complexity of the market process and spontaneous order. It does not sit well with a process-oriented exploration of economic innovation, dynamism, and change. Third, the nationalistic agenda of much great narrative history is well served by this type of nation-centric economic history. As we see in contemporary populist discourse, the *us verus them* idea in economic history and policy is an ever present threat to productive analysis. And finally, it is an approach that even when not deployed for intentionally nationalistic purposes satisfies an easy telling that is familiar, and possibly too deterministic, but hard to break out of.

This last part has been addressed significantly in the analysis of modern economic growth with the emergence of global history approaches to the question of the Great Divergence following the publication of Kenneth Pomeranz book of the same name in 2000.[41] Focusing on nations as the unit of analysis, particularly northwestern European nations, lends itself to easy criticism more recently of not being diverse enough in its outlook and approach; too Eurocentric in a scholarly world increasingly, thankfully, more aware of the problems of lack of diversity—the problem of only looking at a few European and North American countries as the big story.[42] Pomeranz and his coauthors, writing in the inaugural issue of the Journal of Global History, summarize the shift as follows: "Past explanations of globalization and its barbarian foes have relied on grand narratives of the 'rise of the West' and the 'Westernization of the rest,' which have been exposed as flawed and inadequate. Historians are busily quarrying ideas and experiences derived from other traditions, to reach more balanced and satisfactory understandings, even though the Western past remains useful in framing global contrasts and interpretations."[43] The promise of this approach so far has been greater than the payoff.

The response since Pomeranz' 2000 work hasn't so much been to break out of the nation-state-focused narrative as to increase the number of observational units. More recent work, mindful of the criticism that focusing on the Industrial Revolution, or say British economic growth, was Eurocentric, has taken to exploring the topic through more international comparisons. As mentioned above much of the work has focused on what has in the twenty-first-century literature become known as *the Great Divergence*. In this case the divergence doesn't so much refer to the separation of modern economic growth from past economic (mostly) not-growth *within* a country as it does to the divergence of the economic paths of western European and North American economies with the economies of the rest of the world. The focus on the divergence then leads to much interesting analysis of non-European economies, China, India, Japan, Mongol Empire, etc. And directs the historian to look for the great explanation in terms of what was different in those countries relative to Britain. In the case of Pomeranz' China and Britain comparisons the guiding assumption is that the two economies were on the same footing going into the divergence.[44] In the equal footing argument of Pomeranz and others, prior historical experience is not as relevant; therefore focusing on the supposedly unique emergence of commercial culture or institutions in Britain is too Eurocentric and misses the mark. Thus by turning the focus from British economic growth to the great divergence our efforts are directed at cross-sectional analysis rather than time-series analysis. The explanation then becomes that British commercialization and social/cultural historical experience wasn't unique, but that Britons were lucky enough to have at their disposal, by exogenous chance or political machination, the resources, both natural and human exploitation, necessary to make the move to the next level of growth—the ready availability of coal and African slavery, for example.

The great divergence formulation raises a number of interesting questions and opportunities. Particularly, by paying greater attention to non-European experiences it broadens our historical perspectives and allows us to challenge our preconceptions. But it also limits our inquiry by insisting on a hard interpretation of the shortcomings of Eurocentric explanations. This is of course compounded by the continuing nation-state focus of the analysis as well. We have neatly organized the inquiry into groupings that make it all too easy to intentionally, or unintentionally, create *just-so stories*[45] that lead us to misguided conclusions based on a narrow focus on concrete easily delineable differences. The great divergence is a great phrase and a potentially helpful mental model if it is considered as both a cross-sectional *and* time-series question.

In addition to the more recent evidence questioning the equal footing conclusion mentioned above the great divergence approach also fails to adequately take into account the process of *how* that footing was achieved. Economic historians like to look at numbers, sometimes helpfully, sometimes to their detriment. In Poermanz' case relative income per capita and life expectancy to establish the equal footing argument. But those *outcomes* mask the real story. How were they achieved, what methods of economic organization and competition led to the results that are being compared? How did those unique processes differently shape culture, society, and politics in those countries? As Pomeranz' own conclusion shows, undermining his own argument in my mind, very different approaches can be taken to get to certain points—particularly the low-level equilibrium traps that have occurred several times in world history without leading to an explosion of growth and human well-being. He points to Britain's "ruling the seas" as a key to its achievement of the Industrial Revolution—how it started the economy. But China, with a much greater head start, famously abandoned its much earlier mastery of the seas in 1433 leaving the playing field to the Europeans so to speak for hundreds of years.[46] As historian of science Margaret Jacob has observed we need to understand "culture and ideology as vital to the very fabric of historical change."[47] Thus very different societies achieved the low-level economic standards of living present in a few parts of the world in the late eighteenth century identified as key to the equal footings argument. How did their paths to that point direct them into their different future experiences?

By establishing some variation of the equal footing argument and then focusing on variations on traditional *causes* like the relative availability of coal, slavery, the Imperial Navy, colonial agriculture, etc., the global history approach has created a twenty-first-century input/output production function narrative. Land (colonial farming), labor (slavery), and capital (ships, coal, etc.) are the story again; thus the narrative, with a contemporary veneer of cosmopolitanism, has come full-circle. And we are again left scratching our head at the age-old explanation: Nations made stuff with the stuff they had (and the stuff they stole) and from that stuff they made more stuff. And the economy started.

NOTES

1. The idea of delineating sharp breaks in the historic record, of course, is a problem that goes beyond economic history and the origins of modern economic growth. As has been noted in historiographies of the Renaissance, the "Dark Ages," the Enlightenment, etc., clearly identifying beginnings and endings of historic periods, let alone causes, is at best an art more than a science. And even agreeing on whether or not these great epochs occurred in any meaningful sense (outside our own history stories) is even an area of debate. For a diverse overview see, for example: E. H. Carr (1961). *What Is History?* revised edition 1986 Harmondsworth: Penguin. Ernst Mayr, "When Is Historiography Whiggish?" *Journal of the History of Ideas*, April 1990, Vol. 51 no. 2, 301–309. Marc Ferro. 2004. *The Use and Abuse of History* 2nd Edition. And Hewitson (2014). *History and Causality.*Specifically regarding the origins of modern economic growth this trap leads to too much emphasis on "a cause" rather than process or evolution. The logical conclusion is to follow this one cause to outsized conclusions which tend to greatly exaggerate some variable like "cotton" or "coal prices" and relegate markets, institutions, and the competitive discovery process to afterthoughts. See, for examples, in the recent literature Beckert (2014) on the role of cotton even prior to the Industrial Revolution in his *Empire of Cotton: A Global History*, and Allen (2009) on the role of commodity prices in sparking the British Industrial Revolution in his *The British Industrial Revolution in Global Perspectives*. "Global" approaches seem to have become hostage of rather narrow over-specified causality of late.

2. Smith, Adam. 1776 (1994). *An Inquiry Into the Nature and Causes of the Wealth of Nations*. The Classics of Liberty Library, New York.

3. Ludwig von Mises. 1953. Introduction to the 1953 Henry Regnery Co. printing of *An Inquiry Into the Nature and Causes of the Wealth of Nations, Selections*.

4. The former description, *growth*, belying the problem, the later, *performance*, more helpful in terms of approaching the question. Modern macroeconomists since Sollow have utilized "growth models," an approach that was ascendant in recent macroeconomics, displacing temporarily the dominant Keynesian counter-cyclical emphasis of the post–World War II economics agenda. The growth model focus on Lucas and Romer was increasingly influential in macroeconomics from the late-middle 1980s to the late middle first decade of the 2000s, when the sequential shocks of the housing market crisis beginning in 2006, the broader financial crisis of 2008, and the Great Recession, officially dated by the National Bureau for Economic Research, which hands down such decrees, December 2007 to June 2009, sent macroeconomists scrambling back to their Keynesian origins of counter-cyclical inquiry and away from the great question. Romer has since disowned much of the modern macro-growth focus the Lucas and Romer literature (separately authored; Romer was Lucas's PhD student at the University of Chicago) spawned, but on methodological grounds more so than on topical grounds. Much of macroeconomics has been called into question by recent events although the focus seems to still include some acknowledgment of the importance of long-run growth (or performance as we should say) even though the short-sighted (but always popular with the political and rent-seeking classes)

counter-cyclical macro has reared its ugly head again. Romer, Paul M. 2015. "Mathiness in the Theory of Economic Growth." *The American Economic Review* 105, no. 5, 89–93.

5. Smith, of course, needs to be read not only as a student of, but also a product of, his times. Living and studying through the middle and second half of the eighteenth century Smith benefited from having his theoretical boundaries freed by the revolutionary changes he was living through and benefited greatly from his knowledge of previous enlightenment scholars and their predecessors. Even living through a period of great intellectual and economic *change* (or *progress* to use the liberal term) Smith still preceded the most dramatic more narrowly "economic" developments of the Industrial Revolution that have captured the attention of so many of his successors.

6. Much interesting and important work in this area of language and ideas, and the relative nature and social construction of ideas was conducted in the twentieth century by humanists and particularly influential among historians in the emergence of social and cultural history and the over-arching postmodern paradigm. Of course, helpful ideas can be taken too far, and the application of these theories to self-focused reflection has never been the strong suit, to say the least, of much of the resulting outgrowth in history writing. For a critique see, for example, philosopher Stephen Hicks (2014) *Explaining Postmodernism: Skepticism and Socialism from Rousseau to Foucault* (Expanded Edition).

7. One of the popular more recent tactics among progressives and Marxists in history and the humanities is to label economics *itself*, and the economic way of thinking more generally, as the ideological bias, thus providing (very weak) justification for ignoring the pitfalls of non-scarcity informed narratives.

8. Thompson, E. P. (1991). *The Making of the English Working Class*. Toronto: Penguin Books.

9. Braudel, Fernand. *Civilization and Capitalism, 15th–18th Century, Vol. I: The Structure of Everyday Life*; *The Wheels of Commerce: Civilization & Capitalism 15th–18th Century, Vol. 2*; *The Perspective of the World: Civilization and Capitalism 15th–18th Century, Vol. 3*.

10. Of course, any serious student of Adam Smith will note he reached this conclusion much earlier and was far from the caricature of capitalist-apologist some of his less-rigorous advocates and critics alike have suggested.

11. Kenneth Pomeranz. 2000. *The Great Divergence*.

12. Deirdre McCloskey. 2007. *The Bourgeois Virtues: Ethics for an Age of Commerce*.

13. Emma Griffin. 2014. *Liberty's Dawn: A People's History of the Industrial Revolution*. Yale University Press, 10.

14. Earlier commercialization and market-driven agricultural improvements helped overcome the caloric shortcomings more quickly in England and less so the further east one moves in early modern Europe.

15. The idea of *choice* is another crucial component of liberal analysis that has gone increasingly absent, and sometime now even criticized, in contemporary progressive analysis.

16. Emma Griffin. 2014. *Liberty's Dawn: A People's History of the Industrial Revolution.* Yale University Press.

17. Griffin, 1.

18. Griffin, 83.

19. One needs to be very careful here to avoid the conservative or naïve market-apologist approach of trying to write out the misery of the episode. There was by any reasonable standard, particularly relative to our contemporary sensibilities, a great deal of truly horrible nastiness in the human experience for a great many people. The important question is not one of: did it or didn't it happen; but one of: what happened and how was the resulting impact different from the prior social context and how did it change going forward?

20. The critical distinction here being focus on the lived experiences of individuals as found in sources like the rare diary or essay of the working class, poor house records, criminal records, property surveys, clothing stocks, etc.

21. The assumption of one or the other is possibly in many ways the result of virtue signally by scholars and the need to service contemporary ideological objectives.

22. I acknowledge here the need to reject the strong form of the social construction model, which would then deny the thinkers and doers any importance. But it is important to not view intellectual or political history as a unidirectional story of hierarchy (top-down); the influences worked both up and down the social-political strata as recent work on clothing and other social behaviors indicate.

23. On dress and personal autonomy see John Styles. 2008. *The Dress of the People.* Yale University Press.

24. Quoted in John Styles. 2008. *The Dress of the People.* Yale University Press, 190–191.

25. F A Hayek 1974. Nobel Prize Lecture. The Pretence of Knowledge.

26. Alexander Pope quoted on page 62 in Raymond Williams. "Ideas of Nature" in David Inglis, John Bone, Rhoda Wilkie eds. 2005. *Nature: Thinking the Natural, Volume 1* Taylor & Francis, pp: 47–62.

27. Douglass C. North. 1981. *Structure and Change in Economic History.* W.W. Norton and Company.

28. Robert C. Allen. 2009. *The British Industrial Revolution in Global Perspective.* Cambridge University Press.

29. Paul A Samuelson. Foundations of Economic Analysis. 1947 Harvard University Press from his 1941 dissertation of the same name. Samuelson also went on to publish the most successful introductory economics textbooks of the postwar era; one which did not include the word institutions in its first index and continued to tout the great strength of the Soviet economy into the late 1970s. For fuller discussion see Levy and Peart (2011) "Soviet growth and American textbooks: An endogenous past," *Journal of Economic Behavior and Organization* 78, nos. 1–2, 110–125.

30. Williams. 1944. *Capitalism and Slavery.*

31. See specifically Braudel's second volume cited above: *The Wheels of Commerce: Civilization & Capitalism 15th–18th Century, Vol. 2.*

32. O'Brien and Engerman. 1991. "Exports and the Growth of the British Economy from the Glorious Revolution to the Peace at Amiens." In Barbara Solow ed. *Slavery and the Rise of the Atlantic System.*

33. Kenneth Pomeranz. 2000. *The Great Divergence: China, Europe, and the Making of the Modern World Economy*. Princeton University Press.

34. Robert E. Wright. 2017. *The Poverty of Slavery. How Unfree Labor Pollutes the Economy*. New York: Palgrave Macmillan.

35. North. 1981. *Structure and Change in Economic History*, Norton. And North 1990. *Institutions, Institutional Change and Economic Performance*. Cambridge University Press.

36. See, for example, Acemoglu and Robinson. 2011. *Why Nations Fail: The Origins of Power, Prosperity, and Poverty* Crown Publishers. And Acemoglu, Robinson, and Verdier. 2017. "Asymmetric Growth and Institutions in an Interdependent World," *Journal of Political Economy*. Forthcoming.

37. Appleby, Joyce. 2011. *The Relentless Revolution: A History of Capitalism*. WW Norton and Company, 4.

38. As is often the case Smith actually exceeds the accomplishments of those who followed him as his analysis was much more *microeconomic* than *macroeconomic* despite his title.

39. The nation-focused narrative is not only reinforced by the emphasis on national income accounting, but the emphasis on such numbers also masks important aspects lost in such accounting, somewhat ironically, like the social and individual characteristics of society that have evolved but are not represented in such figures.

40. E J Hobsbawm. 1991. *Nations and Nationalism Since 1780: Programme, Myth, Reality*. And Benedict Anderson. 1983. *Imagined Communities: Reflections on the Origin and Spread of Nationalism*.

41. Kenneth Pomeranz. 2000. *The Great Divergence: China, Europe, and the Making of the Modern World Economy*. Princeton University Press. Pomeranz work represents something of the pinnacle of the world systems approach with roots going back at least to Fernand Braudel and Immanuel Wallerstein in the 1970s. See, for example, Braudel (1979) *Civilization and Capitalism, 15th–18th Centuries* published in three volumes 1967–1979. And Wallerstein (1974). *The Modern World-System I: Capitalist Agriculture and the Origins of the European World-Economy in the Sixteenth Century*. New York: Academic Press.

42. As an individual who has personally benefited very greatly from the modern academy's broader acceptance of diversity I want to be very explicit here to acknowledge that I think this is in and of itself a "good thing," unquestionably bound to at least make us question our mental models. I also however want to acknowledge that it can also be misleading if the effort to look beyond the Eurocentric story-telling becomes the *goal* rather than approach to finding better answers. If the story comes back to European origins ultimately it is the responsibility of the scholar to wrestle with those explanations in non-biased ways not hide from them. Here again is where I think liberal *process-oriented* approaches are so important: the *explanation* is *how* the process played out, within a frame work of *universal* human striving for betterment subject to the constraints of scarcity; different places faced different constraints, different competitive processes, and thus outcomes differed. There is no need for a *process-oriented* story to revert to the vulgar *nationalistic* or *triumphalist* narratives of earlier eras, which is a big risk when the unit of analysis is nations or other groups. The *process* of *human action* is not a national or identiational construct it is a *humane*

construct. Economist Elinor Ostrom summarizes the challenge here nicely: "As an institutionalist studying empirical phenomena, I presume that individuals try to solve problems as effectively as they can. That assumption imposes a discipline on me. Instead of presuming that some individuals are incompetent, evil, or irrational, and others are omniscient, I presume that individuals have very similar limited capabilities to reason and figure out the structure of complex environments. It is my responsibility as a scientist to ascertain what problems individuals are trying to solve and what factors help or hinder them in these efforts. When the problems that I observe involve lack of predictability, information, and trust, as well as high levels of complexity and transactional difficulties, then my efforts to explain must take these problems overtly into account rather than assuming them away." *Governing the Commons*, 25–26.

43. Willam Gervase Clarence-Smith, Kenneth Pomeranz, Peer Vries, 2006. "Editorial," *Journal of Global History* 1, no. 1, 1.

44. Pomeranz assertion of equal footing prior to the Industrial Revolution has since come into dispute, see, for example, Huang 2002 "Development or Involution in Eighteenth Century Britain and China?" *Journal of Asian Studies*. Etc.

45. This phrase is of course taken from the great Eurocentrist author Rudyard Kipling. For discussions of his work "Just-So Stories" see, for example, John Hartley, Jason Potts (2014) *Cultural Science: A Natural History of Stories, Demes, Knowledge and Innovation*. Bloomsbury Publishing, London, and the introduction to Lewis Held (2014). *How the Snake Lost its Legs. Curious Tales from the Frontier of Evo-Devo*. Cambridge University Press.

46. Louise Levathes. 1997. *When China Ruled the Seas: The Treasure Fleet of the Dragon Throne, 1405–1433*.

47. Margaret Jacob. 1988. *The Cultural Meaning of the Scientific Revolution*, 253.

Chapter 11

A Non-Manifesto of Liberal History

Alberto Garín

INTRODUCTION

As a researcher and teacher of history I always hope to avoid falling into prejudices that predetermine historical discourse. As far as is possible, history must be released from ideology. For this reason, I hesitate when I think of "liberal history." I wonder, is history the best mechanism to explain the principles of liberty? Is there a particular way of producing "liberal history?" Do Liberals need to rewrite history to make our objectives and achievements more visible? Can we write liberal history while staying honest to the sources? I believe we can. But the kind of history that we must write is different in nature and aims that of the dominant historiographical currents of Marxism, progressivism, and nationalism.

Liberal history is unlike these other perspectives because it does not attempt to impose an ideology on the scientific method. Indeed, no ideology is necessary, if in the end, all I want to do is learn about the action of people as individuals, and if I want to understand how the concept of liberty has evolved or how property rights were developed.

It is the scientific method that allows me to understand how liberal principles emerged, how they developed throughout history and how we can strengthen their impact on the present. So, to write a "liberal history," I do not need a manifesto, a programmatic decalogue, or a party slogan. I need to produce an accurate history that allows me to understand the liberal world.

Of course, history, as we know it today, is not aseptic. We need to understand why we have studied history for centuries, what has been the ultimate goal of creating royal chronicles, historical encyclopedias, and textbooks. History has long been a tool at the service of the State, used to justify power whether it's of a totalitarian nature, an oligarchy, a social democracy or the dictatorship of the proletariat.

This nationalism fuels patriotism on the right and the left, equally among conservatives and Marxists. Liberal principles can best be understood when we decide to move away from history as a story of the rise and fall of nations. Classical Liberals must believe that history begins with the individual, and that history is the record of individuals making choices. Why should we study history? The classical liberal view must be that we study history to better understand ourselves, and to understand how to promote freedom in our time.

WHY STUDY HISTORY?

Most people recognize that we study history because it is necessary according to two familiar maxims. First, following Cicero, we recognize that *historia magistra vitae est*—"history is life's teacher." Second, it follows that understanding past events and circumstances allows us to understand those of the present.[1] But a third reason for studying history is also quite apparent. We study history so that we can guard against others who manipulate the past without our consent. Those who set the agenda of history can establish a narrative that justifies actions that would limit people's liberty in the present. If history were that pragmatic "teacher of life" imagined by Cicero, she would base her instruction on practical cases that would get at life's essential lessons for the here and now. But history teaches different lessons when it is taught as the accumulation of sophisticated data to be memorized and recalled. When historical data is preselected and pre-digested to generate a discourse in agreement with views held by certain authorities, history is no longer a teacher, but a servant of ideology.

Unfortunately, it seems that the dominant mode in history education is not to reflect on history but to internalize the established view without discussion. But with Cicero's dictum in mind, let us consider an example of how history can teach us to challenge our present perceptions. Consider, as an example, the testamentary divisions of certain Hispanic medieval kings. Sancho III of Navarre (990–1035) spent most of his life expanding his kingdom by fighting against his Christian neighbors. Upon his death, he divided his realm among his four sons. These then fought each other to regain the territories that had been ruled by their father. The most successful of these sons was Ferdinand I of León and Castile (1016–1065), who managed to prevail over his brother García III of Navarre. Like his father before him, Ferdinand I wished upon his death that his kingdom would be divided among his sons. And so it was. But the division of Ferdinand's lands gave rise to a new series of civil wars, which only came to end when one of them, Alfonso VI (1047–1109), managed to defeat his brothers.[2]

In considering this story, one might conclude that there is some kind of social principle at work, in which a ruler who divides his assets among his heirs initiates a rivalry among them. Perhaps we could learn from this example and avoid similar mistakes? Should a rule leave political control solely in the hands of a single heir, as was traditionally the case of the Catalan *hereu*?[3] After all, according to some historians of Catalan history, when the eldest son, the *hereu*, laid claim to his father's legacy, the other surviving male heirs were forced to seek new lands and would seek new adventures in life. Some scholar explains that this inheritance tradition in Catalan laid a pattern of entrepreneurship that led to the economic development of the region.

If we translate this historical knowledge to the present, we might have the basis for deciding whether the owner of a business should choose a single heir, or divide his business among multiple heirs.

To make history a teacher of practical lessons, a historian should not only try to narrate the vicissitudes of Hispanic kings or Catalan *hereus*, but should also seek to understand the real consequences of their actions (the division or inheritance) before attempting to extrapolate lessons of the past to our contemporary world. For example, the hereu system did not prevent Barcelona, the capital of Catalonia, from enduring a long period of economic standstill between the 14th and 17th centuries.[4] It is risky to consider that just one element of the past can explain everything about that past. History could be life's teacher if we understand the whole picture, not just the anecdotes.

We arrive, then, at the second function of history: know the past to understand the present. Here also the main risk is to focus only on anecdotes and not to attempt to understand larger historical processes. History designed to guide us in the present may teach us false lessons when political authorities impose their own vision of the past to justify their existence and their actions. Consider the case of Catalonia, where a large part of the population would like to see their region secede from the rest of Spain. To justify secession, leaders of the secessionist movement have aimed at revising history for political gain. The secessionists interpret Iberian history as a longstanding struggle for Catalonia to emerge from the weight of political marginalization and neglect. The Institut Nova Historia,[5] the historical research center funded by the Catalan autonomous government, has made radical and unscientific claims that major historical figures like Miguel de Cervantes, Christopher Columbus, and Leonardo da Vinci were all Catalans and not from Alcalá de Henares, Genoa, and Tuscany. Moreover, the institute has stated that those who deny the Catalan origins of these men must be driven by feelings of hatred that the rest of Spain has directed toward Catalonia since the late 15th century.[6] All this might seem a joke, but it is actually part of a complex political maneuver, the aim of which is not only achieving the independence of Catalonia but strengthening the power of those currently holding political

office. This political element is crucial. Above all else, the main secessionist leaders aspire to seize more authority and to control all the levers of state
power. After years of indoctrination in primary and secondary education
(both public and private), many Catalonians take such historical claims for
truth. The secessionists have generated in Catalonia a historical blindness that
allows their manipulation of a large part of the electorate.[7] History did not
work to explain the present, but to impose a past.

Unfortunately the Catalan case is only one recent example of the abuse of
history to serve state power.[8] In much of the world, history is not only written by the victors but, mainly, by the rulers. Once again, this has been true
from ancient and medieval royal chronicles down to the textbooks of the con-
solidated nation-states of the 19th century. Even in the enlightened West, the
dominant understanding of the nature of history is that it is a story of nation-
states, and that history therefore should give justification of those states.

It is certainly true that an existing state has a greater ability to rewrite history than does a nascent state or a potential one. Counter-narratives written
against the main nationalist thrust of American history speak for the lost
independence of the "California of Californios."[9] But both points of view
reveal a common pattern. For Californios, what prevails in written history is a
collective identity that is opposed to that of others (the Spaniards, Mexicans,
or Americans), a collective identity embodied by those Californios who
achieved a position of power—that is, a state, sometimes under the Mexican
government, sometimes under the U.S. government. In the case of the official
history of the United States, again we find a collective identity fabricated by
way of exclusion: those of European descent who lived on the East Coast are
placed above those who managed to settle in the South or West, with indig-
enous tribes completely marginalized. In traditional histories, group identities
are seen to be in conflict: the inhabitants of the Northeast (Yankees) prevail
against those of the South (Rebels). Next, the political elites in Washington,
DC prevail against the industrialists of the Great Lakes area. Finally, U.S. history becomes a succession of presidents and their respective decisions which
are understood as either against, or in harmony with, the collective activities
of all American citizens.

Let us take two examples from very informative essays. First, the standard
general history of the United States published by *Time-Life* in 1964. These
types of manuals tend to make very few references to recent events. But
President Kennedy (who ruled between 1961 and 1963) receives four whole
pages in the main text and another page in the list of "featured events," where
his assassination is included.[10] The pages dedicated to Kennedy emphasize
everything the president did for his country, ignoring the fact that it is individual citizens who make collective history by living and acting on a daily
basis. By contrast, a personality like George Westinghouse—who, in addition

to inventing the air brake, actually laid the foundations for the use of the alternating current, thus transforming the way we live in tangible ways, who made possible everything from our ability to illuminate our environment at night to our ability to refrigerate our food[11]—is referenced briefly on only three occasions, and never with any explanation as to who he is or what he achieved.[12] And if we jump ahead half a century and consult the *Wikipedia* entry for "History of the United States," John F. Kennedy is now mentioned four times and his brother Robert, twice; Westinghouse gets no mention whatsoever.[13] The "History of the United States" *Wikipedia* page, like the *Time-Life* encyclopedia, includes recent events. There, Obama is mentioned twenty-nine times. Bill Gates and Steve Jobs are not mentioned at all, even though it could be argued that PCs and iPhones brought greater change to the world that did any president's personality and policies.

In-state actors now rule history as the guardians of patriotic essences; the true entrepreneurs matter little or not at all, and never mind the common citizens. We are everywhere confronted by an anachronistic history according to which contemporary statist concepts are imposed on a past in which such concepts were meaningless, and all with the clear objective of "nationalizing" the past. This practice results from, and reinforces, a series of errors.

Error #1: Modern states are held to be the inevitable evolutionary results of human groups bidding to form these states. Thus, we are obliged to speak of the "Renaissance in Spain" when referring to the artistic creations of the 16th century in what were more properly the kingdoms of Castile, León, and Aragon, since Spain as the sole state did not exist (and this is not to mention the misuse of the term "Renaissance").[14]

Error #2: Any group without a current state begins to construct a "common history" as its first step toward gaining authority. Thus, the Catalan case we mentioned earlier. But creating an imaginary collective is not a way to reinforce the identity of each individual composing a group; it only reinforces the need for a national state. Besides Catalonia, the author of these lines has lived in Iraqi Kurdistan (where all Arab heritage is denied), and Hadramut, in the Southeast of the Yemen (where the emphasis on regional uniqueness is used to trump the authorities in Sanaa).

Error #3: The endeavor for a common history overshadows divergence and imposes statist discourse. Whether I imagine myself "Scottish" in my support for independence or fancy myself "English" in my insistence on unity, I still cannot think like myself, John, Mary, or Ramon. In other words, my authentic personality is canceled; all that matters is my nationalist intent.

Error #4: The capacity for action of different peoples is considered to be limited, subject to the will of their respective states. In the current Greek crisis, the culprits are thought to be the totality of Greek citizens. It does not matter whether or not certain Hellenes were actually opposed to the mismanagement of state finances done by the governments of Papandreou (PASOK), Samaras (New Democracy), or Tsipras (Syriza). Similarly, in nationalist history it does not matter if there were Greek entrepreneurs, opposed to the rentier state, who backed truly liberal initiatives. What matters is that all Greeks are the same and therefore all are equally guilty of negligence. A headline that follows this logic was offered by the daily *Libertad Digital*: "Germany Knocks on Greece's Door."[15] The message is clear: Germany, all of Germany, not merely the Merkel government, is making a point to Greece, all of Greece, not just Syriza voters. Individual citizens do not speak, not even Angela Merkel. States have been anthropomorphized and presented as actually communicating. Even more surprising is the fact that we have taken this newspaper headline from a publication put out by an organization that considers itself libertarian. Even there, the image of the state prevails over the reality of individual persons.

These thought patterns exist because human beings can be conditioned by the political arena (state, region, or municipality) in which they are born. You may have a patriotic spirit, usually as a result of the kinds of historical manipulation that we are analyzing here; or I may identify with certain seemingly generic cultural patterns ("we Westerners"). But here are two additional errors:

a. Thinking that what is generic for me is really generic. There are Guatemalans who love marimba music and others hate it. The marimba is not a feature of "Guatemalanness"; it is an attraction for some Guatemalans (and many foreigners).
b. Thinking in terms of generalities that determine my actions as well as those of others. If you were born in Britain, then act, whether you like it or not, as if you are phlegmatic. If you are from Italy, then you will act, inevitably, with excessive passion.

The nationalist histories that we most often find in textbooks accommodate and foment the types of group thinking as follows:

1. They create an exclusive group (the nation).
2. They grant this exclusive group a brilliant past. Even defeats are bright sources of exaltation. It is well known, that Milosevic, with necessary nuances, in his speech at the Gazimestan monument in 1989, used the Serbian defeat at Kosovo in 1389 to indicate the values and purposes of his ultranationalist government.[16]
3. They emphasize that the exclusive group has been offended once, or even several times, forcing it to defend itself, beginning with the drive to unite under a single discourse, that of an authority.

4. They indicate that the main objective of the group is to redress offenses. This will be performed not in the interest of the personal development of each member of the group but, rather, the common, patriotic, social, national, or even tribal interest. In the end, I do not inherit my past; I am enslaved by it.

In the Way of a Liberal History, First, a Correct History

At this point, we might ask if we can do better when researching, teaching, and diffusing history. Can we teach without nationalist history? Let us return to the initial ideas of this chapter. We research, teach, and diffuse history: 1) so as not to repeat past wrongs; 2) in order to understand the present; 3) so that others will not manipulate our past. But and above all, as Liberals, we can research, teach, and diffuse history to demonstrate the ability of the individual to become historical actors, to be accountable, not as an isolated being, but as a part of a society, with the stipulation that this society is not to be one that overrides our individuality but, rather, one which will emphasize it with each step forward.

Once again, we don't try to establish a new methodology to arrive at this history of individuals, like Marxists did to establish the history of social classes. We can focus on individuals after producing a rigorous and scientifically valid history.

The first step toward teaching history better would be to teach it in a practical way, focusing not so much on the facts and the events themselves as on the cause-effect relationships among them. That is, certain events may cause certain results. This is not to predict the future but to understand the parameters that drive human action. A situation of high unemployment or high economic disruption can lead to social tensions, which in turn can lead to a violent revolutionary movement, as the French Revolution. But it can also happen that official, "legal" employment disappears and the employment generated by the "black" market intensifies (as in Spain today, where official unemployment figures are practically meaningless). There is no single pathway to human events, no predetermined, inevitable "unfolding." That is the first lesson that one should take from history.

The present and, even more importantly, the future are as yet unwritten. If we can learn one thing from the past, it is that nothing is predictable. For starters, German industry is now the economic engine of Europe. But this may not be so in a decade. In the 1990s, Germany's economy was slowed by the reunion of the two Germanys, which was difficult to predict. In 1980 few anticipated the fall of the Berlin Wall and its consequences. The lesson is that the economy of the Mediterranean countries can take off and even outpace the German one if their citizens so decide and conditions are right.

Who would have predicted in the 16th century that little, peripheral England would become a world power by the 19th century. The Bedouin tribes of the Arabian Desert in the 6th century could not have imagined the empire that their descendants would build in the 8th century, which would stretch from Morocco to China. The proud Romans of the 2nd century were unable to think that two hundred years later their great capital would pale in comparison to imperial Constantinople, a city that did not even exist in the 2nd century.

History is made according to the will of thousands of individual actors. The future is too. No genetic, racial, cultural, or national reasons prevent any particular group of human beings from progressing or failing. So we have to stop being deceived by this nationalist past. Should Spain and the United States go to war, as they did over Cuba and Puerto Rico in 1898, would we accept that the contributors of this book would also be at odds? What happened in the past can be analyzed and understood, but it cannot justify my ability, or inability, to act in the here and now.

So the question is, once again, when defending the principles of freedom, we should forge a new way of searching, teaching, and diffusing history, whereby we might exalt these principles. In other words, should we practice a form of affirmative action in order to accentuate the value of individuals against their oppression by states or other political groups?

In other words, do we need "A Manifesto of Liberal History" in order to encourage a type of historical research and diffusion that will regard the principles of freedom as our primary goal? Should we privilege our ideological intentions, even at the expense of academic rigor, as has been done with respect to other historiographical tendencies, especially those favored by Marxists?

The answer is obvious: No. To the contrary, it is fundamental that we eliminate as much as possible all biases from our historical investigations.

This does not mean that we should fall into the 19th-century positivist, optimistic point of view that science establishes the valid knowledge.[17] Even in history, even studying the facts of the past (a reality that already happened), we cannot be sure we have all the data and our knowledge will only be valid until we have better knowledge.

As Liberals, we must focus on individual and not collective actors, the latter usually being nation-states. But we often make two mistakes: we confuse individuals with the historical heroes and we underestimate the role of states. If we reduce the Russian Revolution to the actions of famous figures such as Tsar Nicholas II, Kerensky, or Lenin, we get carried away by "historical heroes" and ignore individuals. The Russian Revolution resulted from the actions or inactions of millions of individuals, some of whom are well known, like Nicholas II, Kerensky, and Lenin, but are still not decisive for the final result without the support of all the other individuals alive at that time.

Secondly, whatever we think about them, states are important. This is essentially because millions of people believe in states, work for them, finance them, and support them. It is true that in the end we are still talking about individuals, but millions of individuals often delegate their wills to public officials, from the president of a democratic or totalitarian republic to the functionary behind the window of a bureaucratic agency.

But beyond the value that we give to the specific actions of individuals, or even to the sum of these individuals' actions (as social beings, the value of our actions is that they are related to the actions of other individuals), the key to searching, teaching, and diffusing history correctly remains, as we have just indicated, to eliminate biases.

In what follows, I outline six principles for writing a correct history and, with that, to produce a correct classical liberal history.

1. Avoid historical anachronisms. The principal anachronism is talk of nation-states before the 19th century in order to justify the existence and actions of contemporary nation-states. A common mistake here is to confuse geographical location with the nation-state. Italy has been a geographical reality since Antiquity, but it does not become a solitary state until the 19th century. Moreover, previous Italian states were characterized by long disputes among them. Similarly with Spain, known as Hispania, since the time of the Roman Empire. As a single state, however, it does not take form until the beginning of the 18th century, with "Nueva Planta" decrees signed by Philip V between 1707 and 1716. And it only takes the form of a modern nation-state thanks to the successive liberal constitutions instituted in the 19th century, beginning with the Constitution of Cádiz in 1812. In the 16th century, Spaniards were simply the inhabitants of the Iberian Peninsula. But they belonged to different states: the Kingdom of Portugal, the Crown of Castile, the Crown of Aragon, etc.[18] Nevertheless, and curiously, the difference between geography and political entity, which was quite clear in the 16th century, has become an anachronism at the beginning of the 21st century. For example, we often speak about the Renaissance in 16th-century Spain, using contemporary borders that exclude Portugal.

2. Avoid misguided generalizations. A common example here is to consider that certain principles of individuality, liberty, or property are generic throughout the whole of human history in the ways that we know them today, without being aware that they have progressed and evolved over time. For example, property is not a natural right emanating from all-powerful God or wise Mother Nature; it is the achievement of

contemporary societies, which have provided individuals with the ability to maintain absolute possession of certain goods, and thereby the ability to use, consume, exchange, or destroy those goods.

Property is a social capacity: other members of society recognize an individual's right to property. Thus, there are historical moments in which the absolute right is not given. Feudal lords maintain ownership of a territory, but this is contingent on their service to the monarch who has granted them said territory. As owners, they can use their territory, consume its agricultural products, exchange its parcels, and even raze its forests. But if the feudal lord does not serve the king, the king may withdraw his right to his territory. Why is this so? Is the king the ultimate owner of the property? No, rather, it is because the medieval king is the ultimate administrator of the kingdom. But this too is contingent. If the subjects of the king conclude that the he does not exercise his power correctly, then they can legitimately overthrow him. Are the king's subjects the ultimate owners of the property? No again; they are responsible for choosing the best manager of the property.[19]

Therefore, analyzing the European Middle Ages or the Renaissance by applying contemporary concepts of property rights leads to a serious understanding of how medieval property worked. Again, individual rights are not a natural and eternal principle but, rather, the consequence of the social developments that achieved them. Freedom for Don Quixote, for example, did not mean the absolute freedom to choose for himself but, rather, the freedom to live outside of a prison cell.[20] Recall that Cervantes had been a prisoner in Algiers. The specific freedom that he missed was not to be anyone's prisoner. Therefore, for our Knight of La Mancha, honor was every bit as important as freedom. This is because one way of being free in Algiers was to convert to Islam, but for Cervantes this way to gain freedom was not honorable, not allowed.

3. Avoid using anecdotes and establish historical dynamics. Around 1763, the Spanish army forced the English out of Río Tinto, near Trujillo, on the Caribbean coast of Honduras. It was a success in the war against piracy. Spanish engineer Díez Navarro played an important role in these events and we can use them to write an interesting and adventurous story about the Spaniard.[21]

The important point about piracy is its continuity throughout two centuries. Not just in Honduras, and in the entire Caribbean Sea, but also on the coasts of Brazil, Río de la Plata, and even on the Pacific coast of Hispanic America.

But piracy itself, naval attacks against the Spanish fleet, is also an anecdote when you take in account all the contraband that pirates did. A Spaniard crossing the Honduran forest to get to Río Tinto to engage in black market trade with a British buccaneer would be a curiosity. Thousands of Spaniards trafficking smuggled goods with thousands of British subjects in all of Hispanic America throughout two centuries, and particularly the 18th century, is history, a crucial and historical dynamic. Perhaps, the success of England's Industrial Revolution in the second half of 18th century could explain in this thriving black market across the Atlantic Ocean. Thousands of individuals satisfying their needs over statist monopolies. But this is a thesis for another paper.

The importance of historical dynamics was introduced in the middle of the 20th century by French historian Fernand Braudel, when he spoke about the *longue durée*.[22] In the *longue durée*, the individual is lost not among a social class, but through the passage of the time. After all, in the case of the pirates, the significance is that thousands of people participated in the black market. But it was the individual will of each smuggler that, after two centuries, changed the history of industrial production in Britain. Every smuggler was important.

4. Avoid hagiography. We cannot evaluate the "goodness" of Lincoln according to the criteria of "goodness" in the 21st century. Lincoln actually considered the possibility that black slaves should be sent back to Africa or somewhere in Latin America that could be colonized instead of providing them with rights within the United States.[23] His contemplation of denying slaves the rights of U.S. citizens does not make him a worse person. Rather, he was simply a product of his time, a time when most people, including Lincoln himself, were racists and considered blacks to be displaced Africans who needed to be relocated. More interesting is the fact that, in spite of his racism, Lincoln finally chose to promote the freedom of black slaves.

5. Avoid thinking history is just papers in archives. We need to approach history through every means possible: archives, as well as archaeology and anthropology. Not only because archaeologists and anthropologists are writing history, but also because we need to understand ways of life (from an anthropological point of view) and handle the material culture (from an archaeological point of view) of contemporary societies. And we need to know the territory, not because geography determines personalities, as Montesquieu erroneously claimed, but because the landscape is one of the conditions that influences human action.

We are well aware of the capacity of public authorities or the mass media to distort or manipulate reality. Critical thinking is required to interpret government statements. It is the same with historical sources. If we take literally the information provided in a historical document, we can be misled. We need to check not only with other historical documents, but also with other historical approaches. Using archaeological sources in combination with archival documents could be appropriate when discussing ancient or medieval times. But what about contemporary periods? A famous case was that Benidorm, the tourist city on Spain's Levante coast: how could the actual number of city inhabitants be determined when most of the people were visitors who only spend a few days there per year? The answer came by looking at the tons of garbage produced every year. In a way, it was contemporary archaeology.[24]

6. Finally: Avoid turning historians into fortune-tellers. A good historian understands the dynamics that drove humans in the past. History is not static; societies change continuously. This is true for the simple reason that time, the essence of history, changes. But it is also true because in their social interactions human beings constantly modify their behaviors, whether they do so moderately or radically. With this fluid vision of history in mind, historians must recognize our limitations. We can only establish tendencies. For example, History shows us that a group of people long subjugated by a tyrant can try to overthrow that tyrant. Success is more likely if the subjugated society in question receives important foreign support. But, this does not mean that a historian can predict the last day of Robert Mugabe's regime in Zimbabwe or Kim Jong-un's regime in North Korea. True History, History as a science, aims to understand what happened in the past and what the result has been for the present, but History cannot predict the future.

Some Fields of Research to Build a Liberal History

Liberal history must recover the individual as the main actor in history. It is important to emphasize human action as the result of human will. Why something happened in the past is because a group of individuals decided to carry it out. This group of individuals might be united by kinship, ethnicity, or national sentiment. But they could not be bound by such ties in any absolute sense. The case of the discovery of the human immunodeficiency virus (HIV) by the teams of scientists led by Luc Montagnier and Robert Gallo is an excellent case in point regarding how individuals make history by acting over long periods of time.[25] The discovery was not the result of isolated actions on the part of two scientists in two different countries. Even before either Montagnier or Gallo, hundreds of oncologists, virologists, surgeons, therapists, etc. working in the fight against cancer laid the foundation for the discovery of retroviruses, one of which is HIV. But also, when the AIDS epidemic began in 1981, homosexual lobbies, especially in New York and San Francisco, demanded that health authorities take action in order to understand and find a solution to the disease.[26] That pressure resulted in the allocation of certain funds to teams like Gallo's. What was so strange about the controversy between Montagnier and Gallo was that it was only highlighted when a conflict between the authorities of the United States and France started, a conflict that could then only be terminated when U.S. president Ronald Reagan and French prime minister Jacques Chirac took respective positions on the matter—that is, when the arsonists decided to put out their own fire. In the end, this nationalist confrontation was far more about the efforts of government officials than it was about the efforts of scientists, for the latter passed through different stages of long-distance collaboration over the course of two decades during the 1980s and 1990s, and eventually even published an article together in the 2002 issue of *Science*.[27]

Second, classical Liberals must recognize the roles of everyone who makes up a State organism, from the highest to the lowest official. This does not imply a validation of nationalist creations. Before the 19th century, statist history was, essentially, the history of great leaders. It was clear that most of the inhabitants of a territory, even though they were the real actors in historical events, did not appear in the official chronicles. Since the 19th century, statist history has become the history of nations, and the concept of people appears as the main collective agent of history. A fake agent. The people as a mass is nothing more than a ploy in hands of the nation-State, or in hands of those who want to take control of the nation-State, as in the case of Marxist revolutionary movements.

Without a doubt, a historian who aspires to be rigorous, must begin by distinguishing between the affection he may have for a particular place and the belief that this place generates a common character to all its inhabitants. In the liberal world, there are no equalities beyond the aspiration that everyone be equal under the law. Why then do we think that everyone born in a certain place will have a common character? In other words, how can we rigorously analyze the societies of the past, distinguish between the individuals who formed these societies, if today we persist on throwing ourselves into the arms of culture, homeland, or collective identity?

Only after breaking free from the nationalist corset, can we begin to write good history and, therefore, good liberal history.

Nationalist, state history that leaves out individual action is often incomplete, and often in error. For example, Murdo MacLeod wrote an economic history of colonial Central America based mostly on common export products of the time: cacao, cochineal, and indigo.[28] MacLeod did not take into consideration retail trade, especially that of firewood, which was the main source of fuel at the time,[29] or contraband, the black market moved by pirates that we discussed earlier. Why did not he include them? Because firewood and contraband did not pay taxes, they did not appear in official documents. Once again, MacLeod wrote a statist history.

Why should he have included them? Because human beings used firewood every day to cook, light fires to work in blacksmith shops, or light lamps at night to illuminate the dark. This is the anthropological approach that every good historian needs. Just because the transport and sale of firewood did not pay taxes, does not mean that it ceased to be a necessity. Similarly, if colonial excavations found remains of English pottery, whose trade was prohibited by the Court of Madrid, then it is evident, thanks to archaeology, that American tastes were not subject to official prohibitions; consumer freedom took precedence over the official monopoly. So the economic history presented by MacLeod speaks of the Spanish Crown in America during the colonial period, but makes little reference to individuals, with their free will, who lived in this colonial period. MacLeod wrote a history of the State, not of persons. At the very least, the history he wrote is incomplete.

There are plenty of good examples to consider when writing the history of people which does not coincide with the history of the boundaries of states. Modern states, we know, do not necessarily coincide with the administrative realities of the past. Giuseppe Garibaldi (1807–82), one of the champions of Italian independence, was born in Nice, a city that became part of France in 1860.[30] That such a fervent nationalist was born in a city that changed countries during his lifetime is a good example of how patriotism conforms to historical context and not the other way around. Otherwise, we would have to make the absurd argument that Nice rather suddenly ceased to be very Italian and became a very French one.

A person can live his entire life within the territory of a state, without getting to know the rest of that state and without needing to know anything about that state in order to develop his own intellectual capacities. A famous example is the philosopher Immanuel Kant (1724–1804), who never left his native city of Königsberg (now Kaliningrad), and yet this fact in no way prevented him from expounding a radically advanced philosophical theory.[31]

Many people past and present live transnational lives. If we were to write history according to events in the past century that are restricted to the territory of that republic, then we would have forgotten one of its main economic sectors: remittances from immigrants, mostly those settled in the United States.[32] Some immigrants not only send money but also impose fashions brought from the North, including everything from tastes in clothing and architecture to changes in social relations to variations in family organization (from the uprooting of families to their artificial duplication). All of these elements are transforming Guatemalan social reality, but these are not included in official textbooks. Indeed, a textbook truly worth its salt should include a map of the Republic of Guatemala plus one of those U.S. states that have the highest percentage of Guatemalan immigrants.

The problem of nationalist narrative is easy to see in art history. In the 17th century, Diego Velázquez was the official painter and confidant of King Philip IV, king of Castile, Aragon, and Portugal, as well as Naples, Sicily, and Cerdagne, and lord of Milan, the Netherlands, and Burgundy. So Philip IV was not exclusively the king of Spain, mostly because, as we saw before, Spain did not exist as a state until forty years after the death of Philip IV.

Diego Velázquez met Rubens in Madrid in 1628.[33] Rubens invited Velázquez to Italy to improve his skills as a painter. Rubens himself had been in Italy between 1600 and 1608, studying Titian (1490–1576), among others. When Velázquez arrived in Rome, he met Bernini[34] and admired Michelangelo's (1475–1564).Besides their jobs as artists, Rubens, Velázquez, and Bernini had another thing in common. All three worked for Philip IV, the richest king of his time and who had excellent taste for the beaux arts. Nowadays, in the Art History textbooks,[35] we study Velázquez (1599–1660) as a Spanish painter (even though Spain did not become a state until after 1707); Rubens (1577–1640) as a Belgian painter (even if Belgium was not a state until 1830); and Bernini (1598–1680) as an Italian artist (even when Italy did not become a state until 1871).

Once again, nationalist discourse prevails over individuals and their very fruitful relationships. When artists become part of official history they are no longer recognized as creative geniuses who influenced each other beyond political boundaries. It is true that artists are children of their time, but neither their influences nor the art market are concerned with borders or patriotism. What they are concerned with are human relationships.

To conclude, liberal history is the history of individuals in action. Ancient history only mentions leaders. It is true they were individual persons, but we know more about their anecdotes that the dynamics in which they were involved. Contemporary history is dominated by the masses, by the people, a collective that imposes its ideology and nature on each of its members. It is difficult for history to be life's teacher or to help us understand the present when it is built on incorrect parameters: the hero or the nation-State. To write a correct history we need to give each individual of the past the prominence he or she had. If we can recover the majority of those persons who lived and acted, then we will produce a valid history. And with a valid history, we will be much better prepared to defend the principles of liberty.

NOTES

1. VILAR, Pierre: *Iniciación al vocabulario del análisis histórico*, Crítica, Barcelona, 1982, ch. 1.

2. REILLY, Bernard F: "*Historia de España. Reconquista y Repoblación de la península*," El País, Madrid, 2007, Vol. 7, p. 84.

3. TO FIGUERAS, Lluis: "Señoría y familia: los orígenes del 'hereu' catalán (siglos X–XII)." *Studia historica - Historia medieval*, 11, Universidad de Salamanca, Salamanca, 1993, pp. 57–79.

4. ROIG, Joseph L: *Historia de Barcelona*, Primera Plana, Barcelona, 1995.

5. http://www.inh.cat/

6. SEGURA, Cristian: "Un simposio defiende que Colón, Cervantes o da Vinci eran catalanes," *El País*, El País, Madrid, November 24, 2014.

7. PÉREZ, Fernando J. and Pere RÍOS: "1,8 millones de personas votan por la independencia catalana el 9-N," *El País*, El País, Madrid, November 10, 2014.

8. In the essay coordinated by José Andrés-Gallego, "Historia de la historiografía española" (Encuentro, Madrid, 1999), a series of distinguished historians, among them José María Blázquez and Emilio Mitre, trace discussions about Spain from the earliest sources to the most recent. Obviously, to look for a notion of Spain in antiquity or in the Middle Ages, is, from a political point of view, anachronistic. But these authors are not deterred. They even dedicate several chapters to that other modern political construction, Catalonia, claiming to offer a "balanced" view of history, which nevertheless continues to be a statist vision. By the way, the book was funded by the Spanish Ministry of Culture.

9. See, for example, HUGHES, Charles: "The Decline of the Californios. The Case of San Diego, 1846–1856," *The Journal of San Diego History*, 21, University of San Diego, San Diego, 1975; HUNT JACKSON, Helen: *Ramona: A Story*, Little, Brown, Boston, 1905.

10. LEUCHTENBURG, William E: *The LIFE History of the United States. The Great Age of Change. Volume 12: From 1945*, Time, New York, 1964, vol. 12, pp. 140–143.

11. KLOOSTER, John W: *Icons of Invention: The Makers of the Modern World from Gutenberg to Gates*, Greenwood, Santa Bárbara, 2009, vol. 1, pp. 295ff.

12. MAY, Ernest R: *The LIFE History of the United States. The Progressive Era. Volume 9: 1901–1917*, Time, New York, 1964, vol. 9, p. 9.

13. WIKIPEDIA, *History of the United* States, http://en.wikipedia.org/wiki/History_of_the_United_States, consulted August 22, 2016.

14. WIKIPEDIA, http://en.wikipedia.org/wiki/Spanish_Renaissance, consulted August 22, 2016.

15. LOUREIRO, Maite: "Prensa económica: Alemania señala la puerta a Grecia," *Libertad digital*, Libertad Digital, Madrid, January 5, 2015.

16. GIL WHITE, Francisco: "How Politicians, the Media, and Scholars Lied about Milosevic's 1989 Kosovo Speech. A Review of the Evidence," *Historical and Investigative Research*, www.hirhome.com/yugo/milospeech.htm, September 8, 2005.

17. LARRAIN, Jorge: *The Concept of Ideology*, Hutchinson, London, 1979, p. 197. The more radical positivist position is Ayn Rand's Objectivism and her famous tautology: "A is A." And, probably, the less valid method for a historical research. France is a Republic in 2016. This seems to be an obvious fact, as if to say "A is A." However, thousands of French still consider France to be a Kingdom, and even that there is a rivalry for the throne between the Bourbon line and the Orleans line (GALÁN, Lola: "Luis Alfonso de Borbón, el eterno pretendiente," in *El País*, elpais.com/elpais/2013/11/28/gente/1385661705_797778.html, November 30, 2013). Therefore, "A is A," but not for absolutely everyone.

18. GÓMEZ DÍAZ, Juan: "División territorial de España. Provincias y partidos judiciales. 175 años," in *Toletum: boletín de la Real Academia de Bellas Artes y Ciencias Históricas de Toledo*, no. 55, Real Academia de Bellas Artes y Ciencias Históricas de Toledo, Toledo, 2008, pp. 151–175.

19. LE GOFF, Jacques: *Medieval Civilization 400–1500*, Wiley-Blackwell, Hoboken, 1991.

20. For a contrasting view, see GRAF, Eric C: "Don Quijote: A Fierce Defense of Human Freedom," in *The Canal: Blog of the Panam Post*, blog.panampost. com/editor/2015/11/17/don-quijote-a-fierce-defense-of-human-freedom/, consulted November 17, 2015.

21. GARÍN, Alberto: "L'ingénieur militaire Luis Díez Navarro (1691–1780). De la vielle Europe à la Nouvelle Guatemala," in *Les européen: ces architectes qui on conçu l'Europe (1450–1950)*, Université de Paris-Sorbonne, Paris, 2016.

22. BRAUDEL, Fernand: *On History*, The University of Chicago, Chicago, 1980, p. 25.

23. See MAGNESS, Phillip W. and PAGE, Sebastian N: *Colonization After Emancipation: Lincoln and the Movement for Black Resettlement*, University of Missouri Press, Columbia, 2011.

24. DÍEZ ROS, Rocío, *Generación de residuos urbanos en la provincia de Alicante: la incidencia de la educación ambiental*, Universidad de Alicante, Alicante, 2006, p. 384.

25. COGHLAN, Andy: "Was Robert Gallo Robbed of the Nobel Prize?" *New Scientist*, www.newscientist.com/article/dn14881-was-robert-gallo-robbed-of-the-nobel-prize.html#.VL2l_NKG-Sr, 16 December 2008.

26. SHILTS, Randy: *And the Band Played On: Politics, People, and the AIDS Epidemic*, St. Martin's, New York, 2007.

27. GALLO, Robert C. and Luc MONTAGNIER: "Prospects for the Future," *Science*, 298, www.sciencemag.org/content/298/5599/1730, November 29, 2002, pp. 1730–1731.

28. MACLEOD, Murdo, *Spanish Central America: A Socioeconomic History*, University of California Press, Los Angeles, 1973.

29. GARÍN, Alberto, and OCHAITA, Daniela, "El abastecimiento y consumo de leña en las cocinas coloniales de la Antigua Guatemala," in *XIII Congreso Centroamericano de Historia*, Universidad de Honduras, Tegucigalpa, 2016.

30. Vid GUICHONNET, Paul: *Histoire de l'annexion de la Savoie à la France*, La Fontaine de Siloé, Montmélian, 2003.

31. The biography by Manfred Kuehn (*Kant: A Biography*, Cambridge University Press, New York) breaks our traditional vision of Kant as an ascetic and severe man. But Kuehn's discovery of a young Kant who loved fashion and women does not change the fact that he stubbornly refused to leave the place of his birth.

32. EFE: "Envío de remesas familiares a Guatemala aumentó un 10, 14% en enero de 2014," *América economía*, www.americaeconomia.com/economia-mercados/finanzas/envio-de-remesas-familiares-guatemala-aumento-un-1014-en-enero-de-2014, July 2, 2014.

33. MIRALLES HUETE, Santiago: *Velázquez y Rubens. Conversación en El Escorial*, Turner, Madrid, 2010.

34. FRAGUAS, Rafael, "El cincel de Bernini destella en la calle de Alcalá," in *El País*, Madrid, September 16, 2007.

35. AZCÁRATE RISTORI, José María, *et alii*: *Historia del arte*, Anaya, Madrid, 1980, pp. 493–588; FERNÁNDEZ, Antonio, *et alii*: *Historia del arte*, Vicens-Vives, Barcelona, 1995, pp. 279–336; REYERO HERMOSILLA, Carlos (dir.): *La enciclopedia del estudiante. 17. Historia del arte*, Santillana, Madrid, 2005, pp. 178–199; and WIKIPEDIA, *Art of Belgium*, https://en.wikipedia.org/wiki/Art_of_Belgium, consulted August 22, 2016.

Index

Abbot, Francis Ellingwood, 4, 12
abolition, xv, 3, 9–10, 20, 28–29, 34n6, 56n41, 96, 100, 121, 123, 126. *See also* emancipation
Abzug, Bella, 159
Acemoglu, Daron, 200
Acton, Lord (John Emerich Edward Dalberg-Acton, 1st Baron Acton), 73, 153n1
Addams, Jane, 100
Addick, Barbara, 162
affirmative action, 122–31, 216
African American:
　civil rights, 9, 56n41, 116, 120, 123, 131n4;
　historical accounts, 124–25;
　immigrants, 128;
　life in the Reconstruction era, 129
agency, xix, 54n20, 82, 138, 140–42, 147, 151, 156n41, 200
age of exploration, 63
agricultural innovation, 193, 205n14, 185, 186n1
agrarianism, 11, 78, 192–94
Agricultural Adjustment Administration, 106–13
agricultural revolution, 185
AIDS, 220
Alfonso VI of León and Castile, 210

Ali, Ayaan Hirsi, 161
amendments, of the U.S. Constitution. *See* Constitution, American
American Anti-Imperialist League, 101, 127
American Bar Association, 101
American Economic Association, 98
American Legion, 126
American Library Association, 126
American Revolution, 82
American Sociological Association, 99
anarchists, 4, 162, 168n7, 175, 178
anarchy, 46, 54n19, 162, 174–76, 179, 183–84
anarcho-individualism, 10, 174–75
Andover Theological Seminary, 3
Andrés-Gallego, José, 224n8
Andrew Mellon Foundation, 117
antebellum period, 20–23, 29, 33, 120
anthropology, xi, 60, 152, 214, 219, 222
anti-capitalism. *See* capitalism, opposition to
anti-communists. *See* communism, opposition to
anti-Semitism, 124
anti-slavery. *See* abolition
Appleby, Joyce, xv, 9, 157n56, 200
Aristotle, 173, 183

White, Horace, 96, 103
White, Micah, 70
whiteness, xix, 117–19, 126–28
white privilege, 118, 126
White Rose Society, 163
Wikipedia, 213
Williams, Eric, 199
Williams, "Peg-Leg," 129
Williams, R. Hal, 105
Williams, Stanley, 15
Wilson, Woodrow, 9, 32, 40, 95, 97
Windelband, Wilhelm, 182

wiretapping, 43, 51
Wise, Brownie, 164
Woods, Thomas, 42
Woodward, Vann, 50
working class, 122, 142–45, 151–52,
    191–93, 195, 206n20
World Bank, 201
World War I, 41, 51, 101–3, 126, 129
World War II, 41, 48, 106–7, 116,
    204n4
Wreszin, Michael, 112
Wright, Robert, 199

About the Editors and Contributors

Michael J. Douma is an assistant research professor and the director of the Georgetown Institute for the Study of Markets and Ethics at Georgetown University's McDonough School of Business. He holds a PhD in history from Florida State University and has been a Fulbright Scholar in the Netherlands. His peer-reviewed work includes books and articles on the history of the Dutch around the globe, as well as articles on the American Civil War, the U.S. Constitution, and the philosophy and methods of history. His next book, titled *Creative Historical Thinking* is forthcoming with Routledge.

David T. Beito is a professor of history at the University of Alabama. He received his PhD at the University of Wisconsin. He wrote *Taxpayers in Revolt: Tax Resistance during the Great Depression*; *From Mutal Aid to the Welfare State: Fraternal Societies and Social Services, 1890–1967*; and *The Voluntary City*; and *Black Maverick: T.R.M. Howard's Fight for Civil Right and Economic Power*. Beito's academic research has covered a wide range of topics in American history including civil rights, tax revolts, civil liberties in the New Deal period, the non-governmental provision of infrastructure, and mutual aid.

Hans Eicholz is a historian of economic and political thought and a Senior Fellow with Liberty Fund Inc., an Educational Foundation based in Indiana. He is also the author of *Harmonizing Sentiments: the Declaration of Independence and the Jeffersonian Idea of Self-Government* (2001), and a number of more recent essays on constitutionalism and political economy with particular focus on both the United States and Germany. He is also a contributor to Liberty Fund's Law and Liberty website.

Lenore T. Ealy is President of The Philanthropic Enterprise, Inc., an independent scholarly research institute that seeks to strengthen understanding of how philanthropy and voluntary social cooperation promote human flourishing. She is currently co-editor, with Paul Aligica, of the Lexington Books series *Polycentricity: Studies in Institutional Diversity and Voluntary Governance*. Author of numerous articles, she is also co-editor, with Robert Garnett and Paul Lewis, of *Commerce and Community:Ecologies of Social Cooperation* (Routledge, 2015); co-editor, with Steven Klugewicz, of *History, on Proper Principles: Essays in Honor of Forrest McDonald* (ISI Books, 2010); and co-editor, with Robert C. Enlow, of *Liberty and Learning: Milton Friedman's Voucher Idea at Fifty* (Cato Press, 2006). Ealy also currently serves as Secretary and Executive Director of The Philadelphia Society. Ealy earned a BS from Auburn University, an MA from the University of Alabama, and a PhD in the history of moral and political thought from the Johns Hopkins University.

Jonathan Bean is Professor of History at Southern Illinois University and a Research Fellow at the Independent Institute. He received his PhD in Business History from the Ohio State University in 1994. Bean is the editor and compiler of *Race and Liberty in America: The Essential Reader*, that received praise from *Choice* (American Library Association) and *Diverse Issues in Higher Education* (formerly *Black Issues in Higher Education*). He is also a member of the Illinois State Advisory Panel for the U.S. Commission on Civil Rights. His other books include *Beyond the Broker State: Federal Policies Toward Small Business, 1936–1961* (1996), and *Big Government and Affirmative Action: The Scandalous History of the Small Business Administration* (2001), along with numerous scholarly articles, op-eds, and radio and TV appearances.

Alberto Garín has a degree in Archaeology from the University of París I, Pantheon-La Sorbonne, and a PhD in Architecture from the Universidad Europea de Madrid. He works as the Director of Doctorate Programs and the Explorations on History Program at the Universidad Francisco Marroquín (in Guatemala). He has published several articles about national heritage, and education.

Matthew Brown is an assistant professor in the Department of Business Administration at the University of Illinois-Springfield. He holds a PhD in economics from Florida State University and did graduate work in history at Montana State University. His research interests are in history of economic growth; law and economics, the history, evolution, and impact of economic institutions; and cultural history from an economic perspective.